Abnormal Psychology

Published by:
Saurabh Publishing House

Abnormal Psychology

Samriti Sharma

Saurabh
Publishing House
4735/22, Prakash Deep Building,
Ansari Road, Daryaganj,
New Delhi- 110002

Published by :
SAURABH PUBLISHING HOUSE

Distributed by :
Lotus Press Publishers & Distributors
Unit No. 220, 2nd Floor, 4735/22, Prakash Deep Building,
Ansari Road, Darya Ganj, New Delhi- 110002
Ph.: 23280047, 09811838000
• E-mail : lotuspress1984@gmail.com
www.lotuspress.co.in

Saurabh Publishing House is an imprint of
Lotus Press Publishers & Distributors

Abnormal Psychology

ISBN: 81-89005-09-X

Printed by : **Lotus Press Publishers & Distributors, New Delhi**

PREFACE

Abnormal psychology is the scientific study of abnormal behaviour in order to describe, predict, explain, and change abnormal patterns of functioning. Abnormal psychology in clinical psychology studies the nature of psychopathology, its causes, and its treatments. Of course, the definition of what constitutes 'abnormal' has varied across time and across cultures. Individuals also vary in what they regard as normal or abnormal behaviour. In general, abnormal psychology can be described as an area of psychology that studies people who are consistently unable to adapt and function effectively in a variety of conditions. The four main contributing factors to how well an individual is able to adapt include their genetic makeup, physical condition, learning and reasoning, and socialization.

The part of abnormal psychology has to do with phobias. A phobia is a persistent, abnormal and irrational fear of a specific thing or situation that compels one to avoid it, despite the awareness and reassurance that it is not dangerous. A person suffering from a phobia may find it hard to socialize, work, or go about their everyday life. Phobias belong to a large group of mental problems known as anxiety disorders which includes panic disorders, post-traumatic stress disorders, and obsessive-compulsive disorder (OCD). Phobias can be diagnosed after extensive interview with a mental health professional or someone specializing in abnormal behaviour/ psychology.

Many different professions may be involved in studying mental illness or distress. Most notably, psychiatrists and clinical psychologists are particularly interested in this area and may either be involved in clinical treatment of mental illness, or research into the origin, development and manifestations of such states, or often, both. More widely, many different specialities may be involved in the study of psychopathology. Therefore, someone who is referred to as a psychopathologist may be one of any number of professions who have specialised in studying this area.

This book's matter engaging and innovative systems approach, integrating the biological, psychological, and social perspectives in one concurrent story. Scientific methods are presented in a clear and non-threatening manner, and are based on the most current research. The chapters of the book include personality disorders, eating disorders, substance use disorders, sexual and gender identity disorders, schisophrenic disorders, mood disorders and suicide, treatment of psychological disorders, and more.

Samriti Sharma

CONTENTS

1

Abnormal Psychology: Definition and Meaning

Introduction

All of these difficulties are of concern to psychologists who study abnormal behaviour. However, in addition to these difficulties, two broad classes of conditions have been a focus for psychologists who study abnormal behaviour in childhood. These are disruptive behaviour disorders (such as attention deficit hyper-activity disorder, oppositional defiant disorder, conduct disorder) and emotional disorders (such as anxiety and depression).

In this chapter, disruptive behaviour disorders will be the central focus for three main reasons. First, disruptive behaviour disorders in children and adolescents are particularly prevalent in the community. Second, these disorders are among the most common referrals to child mental health services. Third, in the long-term if left untreated, these disorders are extremely costly both to the children who suffer from them and to society.

After considering the clinical features and epidemiology of attention deficit hyperactivity disorder, oppositional defiant disorder and conduct disorder, theoretical explanations for these problems are presented in this chapter. Each of these specific explanations has been developed within the context of one of four broad theories. These are the biological, psychodynamic, cognitive-behavioural and family systems theories of psychological problems.

Attention Deficit Hyperactivity Disorder

Attention deficit hyperactivity disorder, attention deficit disorder, hyperkinetic disorder, hyperkinesis and minimal brain dysfunction are some of the terms used for a syndrome characterized by persistent overactivity, impulsivity and difficulties in sustaining attention. In this chapter preference will be given to the term attention deficit hyperactivity disorder (ADHD) since this is currently the most widely used.

Case example

Anuj, aged 6, was referred for assessment because his teachers found him unmanageable. He was unable to sit still in school and concentrate on his schoolwork. He left his chair frequently and ran around the classroom shouting. This was distracting for both his teachers and classmates. Even with individual tuition he could not apply himself to his schoolwork. He also had difficulties getting along with other children. They disliked him because he disrupted their games. He rarely waited for his turn and did not obey the rules. At home he was consistently disobedient and according to his father ran 'like a motorboat' from the time he got up until bedtime. He often climbed on furniture and routinely shouted rather than talked.

Family history. Anuj came from a well-functioning family. The parents had a very stable and satisfying marriage and together ran a successful business. Their daughter, Anu, was a well-adjusted and academically able 8-year-old. The parents were careful not to favour the daughter over her brother or to unduly punish Anuj for his constant disruption of his sister's activities. However, there was a growing tension between each of the parents and Anuj. While they were undoubtedly committed to him, they were also continually suppressing their growing irritation with his frenetic activity, disobedience, shouting and school problems. Within the wider family there were few resources that the parents could draw on to help them cope with Anuj. The grandparents, aunts and uncles lived in another locality and so could not provide regular support for the parents. Furthermore, they were bewildered by Anuj's condition, found it very unpleasant and had gradually reduced their contact with Anuj's nuclear family since his birth.

Psychometric assessment and child interview. Psychometric evaluation showed that his overall IQ was within the normal range but Anuj was highly distractible and had literacy and numeracy skills that were significantly below his overall ability level. Anuj perceived himself to be a failure. He believed that he could not do anything right at home or at school and he was sad that the other children did not want to play with him. He believed that his teacher disliked him and doubted his parents' love for him.

Developmental history. There were a number of noteworthy features in Anuj's developmental history. He had suffered anoxia at birth and febrile convulsions in infancy. He had also had episodes of projectile vomiting. His high activity level and demandingness were present from birth. He also displayed a difficult temperament, showing little regularity in feeding or sleeping; intense negative emotions to new stimuli; and was slow to soothe following an intense experience of negative emotion.

Formulation. Anuj was a 6-year-old boy with home- and school-based problems of hyperactivity, impulsivity and distractibility of sufficient severity to warrant a diagnosis of attention deficit hyperactivity disorder. Possible predisposing factors included anoxia at birth, subtle neurological damage due to febrile convulsions in infancy, and a difficult temperament. In Anuj's case ADHD had led to academic attainment difficulties; peer relationship problems; and tension within the family. This wider constellation of difficulties underpinned Anuj's diminishing self-esteem which in turn exacerbated his problems with attainment, peer relationships and family relationships. The absence of an extended family support system for the parents to help them deal with Anuj's difficulties was also a possible maintaining factor. Important protective factors in this case were the commitment of the parents to resolving the problem and supporting Anuj, and the stability of Anuj's nuclear family.

Treatment. Treatment in this case involved both psycho-social and pharmacological intervention. The psychosocial intervention included parent and teacher education about ADHD; behavioural parent training; self-instructional training for the child; a classroom-based behavioural programme, and provision of periodic relief care/

holidays with specially trained foster parents. Anuj was also given stimulant therapy, specifically a twice-daily dose of methylphenidate.

Clinical Features

The clinical features of ADHD in the domains of cognition, affect, behaviour, physical health and interpersonal adjustment are given in Table 1.1. Anuj, in the case example, showed all of these. With respect to cognition, short attention span, distractibility and an inability to foresee the consequences of action are the main features. There is usually a poor internalization of the rules of social conduct and in some instances low self-esteem may be present. With respect to affect, excitability associated with lack of impulse control is the dominant emotional state. This may be coupled with depressed mood associated with low self-esteem in some cases. With ADHD it is the high rate of activity, common comorbid aggressive antisocial behaviour, excessive risk-taking and poor school performance associated with inattention that are the cardinal behavioural features. With respect to physical health in ADHD, in some instances food allergies may be present. Injuries or medical complications associated with antisocial behaviour such as fighting and drug-abuse may also occur. Relationship difficulties with parents, teachers and peers are the principal interpersonal adjustment problems. Difficulties with turn-taking in games due to impulsivity make children with ADHD poor playmates. The failure of children with ADHD to internalize rules of social conduct at home and to meet parental expectations for appropriate social and academic behaviour leads to conflictual parent-child relationships. In school, youngsters with ADHD pose classroom management problems for teachers, and these children invariably have problems benefiting from routine teaching and instructional methods. For these reasons, their relationships with teachers tend to be conflictual.

Historically, a narrow definition of ADHD has been included in the ICD classification system which is widely used in the UK, with great emphasis being placed on the stability of the overactivity problems across home and school contexts. In view of this historical difference in diagnostic practices, it is particularly noteworthy that

Table 1.1. Clinical Features of Childhood Behaviour Disorders

Domain	ADHD	Oppositional defiant disorder	Conduct disorder
Cognition	• Short attention span • Distractibility • Unable to foresee consequences of behaviour • Immature self-speech (internal language) • Low self-esteem • Lack of conscience • Learning difficulties and poor school performance	• Limited internalization of social rules or norms • Hostile attributional bias	• Limited internalization of social rules or norms • Hostile attributional bias
Affect	• Lack of impulse control • Excitability • Low frustration tolerance • Low mood	• Anger and irritability	• Anger and irritability
Behaviour	• High rate of activity • Delay in motor development and poor co-ordination • High level of risk-taking behaviour	• Persistent pattern of defiance towards adults in authority • Aggression • Temper tantrums	• Persistent broad pattern of antisocial behaviour • Defiance • Aggression • Destructiveness • Deceitfulness and theft • Cruelty • Truancy • Running away • Coercive sex • Preadolescent drug use
Physical condition	• Immature physical size and bone growth • Minor physical abnormalities • Allergies • Increased respiratory infections and otitis media		• Physical problems associated with risk-taking behaviour such as fighting, drug abuse or casual unsafe sex
Interpersonal adjustment	• Problematic relationships with parents, teachers and peers	• Problematic relationships with parents	• Problematic relationships with parents, teachers and peers

currently in both the North American DSM IV and the ICD 10 which is used widely in Europe, it is stipulated that symptoms must be present in two or more settings such as home and school for a positive diagnosis of ADHD to be made.

Epidemiology

Reviews of epidemiological studies of ADHD report overall prevalence rates varying from 1 to 19 per cent depending upon the stringency of the diagnostic criteria applied and the demographic characteristics of the populations studied. Using DSM IV criteria a prevalence rate of about 3-5 per cent has been obtained. The prevalence of ADHD varies with gender and age. ADHD is more prevalent in boys than girls and in preadolescents than in late adolescents. Comorbidity for conduct disorder and ADHD is about 20 per cent in community populations and possibly double this figure in clinical populations. Comorbidity for emotional disorders, such as anxiety or depression, and ADHD is about 10 per cent in community populations. In clinical populations the comorbidity rate is maybe twice this figure. Virtually all children with ADHD have attainment problems. However, comorbid severe specific learning difficulties have been estimated to occur in 10-25 per cent of cases. A proportion of youngsters with ADHD have comorbid developmental language delays and elimination problems although reliable epidemiological data are unavailable.

About a third of children with ADHD have a good prognosis, about a third have a moderate prognosis and a third have a poor prognosis. For two-thirds of cases, the primary problems of inattention, impulsivity and hyperactivity persist into late adolescence and for some of these the primary symptoms persist into adulthood. Roughly a third develop significant antisocial behaviour problems in adolescence including conduct disorder and substance abuse, and for most of this subgroup these problems persist into adulthood leading to criminality. Occupational adjustment problems and suicide attempts occur in a small but significant minority of cases.

Etiological Theories

Biological, cognitive-behavioural and family systems theories have been developed to explain the etiology and maintenance of symptomatology in ADHD.

Biological Theories

Biological theories which focus on the role of genetic factors, structural brain abnormalities, neurotransmitter dysregulation, dietary factors and hypo-arousal have guided much research on the etiology of ADHD.

Genetic hypotheses. Genetic theories suggest that a predisposition to hyperactivity is inherited by children who develop ADHD. Twin and family studies support the view that genetic factors play an important role in determining temperamental activity levels in the normal population. However, other environmental factors (either intrauterine or psychosocial) would be required in addition to a genetic predisposition to high activity levels to account for the development of the clinical syndrome of ADHD. It may be that, in some cases, temperamentally overactive children sustain a prenatal or early childhood neurological insult and go on to develop ADHD, whereas others with an overactive temperament develop the syndrome following participation in particular non-optimal types of parent-child interaction. For a small subgroup of children with ADHD, the syndrome appears to be caused by a genetic condition resulting in a generalized resistance to thyroid hormone.

Organic deficit hypothesis. Early work on ADHD was premised on the hypothesis that the syndrome reflected an organic deficit: probably some form of minimal brain damage. Sophisticated neuroimaging studies have failed to reveal a specific structural brain abnormality which typifies cases of ADHD, and neuropsychological studies have failed to reveal a unique pattern of cognitive deficits associated with either localized or diffuse brain damage characteristic of youngsters with ADHD. However, a number of factors which might lead to brain damage during the prenatal or perinatal periods are more prevalent among youngsters with ADHD than normal controls. These include: prenatal difficulties, maternal smoking during pregnancy, maternal alcohol use during pregnancy, low foetal heart rate during delivery, small head circumference at birth, minor physical abnormalities, low birth weight, a high rate of diseases of infancy, lead poisoning and early neurological insult or brain damage. It is important to point out that these factors which may contribute to the development of an organic deficit are not unique to ADHD and occur also in youngsters with other disorders.

Therefore they probably interact with other factors in contributing to the development of ADHD.

Neurotransmitter dysregulation hypothesis. The neurotransmitter dysregulation hypothesis attributes the symptoms of ADHD to abnormalities in neurotransmitter functioning at the synapses affected by psychostimulants which ameliorate the symptomatology of ADHD. McCracken has shown that a dysregulation of the dopamine system in the ventral tegmental areas of the brain and norepinephrine and epinephrine systems in the locus coeruleus may be present in ADHD and it is probably these systems that are influenced by effective stimulant therapy with drugs such as methylphenidate and dextroamphetamine. Approximately 60–90 per cent of children with ADHD respond to these stimulants. They show a reduction in symptomatology and an improvement in both academic and social functioning, although positive effects dissipate when treatment ceases.

Dietary hypotheses. The dietary hypothesis attributes the symptoms of ADHD to children's reaction to certain features of their daily diet. Originally Feingold argued that artificial food additives such as colourants accounted for a substantial proportion of ADHD symptomatology. However, controlled trials of additive-free diets did not support his position. Egger refined Feingold's original allergy theory and argued that particular children with ADHD may have unique allergy profiles and if their diet is modified so as to exclude the precise substances to which they are allergic, then their activity and attention problems may improve. Carefully controlled dietary studies have supported Egger's theory.

Hypo-arousal hypotheses. The hypo-arousal hypothesis explains hyperactivity and inattention as a failure to be sufficiently aroused by signal stimuli to attend to them and regulate activity levels. Hyperactivity may also, according to this hypothesis, reflect stimulus-seeking behaviour. Psychophysiological studies show that ADHD children show reduced psychophysiological responsiveness (as assessed by electroencephalograph (EEG), galvanic skin response (GSR) and heart rate) to novel stimuli with signal value. However, similar unresponsiveness characterizes children with learning disorders and conduct disorders. The use of vivid stimuli in academic settings and highly salient and immediate reinforcers is implicated by the hypo-arousal hypothesis. Reward systems and operant programmes conforming to these specifications have been found to have significant short-term effects.

Cognitive-Behavioural Theories

A number of theories which highlight the importance of deficits in specific cognitive or behavioural processes as the central factor underlying ADHD symptomatology have been proposed. Four of these will be mentioned below. All attempt to show how the overall syndrome of inattention, overactivity and impulsivity may be accounted for by a single underlying core deficit, be it one of the three core symptoms of ADHD or some other cognitive or behavioural process.

Inattention hypothesis. The attentional deficit hypothesis argues that problems with sustaining attention on a single task and screening out other distracting stimuli are the core difficulty that underpins the other symptoms of impulsivity and overactivity in ADHD. That is, youngsters with ADHD at the outset of a task requiring attention will perform at a level equivalent to normal children but, over time, they will show more errors which are directly attributable to the inability to sustain attention. This problem with sustaining attention leads them to change the focus of their attention frequently and this is manifested at a behavioural level as excessive impulsivity and overactivity. On certain laboratory tasks children with ADHD show a gradual deterioration in sustained attention. However, on other tasks they show immediate selective attention problems compared to normals and they also display overactivity while asleep. These findings suggest that a deficit in sustained attention alone cannot fully account for the ADHD syndrome.

Hyperactivity hypothesis. The hyperactivity hypothesis argues that a problem with inhibiting motor activity is the core deficit that underpins the ADHD syndrome and can account for inattention and impulsivity. There is a large body of evidence which shows that hyperactivity is unique as a symptom to children with ADHD compared to children with other psychological problems and that hyperactivity as a construct correlates with many academic indices of attentional problems.

Impulsivity hypothesis. This hypothesis argues that a core problem in inhibiting cognitive and behavioural responses to specific stimuli leads to poor performance on tasks apparently requiring good attentional abilities and also on tasks requiring careful regulation of behaviour. Thus the central problem in ADHD according to this hypothesis is with cognitive and behavioural impulsivity or disinhibition. According to this theory, with academic tasks apparently requiring high levels of sustained attention, children with ADHD have problems using systematic cognitive problem-solving strategies because they are cognitively impulsive. Also, in both academic and social situations, children with ADHD engage in careless work practices in school and engage in socially inappropriate behaviour with peers, parents and teachers because they are behaviourally impulsive. There is some evidence to show that, while children with ADHD may know and understand problem-solving skills and social skills, they fail to use them appropriately in academic and social situations.

Rule-following deficit hypothesis. Barkley posits a difficulty in rule-following as the central problem in ADHD. This rule-following deficiency is due to an inability to use inner and outer speech as a discriminative stimulus to cue particular responses. In addition to the extensive evidence for developmental language delay in children with ADHD, there is some support for the delay in the development of internal speech in children with this condition.

To compensate for deficits in attention, regulation of motor activity, impulsivity and rule-following, various skills training programmes have been developed, largely within the cognitive-behavioural tradition. Self-instructional training for managing academic tasks and social skills training to manage relationship problems (particularly those involving peers) are the main types of skills taught within these programmes. Because of the negligible impact that such programmes have when conducted in isolation, they are now offered as one element of a multimodal package involving stimulant medication, family intervention and school intervention. Hinshaw has argued that it is probable that compensatory problem-solving and social skills training programmes can have optimum effects when offered after a consistent home- and school-based contingency management programme has been established and stimulant treatment is in progress.

Family Systems Theory

Family systems theories have focused largely on the role of the family system or the wider social context in the etiology and maintenance of ADHD. With respect to family problems, parental psychological problems such as depression, aggression or alcohol abuse, exposure to marital discord, overintrusive parenting during infancy, and coercive parent-child interactions in childhood and adolescence have all been found to have associations with ADHD. With respect to the wider social system the following factors have been found to be associated with ADHD: low socio-economic status, institutional upbringing, peer relationship problems and relationship problems with school staff. A problem with much of the research on psychosocial factors in the etiology and maintenance of ADHD is the fact that in many cases comorbid conduct disorders are present, and the risk factors that are identified, which bear a close resemblance to those identified for conduct disorders, may primarily be associated with the etiology of conduct problems rather than ADHD. A second difficulty is untangling the causal chain and establishing which family and relationship difficulties precede the development of ADHD and are predisposing factors; and distinguishing these from relationship difficulties that evolve in response to ADHD and possibly maintain or exacerbate the condition.

Family-based interventions and multisystemic intervention programmes involving the child's wider social network have evolved from family systems theories of ADHD. These programmes focus on improving parenting skills and enhancing the child's relationships with members of the family and the wider network. Such programmes have been shown to have positive short-term effects on both symptomatology and social adjustment.

Intervention

There is a growing consensus within the field that single-factor theories are unlikely to be able to explain the complex and heterogeneous population of youngsters who qualify for a diagnosis of ADHD. It is probable that a variety of biological and psychosocial factors interact in complex ways to give rise to the syndrome and that problems with a number of psychological processes, particularly those involved in regulating both cognitive and motor responses, underpin symptomatology. The symptomatology is probably partially maintained and exacerbated by problematic relationships within the family, the peer group and the school. In view of this integrative formulation, it is not surprising that multimodal treatment packages that include behavioural parent training, self-instructional training and school-based contingency management combined with stimulant therapy have been found to be most effective. With behavioural parent training, parents are coached in how to consistently reinforce socially appropriate behaviour and extinguish inappropriate behaviour. School-based contingency management programmes extend this type of approach into the child's classroom environment. In self-instructional training, children with ADHD are coached in the use of self-instruction to control the way in which they deploy their attention and control their impulses to engage in high levels of activity. With stimulant therapy, children receive regular doses of methylphenidate or dextroamphetamine.

Conduct Disorder and Oppositional Defiant Disorder

Conduct problems constitute a third to a half of all clinic referrals, and chronic conduct problems are the single most costly disorder of adolescence for three reasons. First, they are remarkably unresponsive to traditional individual approaches to treatment. Positive outcome rates for routine treatments range from 20 to 40 per cent. Second, about 60 per cent of adolescents with conduct problems have a poor prognosis.

Adolescents with chronic conduct disorder turn to adult criminality and develop antisocial personality disorders, alcohol-related problems and a variety of psychological difficulties. They also have more problems with health, educational attainment, occupational adjustment, marital stability and social integration. The third reason for the high cost of conduct problems is the fact that they are intergenerationally transmitted. Adults with a history of conduct disorder rear children with a particularly high prevalence of conduct difficulties.

Case example

Rahul, aged 11, was referred by his social worker for treatment following an incident in which he had assaulted neighbours by climbing up onto the roof of his house and throwing rocks and stones at them. He also had a number of other problems, according to the school headmaster, including academic underachievement, difficulty in maintaining friendships at school and repeated school absence. He smoked, occasionally drank alcohol, and stole money and goods from neighbours. His problems were longstanding but had intensified in the six months preceding the referral. At that time his father, Pramod, was imprisoned for raping a young girl in the small rural village where the family lived.

Family history. Rahul was one of five boys who lived with their mother, Rita, at the time of the referral. The family lived in relatively chaotic circumstances. Prior to Pramod's imprisonment, the children's defiance and rule-breaking, particularly Rahul's, were kept in check by their fear of physical punishment from their father. Since his incarceration, there were few house rules and these were implemented inconsistently, so all of the children showed conduct problems, but Rahul's were by far the worst. Rita had developed intense coercive patterns of interaction with Rahul and Jimmy (the second eldest). In addition to the parenting difficulties, there were also no routines to ensure bills were paid, food was bought, washing was done, homework completed or regular meal and sleeping times were observed. Rita supported the family with welfare payments and money earned illegally from farm-work. Despite the family chaos, she was very attached to her children and would sometimes fake them to work with her rather than send them to school because she liked their company.

At the preliminary interview, Rita said that 'her nerves were in tatters'. She was attending a psychiatrist intermittently for pharmacological treatment of depression. She had a longstanding history of conduct and mood regulation problems, beginning early in adolescence. In particular she had conflictual relationships with her mother and father which were characterized by coercive cycles of interaction. In school she had academic difficulties and peer relationship problems.

Rita had been ostracized by her own family when she married Pramod whom they saw as an unsuitable partner for her, since he had a number of previous convictions for theft and assault. Pramod's family never accepted Rita, because they thought she had 'ideas above her station'. Rita's and Pramod's parents were in regular conflict, and each family blamed the other for the chaotic situation in which Pramod and Rita had found themselves. Rita was also ostracized by the village community in which she lived. The community blamed her for driving her husband to commit rape.

Pramod, the father, also had longstanding difficulties. His conduct problems began in middle childhood. He was the eldest of four brothers, all of whom developed conduct problems, but his were by far the most severe. He had a history of becoming involved in aggressive exchanges that often escalated to violence. He and his mother had become involved in coercive patterns of interaction from his earliest years. He developed similar coercive patterns of interaction at school with his teachers, at work with various foremen and also in his relationship with Rita. He had a distant and detached relationship with his father.

Developmental history. From Rahul's developmental history, it was clear that he was a difficult-temperament child who did not develop sleeping and feeding routines easily and responded intensely and negatively to new situations. His language development had been delayed and he showed academic difficulties right from his first years in school. On the positive side, Rahul had a strong sense of family loyalty to his brothers and parents and did not want to see the family split up.

Psychometric assessment. From the Child Behaviour Checklists completed by Rita, it was clear that Rahul and his three brothers had clinically significant conduct problems and that Rahul's were by far the most extreme. A similar pattern emerged from behaviour checklists completed by the boys' teachers. A psychometric evaluation of Rahul's abilities and attainments showed that he was of normal intelligence, but his attainments in reading, spelling and arithmetic fell below the 10th percentile. From his subtest profile on the psychometric instruments, it was concluded that the discrepancy between attainment and abilities was accounted for by a specific learning disability.

School report. The headmaster at the school which Rahul and his brothers attended confirmed that Rahul had academic, conduct and attainment problems, but was committed to educating the boys and managing their conduct and attendance problems in a constructive way. The headmaster had a reputation (of which he was very proud) for being particularly skilled in managing children with behaviour problems.

Formulation. Rahul was an 11-year-old boy with a persistent and broad pattern of conduct problems both within and outside the home. He also had a specific learning disability and peer relationship problems. Factors which predisposed Rahul to the development of these problems included a difficult temperament, a developmental language delay, exposure to paternal criminality, maternal depression and a chaotic family environment. The father's incarceration six months prior to the referral led to an intensification of Rahul's conduct problems. The conduct problems were maintained at the time of the referral by engagement in coercive patterns of interaction with his mother and teachers; rejection of Rahul by peers at school; and isolation of his family by the extended family and the community. Protective factors in the case included the mother's wish to retain custody of the children rather than have them taken into foster care; the children's sense of family loyalty; and the school's commitment to retaining and dealing with the boys rather than excluding them for truancy and misconduct.

Treatment. The treatment plan in this case involved a multisystemic intervention programme. The mother was trained in behavioural parenting skills. A series of meetings between the teacher, the mother and the social worker was convened to develop and implement a plan that ensured regular school attendance. Occasional relief foster care was arranged for Rahul and Jimmy(the second eldest) to reduce the stress on Rita. Social skills training was provided for Rahul to help him deal with peer relationship problems.

Clinical Features

It may be seen that a distinction is made between oppositional defiant disorder, and conduct disorder with the former reflecting a less pervasive disturbance than the latter. In a proportion of cases oppositional defiant disorder is a developmental precursor of conduct disorder. The main behavioural feature of conduct disorder is a pervasive and persistent pattern of antisocial behaviour which extends beyond the family to the school and community; involves serious violations of rules; and is characterized by defiance of authority, aggression, destructiveness, deceitfulness and cruelty.

Youngsters with conduct disorder show a limited internalization of social rules and norms and a hostile attributional bias where the youngster interprets ambiguous social situations as threatening and responds with aggressive retaliative behaviour. Anger and irritability are the predominant mood states. Problematic relationships with significant members of the child's network typify children with conduct disorder. Negative relationships with parents and teachers typically revolve around the youngster's defiant behaviour, and with peers the problems typically centre on aggression and bullying which is guided by the hostile attributional bias with which conduct-disordered youngsters construe many of their peer relationships. With conduct disorders there may also be problematic relationships with members of the wider community if theft or vandalism has occurred. Multiagency involvement with juvenile justice or social work agencies is common. Also, because conduct disorder is associated with family disorganization, parental criminality and parental psychological adjustment difficulties, professionals from adult mental health and justice systems may be involved.

With both conduct disorder and oppositional defiant disorder three classes of risk factors increase the probability that conduct problems in childhood or adolescence will escalate into later life difficulties that is, personal characteristics, parenting practices, and family organization problems. Difficult temperament, aggressiveness, impulsivity, inattention and educational difficulties are the main personal characteristics of children and adolescents that place them at risk for long-term conduct problems. Ineffective monitoring and supervision of youngsters, providing inconsistent consequences for rule violations, and failing to provide reinforcement for prosocial behaviour are the main problematic parenting practices that place children and adolescents at risk for the development of long-term anti-social behaviour patterns. The family organization problems associated with persistence of conduct problems into adulthood are parental conflict and violence, a high level of life stressors, a low level of social support and parental psychological adjustment problems such as depression or substance abuse.

Epidemiology

Overall prevalence rates for conduct disorder vary from 4 to 14 per cent depending upon the criteria used and the population studied. Conservative estimates of prevalence range from 2 to 6 per cent. Conduct disorder is more prevalent in boys than in girls with male:female ratios varying from 4 : 1 to 2 : 1. Comorbidity for conduct problems and other problems, such as ADHD or emotional disorders, is quite common, particularly in clinic populations. The comorbidity rate for conduct disorder and ADHD in community populations is 23 per cent. The comorbidity rate for conduct disorder and emotional disorders in community populations is 17 per cent for major depression and 15 per cent for anxiety disorders.

Many theoretical perspectives attempt to explain development, among the most prominent are: Jean Piaget's Stage Theory, Lev Vygotsky's Social Contextualism (and its heir, the Ecological Systems Theory of Urie Bronfenbrenner), and especially the information processing framework employed by cognitive psychology.

The empiricist position on the issue of language acquisition suggests that the language input does provide the necessary information required for learning the structure of language and that infants acquire language through a process of statistical learning. From this perspective, language can be acquired via general learning methods that also apply to other aspects of development, such as perceptual learning. There is a great deal of evidence for components of both the nativist and empiricist position, and this is a hotly debated research topic in abnormal psychology.

Etiological theories

Biological, psychodynamic, cognitive-behavioural and social systems theories have been put forward to explain the development of conduct problems and to guide the development of treatment programmes. Since the distinction between oppositional defiant disorder and conduct disorder is a relatively recent development, most theories in this area have been developed with specific reference to conduct disorder, but have obvious implications for oppositional defiant disorder which is probably a developmental precursor of conduct disorder in many cases.

Biological theories

Biological theories have focused on the roles of genetic factors, hormonal factors, arousal levels and neuropsychological deficits in the etiology of conduct problems.

Genetic theories. There are many lines of research which focus on genetic and constitutional aspects of children with conduct disorder, and these are guided by the hypothesis that biological factors underpin antisocial behaviour in youths. The predominance of males among youngsters with conduct disorders and the observation that the concordance rate for conduct problems among monozygotic twins (87 per cent) is higher than that for dizygotic twins (72 per cent) point to the importance of some constitutional factors in the etiology of conduct disorders. Early reports of a causal link between XYY syndrome and conduct problems have not been supported by later research. The association between XYY syndrome and conduct problems appears to be due to the high rates of parental separation and maternal psychological problems that characterize the families of XYY children.

Hormonal theories. One of the more promising leads in the search for biological factors associated with conduct problems is a link between aggressive behaviour and elevated testosterone levels in male teenagers.

Arousal theory. Children with conduct disorders have lower arousal levels than normal children, according to this theory, and so are less responsive to rewards and punishments. They have an impaired capacity for responding to the positive reinforcement that often follows prosocial behaviour or for avoiding punishments associated with antisocial behaviour. Thus, they fail to learn prosocial behaviour or to avoid antisocial behaviour. It is assumed that this abnormally low arousal level is inherited and the results of twin studies partially support this. Treatment based on this hypothesis must involve highly structured and intensive learning situations if social rules are to be learned. The positive and negative reinforcers used must be highly valued and delivered immediately following responses. All rule infractions must lead to immediate withdrawal of desired stimuli. Rule-following should be immediately and intensely rewarded on a variable interval schedule, since this leads to learning that is maximally resistant to extinction. These treatment implications of arousal theory have been incorporated into the design of residential token economies for delinquent adolescents; behavioural parent training programmes; school-based behavioural programmes; and treatment foster care.

Neuropsychological deficit theory. Neuropsychologically-based deficits in verbal reasoning and executive functioning, according to this position, underpin self-regulation difficulties that contribute to conduct problems. They may also lead to underachievement which leads to frustration and this contributes to aggressive behaviour. This position is supported by a substantial body of evidence that documents verbal reasoning and executive function deficits in children and teenagers with conduct problems, by studies that confirm a strong association between reading difficulties and conduct problems, and by studies that show that unsocialized conduct problems are associated with self-regulation problems. Remedial interventions that facilitate the development of language and academic skills are the principal types of treatment deriving from this theory.

Psychodynamic theories

Classical psychoanalytic theory points to superego deficits and object relations theorists highlight the role of disrupted attachments in the development of conduct problems.

Superego deficit theory. Within psychoanalysis it is assumed that societal rules and expectations are internalized through identification with the parent of the same gender. This internalization is referred to as the superego. Aichorn argued that anti-social behaviour occurs because of impoverished superego functioning. The problems with superego functioning were thought to arise from either overindulgent parenting on the one hand or punitive and neglectful parenting on the other. With overindulgent parenting, the child internalizes lax standards and so feels no guilt when breaking rules or behaving immorally. In such cases any apparently moral behaviour is a manipulative attempt to gratify some desire. With punitive or neglectful parenting, the child splits the experience of the parent into the *good caring parent* and the *bad punitive/neglectful parent* and internalizes both of these aspects of the parent quite separately with little integration. In dealing with parents, peers and authority figures, the child may be guided by either the internalization of the good parent or the internalization of the bad parent. Typically at any point in time such youngsters can clearly identify those members of their network who fall into the good and bad categories. They behave morally towards those for whom they experience a positive transference and whom they view as good, and immorally to those towards whom they have a negative transference and view as bad. Residential group-based milieu therapy where staff consistently and compassionately enforce rules of conduct which reflect societal standards is the principal treatment to evolve from this theoretical perspective. Within such a treatment programme children gradually internalize societal rules, integrate the *good* and *bad* parental introjects, and develop a more adequate superego.

While there is little evidence for the effectiveness of psychoanalytically-based treatment for conduct disorders, it has provided important insights into the impact of working with such youngsters on the dynamics within multidisciplinary teams. For example, in my clinical experience, conduct-disordered youngsters who have internalized good and bad parental representations into the superego typically project good parental qualities onto one faction of the multidisciplinary team (typically the least powerful) and bad parental qualities onto the other team members (typically the most powerful). These projections elicit strong countertransference reactions in team members, with those receiving good projections experiencing positive feelings towards the youngster and those receiving bad projections experiencing negative feelings towards the youngster. Inevitably this leads to team conflict which can be destructive to team functioning if not interpreted, understood and worked through.

Attachment theory. Bowlby pointed out that children who were separated from their primary caretakers for extended periods of time during their first months of life failed to develop secure attachments and so, in later life, did not have internal working models for secure trusting relationships. He referred to such children as displaying affectionless psychopathy. Since moral behaviour is premised on functional internal working models of how to conduct oneself in trusting relationships, such children behave immorally. Treatment according to this position should aim to provide the child with a secure-attachment relationship or corrective emotional experience which will lead to the development of appropriate internal working models. These in turn will provide a basis for moral action.

While the provision of a secure attachment experience within the context of outpatient weekly individual therapy is an ineffective treatment for children with conduct disorder, a secure attachment relationship is a central treatment component in some effective interventions, such as treatment foster care. Here, the foster parents provide the child with a secure-attachment experience and couple this with good behavioural management.

Autopoietic Theory and Social Systems

The aspect of autopoietic theory most important to enterprise researchers is its attitude and application to the study of human (inter-) activity and the social systems within which this occurs. This point of intersection has already been employed in social / management analyses of enterprises and / or their information technology needs. In the information technology (IT) community, Winograd and Flores are the most widely known and cited authors who invoke autopoietic theory in analyzing enterprise activities. Morgan makes extensive use of autopoiesis in discussing the form, function, and character of enterprises. Von Krogh and Roos apply principles from autopoietic theory in laying out a schema for corporate knowledge building. Mingers analyzes the points of similarity between autopoietic theory and sociologist Anthony Giddens' structuration theory, which is becoming popular in MIS and CSCW circles under the label Adaptive Structuration Theory (AST).

The issue of how autopoiesis can or should be applied to social systems is an ongoing topic of debate. In the sections below, some of the key issues to date will be reviewed. This overview will necessarily be brief and shallow. Further information on these topics can be obtained through the references and resources provided.

For our purposes, it's enough to note there are two primary approaches in applying autopoiesis to social systems. The first applies the formal aspects of autopoietic theory (e.g., organization; autopoiesis) to the social system itself. The second derives an explanation of the social system from the phenomenological aspects of the theory (e.g., the observer;

languaging). These two approaches have demarcated the lines of debate over the years. Before reviewing these alternatives in more detail, we shall briefly review what Maturana and Varela themselves have to say about social systems.

Maturana and Varela on Social Systems

Maturana considers social systems as emergent from or constituted by the interactivity of their participants, not as a priori abstract units. To Maturana, social systems are realized primarily in linguistic (consensual) domains. The character of a social system is dependent on the specific interactions among its participants and varies with changes in those interactions (e.g., regarding frequency, connectivity, membership). As a medium, the social system exerts influence upon individual participants through affordances for and regularities in their interactivity, and this influence is recursively exercised upon the emergent social system through the participants' ongoing interactions. The participants may operate in multiple social systems (e.g., teams, clubs), although within each one they function as if engaged in a distinct domain of interactions. Distinctions (to an observer) among behaviours in different such settings are construed as roles delineating individual activity within the respective social domains. Because these roles are dynamic descriptions, the participant (as an observer) may recursively distinguish among them, allowing her to differentiate among (and realize) multiple such roles within one such social domain.

Social Systems Theories

Systems theories highlight the role of family systems and broader social systems in the etiology and maintenance of conduct problems.

Family systems theory. Within the family therapy tradition, the structural, functional and strategic schools have been most influential in offering a framework for understanding how conduct disorders are maintained by patterns of family interaction and how they may be resolved by intervening in these patterns. At a structural level, families with youngsters who have conduct problems are more disorganized than other families. Rules, roles and routines are unclear. Communication is indirect, lacking in empathy and confusing. There is also an absence of systematic family problem-solving skills. The members are more emotionally disengaged from each other in comparison with other families. In addition, families with youngsters who display conduct problems have difficulties maintaining clear unambiguous intergenerational hierarchies and negotiating lifecycle transitions.

With respect to ambiguous hierarchies, conduct problems are maintained if a youngster becomes involved in conflicting overt and covert hierarchies with the parents. The overt hierarchy in most families involves a spoken acceptance that both parents share a strong coalition around which there is a boundary which separates the parents hierarchically from the child so that the child is to some degree subservient to the wishes of both parents. Where children have conduct problems, in addition to this overt hierarchy, there is typically a covert hierarchy in which the child and one parent share a strong cross-generational coalition around which there is a covert boundary which separates them hierarchically from the other parent. This covert hierarchy is not spoken about or denied. Usually it is the mother and child who share the covert coalition and the father who is hierarchically inferior to this dyad. Haley refers to this family structure as the pathological triangle. Not surprisingly, parents in families with this organizational problem often have marital difficulties.

With respect to lifecycle transitions, many families in our culture evolve through a series of predictable stages of the life-cycle. Haley has argued that some families with youngsters who have conduct problems become stuck at the stage of being a family with adolescents living at home and have difficulty making the transition to being a family in the empty nest stage of development. These families often display the structure described as the pathological triangle. The delinquent behaviour may serve the function of preventing the family from splitting up.

Family therapy based upon structural and strategic systems theory aims to help families become more coherently organized. There is some evidence that family therapy based on these structural and functional principles is a more effective treatment for preadolescents and young adolescents with conduct problems than either non-directive family therapy or individual therapy.

Sociological theories. A variety of sociological theories have posited a causal link between deviant antisocial behaviour typical of conduct disorders and aspects of the wider sociocultural context within which such behaviour occurs. Anomie theory is a commonly cited exemplar of this body of theories. According to anomie theory, theft and other related antisocial behaviour such as mugging and lying are illegitimate means used by members of a socially disadvantaged delinquent subculture to achieve material goals valued by mainstream culture. Anomie is the state of lawlessness and normlessness that characterizes such subcultures. Treatment premised on this theory must provide delinquents and their peer groups with legitimate means to achieve societal goals. Remedial academic programmes, vocational training programmes, and treatment foster care are the main treatment approaches implicated by this theory. There is some evidence for the efficacy of treatment foster care. *Multisystemic ecological theory.* This position entails the view that multiple systems (including the individual, the family, the school and the community) are involved in the genesis and maintenance of conduct problems and consequently effective treatment must target multiple systems rather than any single system. Bronfenbrenner's model of ecologically nested systems is the foundation for this theory. Conduct disorders, it is argued, are maintained by multiple factors in these multiple ecologically nested systems. Important individual factors include difficult temperament, early separation experiences, hostile attributional bias, poor social skills, difficulties learning prosocial behaviour from experience, and academic learning difficulties. Family factors include family disorganization, ambiguous family hierarchies, parent-child attachment difficulties, parenting and discipline problems, marital discord and difficulty negotiating family lifecycle transitions. School factors include patterns of inter-action that maintain school-based discipline problems, attainment difficulties and lack of educational resources. Community factors include involvement with deviant peers, drug abuse and involvement in poorly co-ordinated multiagency networks. Treatment based on this model must be individually tailored and based on a multisystem ecological assessment. Treatment packages should include:

- Individual and group cognitive and social skills training
- Family therapy to reduce family disorganization
- School-based interventions to deal with interactional patterns that maintain school-based conduct problems and under-achievement
- Peer-group-based interventions to enhance prosocial peer relationships and reduce involvement in deviant peer groups.

Intervention

Personal characteristics of children and adolescents and psychosocial factors within the family and the wider system may predispose youngsters to develop conduct problems. Once these develop, they may remain confined to the home in the case of oppositional defiant disorder or spread to the community in the case of conduct disorder. The degree to which conduct problems escalate depends upon the degree to which there are problem-maintaining factors within the family, school and peer group. Despite their complexity, conduct problems are not completely refractory to treatment. Available evidence from empirical studies permits treatments of choice to be identified for preadolescent behaviour problems and more pervasive difficulties in adolescence.

For the circumscribed conduct problems, typical of children with oppositional defiant disorder, behavioural parent training is currently the treatment for which there is greatest empirical support. Behavioural parent training involves coaching parents to target and reinforce their children's prosocial behaviour while extinguishing their antisocial behaviour.

For pervasive conduct problems, typical of children with conduct disorder, family therapy, multisystemic therapy and treatment foster care are currently the treatments for which there is greatest empirical support. Family therapy involves helping parents, adolescents and other family members develop patterns of interaction that promote prosocial behaviour, better communication and family problem-solving. Multisystemic therapy extends beyond the family and includes intervention in the school and peer group and also at the individual level, so that problem-maintaining factors in all of these systems are modified. Multisystemic intervention may also involve addressing parents' personal difficulties such as depression or alcohol problems. Where parents' personal difficulties are too severe to permit them to engage effectively in multisystemic treatment, treatment foster care is the intervention of choice. Here, the conduct-disordered youngster is placed with a specially trained foster family who work collaboratively with the child's natural parents in implementing a behavioural programme which allows the youngster to develop prosocial behaviour and disengage from patterns of antisocial behaviour and interaction. With respect to service development, it may be most efficient to offer services for adolescent conduct disorder on a continuum of care. Less severe cases may be offered family therapy. Moderately severe cases and those that do not respond to circumscribed family interventions may be offered multisystemic therapy. Extremely severe cases and those that are unresponsive to intensive multisystemic therapy may be offered treatment foster care.

There are many other treatments for conduct disorders besides those highlighted in this chapter. Some are empirically untested so we do not know if they are effective. Some have been tested and found to be ineffective. And, most importantly, there are those treatments which have been tested and found to be harmful. There is now considerable evidence that intervention programmes which bring youngsters with conduct disorders together in groups lead to an increase in conduct problems. This may occur because youngsters reinforce each other's deviant behaviour and share a commitment to a deviant set of values and ideology. The fact that interventions which aggregate conduct-disordered youngsters are harmful unfortunately has not had a major impact on policies for dealing with juvenile delinquents. Indeed, many of our current policies in this domain exacerbate rather than ameliorate the problem.

Controversies

There are many controversies in the scientific study and clinical treatment of abnormal behaviour in childhood. A controversy concerning the diagnosis of conditions such as dyslexia (specific reading disability) or ADHD deserves particular mention because it highlights many of the ethical dilemmas psychologists have to face when studying and treating abnormal behaviour in childhood. There is a view that disorders such as ADHD or dyslexia are invalid fabrications and that giving children these diagnoses meets particular needs of parents, health or educational professionals, the pharmaceutical industry or society. For example, parents who have children with literacy problems may prefer to view their youngsters as 'bright but dyslexic' rather than 'slow learners'. Educational professionals may also support the diagnosis of dyslexia because they have an investment in developing programmes for dyslexic children and having these resourced through state funding. With ADHD, parents or schools may have difficulty meeting children's needs for intellectual stimulation, nurturance and clear limit-setting and so their children become aggressive and disruptive. In response these parents or educational professionals may prefer children in their care to receive a diagnosis of ADHD and a prescription for stimulant therapy, such as Ritalin (methylphenidate), rather than exploring ways to better meet the children's needs for intellectual stimulation, nurturance and clear limit-setting. In such instances pharmaceutical companies may support the diagnosis of ADHD, because they may stand to gain financially from offering a pharmacological treatment for behaviour problems.

There is an important ethical dimension to this position which views diagnoses as invalid fabrications designed to meet the needs of specific constituencies. For example, there are serious ethical problems with the diagnosis of a condition which is an invalid fabrication if the treatment for the condition (such as prescribing Ritalin) has harmful effects. Currently, the long-term effects of Ritalin or other stimulant therapies are unknown. Furthermore, if dyslexia and ADHD are invalid fabrications, then it is difficult to ethically justify committing public resources to funding their treatment when these resources might be better used to deal with the more fundamental problems which lead to society wanting to believe in diagnoses such as dyslexia and ADHD. These problems might be the stigmatization of slow learners or the reticence of society in supporting parents and teachers in developing ways to meet their children's needs for intellectual stimulation, nurturance and clear limit-setting.

An alternative to this viewpoint is that there is a large body of scientific evidence which supports the validity of diagnoses such as dyslexia and ADHD. There is evidence which shows that many children with dyslexia score high on IQ tests but poorly on measures of visual and auditory sequential memory. Such children have difficulties processing symbolic information and these difficulties are subserved by abnormal neurophysiological processes. Advocates of this viewpoint accept that dyslexia is a well-defined syndrome which deserves further scientific investigation. They also view the development and resourcing of remedial teaching programmes for dyslexic children as essential and argue that to fail to do this is discriminatory and unethical.

Similarly psychologists who study ADHD have shown that these children have difficulties sustaining attention and regulating their activity levels and these difficulties are subserved by abnormal neurophysiological processes. Furthermore, many children with a diagnosis of ADHD come from families in which parents have demonstrated good parenting skills with other siblings, so it may be argued that ADHD is not the outcome of poor parenting. Advocates of this viewpoint accept that ADHD is a well-defined syndrome requiring further scientific investigation and argue that it would be unethical to withhold pharmacological treatments such as Ritalin (or other stimulant therapies) for children with this disability.

In order to further our understanding of abnormal behaviour (such as literacy problems, attention difficulties and overactivity) continued scientific study is essential. In so far as the use of diagnostic categories as working hypotheses supports this, diagnoses such as dyslexia and ADHD are valuable. However, it is also valuable to study the social psychological processes that underpin diagnosis in clinical practice and to be vigilant for ethical problems that this may entail.

Summary

Attention deficit hyperactivity disorder is currently the most common term used for a syndrome characterized by persistent overactivity, impulsivity and difficulties in sustaining attention. Between 1 and 5 per cent of children have this syndrome, which is typically lifelong. Comorbid developmental language delays, specific learning difficulties, elimination disorders, conduct disorders and emotional disorders are quite common. A poor outcome occurs for about a third of cases who typically have secondary conduct and academic problems. Available evidence suggests that a marked genetic predisposition for an overactive temperament, which finds expression as a result of exposure to physical and psychosocial environmental risk factors during the pre- and perinatal periods and early infancy, causes the syndrome. Adjustment problems shown by youngsters with ADHD are in part maintained by problematic relationships within the family, school and peer group. Multimodal treatment includes behavioural parent training, school-based contingency management, self-regulation skills training, dietary control where food intolerance is present, and stimulant therapy. In addition assessment and treatment of comorbid problems may be required.

Conduct disorders are the most common type of childhood psychological problems. Children with conduct problems are a treatment priority because the outcome for more than half of these youngsters is very poor in terms of criminality and psychological adjustment. In the long-term the cost to society for unsuccessfully treated conduct problems is enormous. Up to 14 per cent of youngsters have significant conduct problems and these difficulties are far more common among boys. Comorbidity for conduct disorders and both ADHD and emotional problems such as anxiety and depression is very high, particularly in clinic populations. The central clinical features are defiance, aggression and destructiveness; anger and irritability; pervasive relationship difficulties within the family, school and peer group; and difficulties with social cognition. Specifically, there is a failure to internalize social norms and a negative bias in interpreting ambiguous social situations. Biological theories have focused on the roles of genetic factors, hormonal factors and arousal levels in the etiology of conduct problems. Classical psychoanalytic theory points to superego deficits, and object relations theorists highlight the role of disrupted attachments in the development of conduct disorders. Problems with social information processing and social skills deficits are the principal factors highlighted in cognitive theories of conduct problems. Modelling and coercive family processes have been identified by social learning theory as central to the development and maintenance of conduct difficulties. Systems theories highlight the role of characteristics of family systems, broader social network systems and societal systems in the etiology and maintenance of conduct problems. With oppositional defiant disorders in preadolescent children whose problems are confined to the home, behavioural parent training is the treatment of choice. With older children and adolescents who present with pervasive conduct problems, a multisystemic intervention programme targeting specific problem-maintaining processes or potential problem-resolving processes within the child, the family and the school is the most effective approach to treatment.

2

CLASSIFICATION, ASSESSMENT AND DIAGNOSIS

Introduction

One of the key features of the scientific approach to any subject is that it is systematic. The subject matter is grouped into categories of items that share similar features, or subjected to some other form of logical organization that makes it easier to see patterns or consistencies in what is observed. The natural sciences have long employed classification systems of various sorts, such as the periodic table of the elements used in chemistry or the phylogenetic systems of the biological sciences. Medical science began to make progress by identifying different illnesses and providing different forms of treatment for them. By comparison, there was very little consistency in the approach to abnormal behaviour. In Britain, a classification scheme was produced by the Statistical Committee of the Royal Medico-Psychological Association, but never utilized by the members.

One of these early schemes was that produced by Kraepelin, who is often regarded as the founder of modern psychiatry. His system identified symptom groups or syndromes, which he considered to have organic causes, *i.e.* they were physically based. For example, severe mental illnesses were divided into dementia praecox (now known as schizophrenia), which was thought to result from a chemical imbalance, and manic-depressive psychosis, which was thought to result from metabolic irregularities. Kraepelin's system was the basis from which modern diagnostic schemes developed.

There are two major schemes in use at present. These are: the *Diagnostic and Statistical Manual of Mental Disorders* (DSM), originally produced by the American Psychiatric Association in 1952 and now in its fourth revision; and the *International Classification of Diseases* (ICD) produced by the World Health Organization in 1948 to cover both physical and mental illness, and now in its tenth version. In both cases, the aim is to categorise mental disorder and thereby to provide diagnoses that can be linked with explanations and treatments. In the sections that follow we will examine these in more detail, with examples of cases that fit some of the categories. The procedures used to carry out the diagnosis, and an evaluation of the systems.

Diagnostic and Statistical Manual of Mental Disorders (DSM)

DSM IV is a multi-axial system, that is, it suggests that each individual who presents with abnormal behaviour can be assessed on five different axes of functioning representing different aspects of the person's life. Axes I and II represent the clinical syndromes. Axis III covers general medical conditions that may affect behaviour. Axis IV covers psychosocial and environmental problems, such as adverse life events. Axis V is a global assessment of psychological, social and occupational functioning. We will look at each of these in turn, but note that only the first three are compulsory for diagnosis. Looking at all of them, however, in the course of a clinical assessment, should give a much better basis for treatment than simply providing an Axis I or Axis II diagnosis, as used to be the case. This is partly because the medical (Axis III) and social (Axis IV) problems that the individual has can also be given attention. It is also obvious that overall functioning (Axis V) may not always be closely linked with symptoms. Anxiety, for example, may or may not impair ability to work, depending on the nature of the person's job.

Axis I covers the major syndromes, and Axis II covers more chronic conditions that can either underlie them or occur separately. Most people would receive a diagnosis on one axis or the other, but it is possible to have both. Eating disorders and mental retardation, for example, can occur separately or together. Axis II is divided into two categories: personality disorders and mental retardation. Both are chronic problems that may underlie Axis I syndromes. Personality disorders are long-term, rigid and maladaptive ways of behaving that cause stress and impair functioning.

Mental retardation is associated with intellectual functioning that is below average by the age of 18 years, and associated deficits in functioning. It is divided into four groups. The most common form is mild retardation, which usually results from lack of early stimulation or inadequate early relationships. Moderate, severe and profound retardation are generally biological in origin. They include Down's syndrome (which results from a chromosomal abnormality), foetal alcohol syndrome (which results from maternal alcoholism), cretinism (the result of endocrine malfunction) and disorders due to brain damage or disease in childhood.

For each of the syndromes or conditions identified on the axes described, DSM gives details of diagnostic features, prevalence and diagnostic criteria. For some, there is also information about cultural differences, aetiology and treatment. In the next section, we will look at some of the major categories in more detail.

Axis III aims to draw the clinican's attention to the possible behavioural consequences of some medical conditions. An apparently psychological disorder may prove to have a medical cause and may respond better to medical treatment. For example, hormone problems could result in mental retardation. Pregnancy complications or hormonal changes could lead to anxiety or a depressive disorder. In such cases, physical treatment may be more appropriate, and/or treatment may take a different form from that which would be given for anxiety or depression that has other origins. The conditions mentioned on Axis III include: infectious and parasitic diseases; endocrine, nutritional, metabolic and immune system disorders; diseases of the blood, circulatory, respiratory, digestive, nervous, genito-urinary, skin and musculoskeletal systems; complications associated with pregnancy and the perinatal period, and injury and poisoning.

Table 2.1. DSM IV: The Major Clinical Syndromes of Axis I

- Schizophrenia and other psychotic disorders (marked by disturbances of thought, emotion, perception, loss of contact with reality, delusions and hallucinations)
- Mood disorders (major depression, mania and bipolar disorder, *i.e.* swings between the two)
- Anxiety disorders (excessive fears, phobias, obsessive-compulsive disorder, panic attacks, post-traumatic stress disorder and generalized anxiety)
- Dissociative disorders (changes in normal consciousness such as loss of memory [amnesia] and identity [multiple personality disorder])
- Psychoactive substance abuse disorders (problems related to the use of alcohol, nicotine or other psychoactive drugs)
- Eating disorders (excessive concern about body weight and inability to regulate eating, as in self-starvation [anorexia] and alternate bingeing and purging [bulimia])
- Somatoform disorders (excessive worry about health, and illness such as paralysis for which no physical cause can be found)
- Factitious disorders (claims of illness leading to excessive help-seeking, as in Munchausen's syndrome)
- Sexual and gender identity disorder (problems of identity, such as transsexualism, and of arousal, such as impotence, fetishism and voyeurism)
- Sleep disorders (insomnia, apnea, narcolepsy and sleepwalking)
- Delirium, dementia, amnestic and other cognitive disorders (resulting from ageing, poisoning or disease of the brain, such as Alzheimer's disease)
- Disorders of infancy, childhood or adolescence (autism, attention deficit hyperactivity disorder or ADHD and learning disorders)
- Impulse control disorders (pyromania or fire-setting, gambling, kleptomania)
- Adjustment disorders (excessive anxiety and depression resulting from life stresses such as bereavement)

Table 2.2. DSM IV: Personality Disorders of Axis II

- Antisocial personality (indifference to the feelings of others, criminal behaviour, lack of self-control and irresponsibility)
- Obsessional personality (excessive adherence to rules and detail, striving for perfection, lack of emotional response)
- Paranoid personality (tense, self-important, suspicious, sensitive to criticism) Schizoid personality (solitary, withdrawn, poor social skills and limited emotional expression)
- Histrionic personality (sociable, but egocentric, insincere and shallow, with emotional displays)
- Narcissistic personality (self-important, attention-seeking, exhibitionistic, fantasises about success and power)
- Dependent personality (lack self-esteem, cannot cope with everyday life, cannot assume responsibility)

Axis IV is not compulsory, meaning that clinicians are not required to use this axis as part of their diagnostic process. However, it is useful because it draws attention to other aspects of functioning that may have contributed to the individual's problems, or may be the result of their behavicural difficulties. Either way, they may also need to be addressed in the course of treatment. In general, clinicians are encouraged to note only the problems that have arisen during the previous year, although there are cases (*e.g.* post-traumatic stress disorder) where a longer view may be necessary.

Table 2.3. Axis IV of DSM: Psychosocial and Environmental Problems

Type of problem	Examples
Primary support group	Death or ill-health of family member; sibling rivalry; sexual or physical abuse; divorce, remarriage or separation
Social environment	Lack of social support, loss of friendships, discrimination, retirement or other transition
Educational	Illiteracy, academic problems, conflict at school, bullying

(Contd.)

Type of problem	Examples
Occupational	Stress, dissatisfaction or discord, unemployment or threats of redundancy
Housing	Homelessness, poor housing, discord with neighbours
Economic	Poverty, lack of welfare support
Health care	Inadequate services or insurance, lack of transport
Legal	Arrest or imprisonment, being a victim of crime or being involved in litigation

Axis V is the Global Assessment of Psychological, Social and Occupational Functioning (GAF scale). This provides a 100-point rating scale from 'superior functioning' down to 'unable to function' across all of the areas mentioned. Physical or environmental impairments are not included. A summary of the ratings is given in Table 2.4. There are also individual scales for measuring social and occupational functioning (SOFAS) and relationship functioning (GARF). The legal criteria, as well as many of the DSM diagnostic criteria, may require these areas to be assessed. Some individuals with severe problems can nevertheless function well; others with comparatively mild problems may be completely unable to function.

Table 2.4. The Global Assessment of Functioning Scale from DSM IV

Rating band	Description of functioning
100-91	Superior across a wide range of activities
90-81	Good in all areas, generally satisfied with life, minimal symptoms, only everyday problems
80-71	Transient symptoms in response to stress, only slight impairment in functioning
70-61	Mild symptoms (*e.g.* insomnia) or difficulties in functioning, but able to maintain personal relationships
60-51	Moderate symptoms (*e.g.* panic attacks) or difficulties in functioning (*e.g.* conflicts with others)

Rating band	Description of functioning
50-41	Serious symptoms of impairments (*e.g.* suicidal, unable to keep job)
40-31	Major impairment in several areas or impairment in communication
30-21	Serious impairment in communication (*e.g.* incoherent) or delusions, or inability to function in most areas (*e.g.* no job, home or friends)
20-11	Some danger of hurting self or others, or occasional failure to maintain personal hygiene, or extremely impaired communication (*e.g.* mute)
10-1	Danger of severely hurting self or others (suicidal or violent) or no personal hygiene

After using all of the scales to assess an individual, a clinician might come up with the following diagnosis:

Axis I : Generalised anxiety disorder
Axis II : Dependent personality disorder
Axis III : HIV positive
Axis IV : Problem related to occupation (lost job)
Axis V : GAF = 35

This is a relatively simple case; many individuals will have more than one identifiable problem—for example, there may be a somatoform disorder as well as an anxiety disorder.

Progress exercise. Link each one of the behavioural problems on the left with one of the categories given on the right. Check your answers against Table 2.1 when you have finished.

Loss of contact with reality	Mood disorders
Excessive alcohol consumption	Impulse control disorders
Starving oneself	Schizophrenia and other psychotic disorders
Swinging between elation and depression	Anxiety disorders
Excessive fear some time after a traumatic experience	Psychoactive substance abuse disorders
Changing from one personality to another	Somatoform disorders
Gambling to excess	Dissociative disorders
A physical problem with no physical cause	Eating disorders

Axes I and II: Major Categories

In this section, we will be taking a closer look at the DSM IV diagnostic criteria for just five of the conditions listed in Axes I and II. These categories are based on the presence of clusters of symptoms, an approach endorsed by the medical model. Note that other models (*e.g.* the humanistic approach) may not accept this way of dealing with mental disorder. The conditions that we will be looking at here are: schizophrenia; major depression; obsessive-compulsive disorder; bulimia nervosa; antisocial personality. Space limitations preclude any more coverage than this, but the interested reader is referred to more detailed texts at the end of this chapter. A case study is also provided for each condition by way of illustration.

Schizophrenia

John was referred to a psychiatrist at the age of 22, after leaving home to go to college. Prior to that, he lived at home with his mother and sister, and had always had problems making friends. Living in a shared house with other students proved to be difficult, and he spent increasing amounts of time in his room. He began to think that the other people in the house were plotting against him, and imagined that they were standing outside his door and shouting abuse. As his work began to suffer, he began to have paranoid thoughts about his college lecturers. This eventually extended to the belief that MI5 had bugged the house with microphones hidden in the walls. After he left college and returned to the family home, he had little energy and no interests. He remained unemployed and continued to avoid contact with anyone outside the home.

This is an example of a psychotic disorder, a group of conditions that share the feature of being divorced from reality and lacking any insight into the condition. The symptoms vary widely, and hence DSM gives details of five subtypes—catatonic, paranoid, disorganized, undifferentiated and residual. Here we will just be looking at the general picture. Broadly speaking, there are two groups of symptoms the positive symptoms; which consist of excessive behaviours, and the negative symptoms, which consist of behavioural deficits. The behaviours affected may be cognitive, emotional and psychomotor.

Positive symptoms include thought disturbances such as delusions. These are thoughts that appear to most people to be misinterpretations of reality, for example, delusions of persecution or of grandeur, or a conviction that thoughts are being inserted into the mind by aliens. Thoughts, and their expression in language, are frequently confused, leading to loose associations (shifting from one topic to another), and perseveration (repetition of statements). Hallucinations (perceptions that occur in the absence of the appropriate external stimuli), particularly the hearing of voices, may occur. Movements may be excessive in style or amount. Emotions are often inappropriate to the occasion, such as laughing at bad news.

Negative cognitive symptoms may include a tendency to say very little (alogia). Emotionally, the person may report an inability to feel pleasure (anhedonia), display very little emotion (blunted or flat affect), or show inappropriate emotional responses. There may be social withdrawal, and loss of volition leading to apathy. Movement may become repetitive, or there may be no movement at all, a state known as catatonia.

Table 2.5. Diagnostic Criteria for Schizophrenia

The criteria have been identified as involving the presence of two or more of the following characteristic symptoms for a significant proportion of the time during a 1-month period:

- delusions;
- hallucinations;
- disorganized (*e.g.* incoherent) speech;
- grossly disorganized or catatonic behaviour;
- negative symptoms such as lack of emotion, speech or motivation.

This must be associated with marked inability to function in at least one major area, such as work, relationships and self-care. Signs of disturbance must continue for at least 6 months, and must not be due to mood disorder, schizoaffective disorder, substance abuse or medical conditions. There are also four subtypes: paranoid (delusions and hallucinations predominate); catatonic (motor disturbance predominates); disorganized (emotional disorder and disorganization of speech and thought predominate); and undifferentiated (apathy, loss of interest and social withdrawal).

Major Depression

Monica was persuaded by a priest (whom she had gone to see about her relationship difficulties) that she needed to see a counsellor. She had experienced problems with relationships, including parental, since childhood. She had never known her father, felt distant from her stepfather, and had a mother who used alcohol to alleviate her own relationship problems. After an initial abusive relationship, she had found herself a more suitable partner. All seemed to be well until he began to pay less attention to her and became more absorbed in his job. At the same time, she had lost her job, and showed little inclination to find another. She started to become less interested in her old activities, and neglected her friends. She felt useless, and often stayed in bed all day crying, particularly when her partner was away on business, which increased her feelings of being unable to cope. Despite being presented with evidence to the contrary, she felt that her friends and family disliked her. Finally, she began to think about committing suicide.

This is one of a group of disorders characterised mainly by emotional disturbance. Other areas of functioning that may be affected include cognitive, motivational, behavioural and physical. The mood changes are severe and long-lasting, and include feelings of intense sadness and emptiness, and loss of pleasurable feelings such as affection and enjoyment. Cognitively, patients have a very negative view of life, present and future, and of themselves. They may feel so worthless that they think they would be better off dead. There may be confusion and memory impairment. Their motivation to carry out everyday activities is considerably reduced, and to do anything is a great effort. Activity levels are low, movements slow, and they may stay in bed all day. There are also physical symptoms such as loss of appetite, constipation, loss of sexual drive, intolerance of noise and bright lights, and weight changes.

These symptoms should cause significant impairment in key areas of functioning, and should not be attributable to substance abuse, medical conditions or bereavement within the last 2 months.

Table 2.6. Diagnostic Criteria for Major Depression

Five or more of the following (including at least one of the first two) must be present most of the time during the same 2-week period:

- depressed mood;
- loss of interest or pleasure in most activities;
- changes in weight or appetite;
- reduced or increased sleep;
- restlessness or lethargy;
- feelings of worthlessness or guilt;
- inability to concentrate or make decisions;
- recurrent thoughts of death and suicide.

Obsessive-compulsive Disorder

Phillip's father was the manager of a health food shop. Even as a child, Phillip was very tidy, unlike his brother. As he grew up, he became more particular about cleanliness and tidiness issues. His college work was always very neatly done, and he washed his hands several times each day. He was particularly upset by having to share a toilet seat with flatmates when he went to college. Several relationships with women had ended due to his hoarding and obsessive behaviours. Every morning, he had to carry out several rituals in the bathroom, which necessitated him getting up at 4.30 am. His shaving equipment was laid out precisely, all items facing the right direction and in the correct order and position, and he shaved according to an exact pattern. Any error or interruption meant that he had to repeat the process from the beginning. When driving to work, if he travelled over a bump in the road, he would have to go back and make sure that he had not hit anybody. The journey would generally take twice as long as it should have, and he would be late for work. As a result, he had already lost one job and was having difficulties with the current one.

This is an example of the group of conditions known as the anxiety disorders. The characteristic feature of the group is, as the name implies, fear and anxiety that appear to be groundless. Although anxiety may be observed in some other disorders, such as schizophrenia, in this case the individual is aware that the behaviour is unreasonable but simply cannot control it; such insight is not found in the more severe conditions. Obsessions are recurrent thoughts, images or impulses that invade consciousness and are very difficult to control. They may take the form of doubts (*e.g.* about whether the door was locked when the person left the house), fears about doing things that are prohibited (*e.g.* dancing on a gravestone), persistent images (*e.g.* of a baby being flushed down a toilet), impulses (*e.g.* to drink a pot of ink), or thoughts about the future. Compulsions are repetitive, stereotyped behaviours that have to be performed, often in response to the obsessive thoughts, in order to keep anxiety at bay. They usually take the form of counting (*e.g.* paving stones on the way to work), cleaning (*e.g.* wiping door handles after every use), checking (*e.g.* that doors and windows are locked several times before leaving home) or avoidance (*e.g.* refusing to touch any other member of the family).

The diagnostic criteria for obsessive-compulsive disorder are shown in Table 2.7. These must interfere significantly with normal functioning, must take up more than 1 hour per day and must be distressing. They must not be due to another Axis I disorder or to substance abuse or medical conditions.

Table 2.7. Diagnostic Criteria for Obsessive Compulsive Disorder

Obsessions or compulsions must be present, and the individual must be aware that they are unreasonable. Obsessions are defined by:

- recurrent, intrusive thoughts, impulses or images that cause anxiety;
- these must extend beyond everyday worries;
- the individual must recognize that they are produced by his/ her own mind and must try to suppress or neutralise them.
- Compulsions are defined by:
- repetitive behaviours that the person feels compelled to carry out;
- they are carried out with the aim of reducing distress but are excessive or not logically related to the problem concerned.

Bulimia Nervosa

A child of two successful parents, Devika was persuaded to see a psychologist when her boyfriend found her vomiting after a bingeing session. Her father was a lawyer, obsessed with success, and her mother was a very attractive woman who was obsessed with appearances. Devika had never felt able to satisfy either of them. Weight control had always been an issue since she was teased about it as a child, and she had learnt about controlling it by vomiting from a friend. She had also seen a psychiatrist for depression in the past, and regularly abused several drugs including alcohol. By the age of 22, she had reached the stage where she was bingeing and purging several times a day, and often had to shoplift the food needed as she could not afford to buy it. She believed that she was overweight, although she was not, had not had a period for several years and had no interest in sex.

This is part of a group of eating disorders. It usually occurs in females, after a period of intense dieting, and involves episodes of uncontrolled overeating (binges) followed by purges (*e.g.* self-induced vomiting, use of laxatives or diuretics, excessive exercise or fasting) by way of compensation. Weight usually stays within the normal range, although it may fluctuate noticeably. The binges may be triggered by tension or depression, possibly as the result of some upsetting event. Typically, there will be about 10 episodes in a week. Massive amounts of high-calorie, 'forbidden' foods will be gobbled down in secret without even tasting them; this will be followed by feelings of guilt and depression, together with fears about weight gain.

Bulimics often have a history of mood swings and low tolerance for frustration and boredom. They find it difficult to control their impulses, are generally quite emotional, and may also abuse alcohol and other drugs. The physical consequences of bulimia are considerable in severe cases: tooth decay may result from the acidic content of vomit; potassium deficiency may result in heart or intestinal problems; acute dilation or rupture of the stomach is possible; and callouses may develop on the back of the hand where it rubs against the teeth when inducing vomiting. There are also social consequences, since social activities may be restricted as a result of the amount of time and money devoted to bingeing and purging. The diagnostic criteria for bulimia nervosa are given in Table 2.8.

Table 2.8. Diagnostic Criteria for Bulimia Nervosa

- Recurrent episodes of binge eating, which is identifiable as eating more food than most people would over a specific period of time, with a feeling of lack of control over the eating.
- Recurrent compensatory behaviour (*e.g.* vomiting, laxative use, fasting, exercising to excess) to prevent weight gain (subtypes of purging and non-purging are identified by the nature of the compensatory behaviours).
- Bingeing and compensating should occur at least twice weekly for 3 months.
- Self-evaluation is overly influenced by body shape/weight
- These behaviours do not occur solely during anorexic episodes.

Antisocial Personality Disorder

Following the divorce of their parents, Kanth and his brother both suffered physical abuse at the hands of their father before being returned to the custody of the mother. She was a heavy user of drugs and alcohol. Problems at school led to him being expelled, and eventually being categorised as severely emotionally disturbed. At the age of 12, he was caught shoplifting. By 14 he was committing burglaries. After running away from home, he lived by theft and drug-dealing, and was eventually put into a home for juvenile offenders until he was 18. On his release, drug-dealing became his main source of income, and he continued to be arrested for minor offences. Relationships with females were short-lived. He came to the attention of the authorities again when, after several episodes of domestic violence, he stabbed his current girlfriend and was convicted of attempted murder. He was hostile to the psychologist and refused to answer any of the questions put to him. The psychologist found that he had little tolerance for stress and felt inadequate. He had come to deal with all his problems by using drugs and violence, neither of which he could control. His own satisfaction was his sole motivation, and he had little regard for the feelings of others.

This is one of a group of personality disorders in which the behaviour problem impairs social or occupational functioning. The antisocial personality is also referred to as sociopathic or psychopathic. The main characteristic is that they cause a great deal of distress to others, rather than feeling distressed themselves. Repeated criminal behaviour is likely, although not all criminals have an antisocial personality, nor are all antisocial personality cases criminals. Offences often include violence, prostitution, theft, drugs- or alcohol-related offences. Behaviour is irresponsible in a variety of ways. For example: regular employment is unlikely; there may be little or no evidence of parental behaviour; relationships may be limited to short-term sexual liaisons; lying and impulsivity may be evident, and may lead to financial problems; there may be little evidence of any feelings of guilt or remorse. The diagnostic criteria are given in Table 2.9.

Table 2.9. Diagnostic Criteria for Antisocial Personality Disorder

- The individual should be at least 18 years old, with previous history of conduct disorder before the age of 15.
- Since 15, there should be evidence of disregard for the rights of others, as shown by at least three of the following: repeated unlawful acts; deceitfulness; impulsivity; physical aggression; disregard for the safety of self or others; irresponsible behaviour; lack of remorse.
- This should not be part of a schizophrenic or manic disorder.

Progress Exercise

Consider each of the five case studies presented in the chapter in the light of the five DSM axes, and present as full a diagnosis as you can. Note for each of them which Axis I and II criteria their symptoms may fulfil, and whether any Axis III and IV problems may be present. Then suggest a rating for Axis V

International Classification of Diseases (ICD)

ICD 10 has a section devoted to mental disorders; the main categories are given in Table 2.10. There is also a multiaxial system for mental disorders that affect children and adolescents. According to this, Axis II is specific delays in development, Axis

III is intellectual level, Axis IV is medical conditions, Axis IV is abnormal psychosocial conditions and Axis VI is the global assessment of functioning.

Table 2.10 ICD 10: Major Categories of Mental Disorder

Category	Examples
Organic disorders	Alzheimer's and amnesia due to organic damage/disease
Schizophrenia, schizotypal and delusional disorders	Schizophrenia
Psychoactive substance use disorders	Alcohol and drug-related problems
Mood (affective) disorders	Depression, mania and manic depression
Neurotic, stress-related and somatoform disorders	Phobias, generalised anxiety, obsessive-compulsive disorder, multiple personality
Behavioural disorders associated with physiological and physical factors	Eating disorders, sexual dysfunction not organically caused
Disorders of adult personality and behaviour	Personality disorder, habit and impulse disorder, disorders of gender, identity and sexual preference
Mental retardation	Mild, severe and profound
Disorders of psychological development	Disorders of speech, language and learning, autism, Asperger's syndrome
Disorders with onset in childhood and adolescence	Attentional and conduct disorders, tics, enuresis, stuttering
Unspecified	

Comparing DSM and ICD

As both ICD and DSM are classifying the same behaviours, it should not be too surprising that they are very similar. Both, for example, have a category for psychoactive substance-related disorders, for mental retardation and for personality disorders. However, there are some differences worth pointing out here. The most obvious difference is that (adult) ICD has only one axis, whereas DSM has five. ICD also appears to have fewer categories; for example, ICD groups neurotic, stress-related and somatoform disorders into one group, whereas DSM has four groups (anxiety, dissociative, adjustment and somatoform disorders) covering the same behaviours. Similarly, ICD has one group for disorders of adult personality and behaviour, whereas DSM has four (personality disorder, sexual and gender identity disorders, impulse control disorders and factitious disorders). On the other hand, DSM has one group for disorders first diagnosed in infancy, childhood or adolescence, whereas ICD has two (behavioural and emotional disorders with onset usually occurring in childhood or adolescence, and disorders of psychological development).

Clinical Assessment Procedures

Following referral, assessment by clinicians will be the first step in the process of helping persons suffering from mental disorder. It will take different forms depending on the training and biases of the clinician (for example, a counsellor assesses but does not diagnose) but the basic principles will remain the same. In this section we will look at the general principles and then the range of methods that may be used.

Principles of Assessment

What is clinical assessment and why is it used?

Clinical assessment is the process of gathering information about a client in order to gain a better understanding of the person. An assessment method (or methods) will be chosen by the clinician, and the results interpreted and written up in a report. Assessment will be carried out for three main reasons (although not all assessments will involve all three):

- **Diagnosis and screening.** Diagnosis is the process of outlining the symptoms of the patient and seeing how they fit the syndromes detailed in the classification system. To identify the client's problem is an important first step in deciding on the correct treatment. Diagnosis may also be required in order to determine whether or not the client is to be judged sane for legal purposes. Screening may be needed to select clients who would be most appropriate for particular treatment programmes.
- **Evaluation of therapeutic interventions.** It is important to measure the behaviours that are being targeted before the intervention begins, in order to have a baseline against which post-intervention measures can be compared.
- **Research.** Quantitative or qualitative measurement is essential to any programme that is attempting to test hypotheses about

the causes of behaviour problems, such as the link between media violence and aggression in children for example.

What are the properties of a good assessment system?

As has already been made clear, assessment needs to provide a measurement of the behaviours concerned. This may be qualitative (simply indicating what type of behaviours are displayed), or quantitative measurement (indicating how much of the behaviour is shown). The latter is usually preferred because it is more precise. In order to be considered scientific, the measurement must also be objective; this means that it should not be influenced by anything other than the behaviour under consideration. In particular, it is important to rule out the influence that the clinician may have at all stages of the assessment process. It is also necessary in some cases to compare the person being assessed with the population at large in order to see if they are abnormal. In order to do this, the test or procedure used must provide some idea of population norms for that behaviour. The procedure by which this is done is referred to as standardization, and involves giving the test to a large sample of the population in order to find the average score.

The key issues to consider when evaluating an assessment system are reliability and validity. By implication, these issues also relate to the classification system (*i.e.* DSM or ICD) that is used in conjunction with assessment, since they cannot be evaluated independently. We will be returning to reliability and validity throughout the chapter, so it is important to explain their meaning at this stage. You need to bear them in mind as we explore the assessment techniques.

Reliability

A reliable test is one on which an individual will achieve the same score each time he or she is tested. This means that it must be stable across time (**test-retest reliability**) – assuming of course that the behaviour concerned is stable. Anxiety, for example, may be expected to fluctuate, whereas compulsive behaviours should be stable. It must also yield the same results irrespective of who administers the test (known as interscorer or **interrater reliability**); this requires the scoring system to be clear-cut, so that it cannot be interpreted differently by different users. Finally, it must show internal consistency, in that all of the test items must be good indicators of the behaviour concerned (measured by Cronbach's alpha or **split-half reliability**). If some are not, they may erroneously inflate scores on the test.

Validity

Validity refers to whether or not the test actually measures what it claims to measure. A personality test may be reliable, in the sense of being consistent, for example, but it may be a test of intelligence or literacy rather than personality if the questions are too difficult to understand. It follows that a test may be valid for one purpose, but not for another. A PET scan, for example, is a valid measure of brain activity but not of intelligence. There are several different types of validity. **Face validity** refers to whether the items in the test seem to be good examples of the behaviour concerned. If we are considering aggression, for example, is it appropriate to include items about verbal as well as physical aggression? **Construct validity** requires the test to be based on a theory for which there is some support. Many tests of personality, for example, are based on particular theories; the same is not true of tests of intelligence, where the tests often preceded the theories and the theories are general rather than specific. Validity can also be shown by the test being correlated with another measure of the same thing (sometimes called **criterion validity**). If this is carried out at the same time, this is known as **concurrent validity**. A PET scan, for example, can be used as an indicator of Alzheimer's disease, against which other assessment procedures can be validated. If the other measure is given later, it is called **predictive validity**; thus an intelligence test score may be related to future academic progress.

Both reliability and validity will be affected by the applicability of the test used to the people it is used with (in terms of factors such as culture and age, for example), and by other biases such as responses to any emotional content in the test, complexity of questions and general response biases.

In practical situations, it is also necessary to consider the test's **clinical utility**. This can be described as its 'hit rate' – how often it identifies correctly that someone has a particular problem or is clear of it. A good test should lead to a high proportion of correct diagnoses and should do this more quickly and cheaply than other methods. A weak test may incorrectly miss people with problems (false negatives) or give positive diagnoses to those who do not have problems (false positives), both of which can be harmful. Cost-effectiveness assessments have to bear this in mind. A particularly good example is given by the case of child abuse, where mistakes can have grave consequences. Errors are particularly likely if the condition concerned is rare, *i.e.* it has a low base rate.

Progress Exercise

Define the meaning of the following: test-retest reliability; interrater reliability; split-half reliability; face validity; construct validity; concurrent validity; predictive validity.

When you have finished you can check your answers against the terms given in the glossary.

Methods of Assessment

A variety of methods are available to clinicians, all of which have advantages and disadvantages. All measurement is subject to errors, so we need to know the tolerance limits of each method and the best circumstances in which to apply it. Some methods are more suitable for certain aspects of functioning, therefore to obtain an overall picture a combination will be used on any particular case. The assessment needs to cover the case history (often known as the core assessment), behaviour, social and cognitive functioning, personality and mood, and neuropsychological functioning, although not all of these will be required in every case.

Clinical Interviews

Talking to the client is often the first stage of the assessment process. As well as gathering information about the presenting problem, including current feelings and concerns, relationships, employment and family issues, and personal history, the interview can tell the clinician a great deal in an indirect manner by providing an opportunity to observe the way that the client interacts. Posture, gestures, facial expressions, eye contact etc., can all provide useful information. Encouraging openness and free communication is essential if the interview is to be useful, so establishing rapport with the client and giving assurances of confidentiality are crucial at the outset. Computers have been introduced by some clinicians to conduct initial interviews. This obviously saves money and the clinician's time, but in turn reduces the opportunities for gathering information about nonverbal communication. In the medical sphere, it has been found that people will sometimes reveal more to a computer than to a doctor (presumably because they are less embarrassed), so computers may have advantages with some clients.

Clinicians from different persuasions will focus on different areas during the interview: for example, psychodynamic theorists may be more concerned with childhood experiences than behaviourists would be; socio-cultural theorists may be more interested in social conditions.

There are many different types of interview. One important distinction is between unstructured and structured interviews. In a structured interview, the client is asked open-ended questions and allowed to discuss whatever she or he feels is important. This has the advantage that the client, rather than the clinician, can determine the direction that the conversation takes. In the latter, the clinician uses a prepared list of questions, which has the advantage of allowing comparisons to be made between the responses of different individuals. It also ensures that no important issues or aspects of behaviour are omitted. Panic disorder, for example, may be explored by initally asking a screening question ('Have you ever felt anxious in a situation where most people would not feel afraid?'), followed by precise questions to assess severity ('Did you sweat?'). There are also versions for children, *e.g.* the DIS-C. The model that the clinician subscribes to may well dictate preference for one type of interview over another—a psychodynamic or a humanistic theorist may prefer an unstructured interview, for example, and behavioural, cognitive and medical theorists may prefer structured interviews.

A **mental state** interview may also be used, which aims to evaluate the current functioning of the client. It is presented in a structured form to ensure that particular areas are covered. Appearance, general behaviour, speech, mood, thought content, abnormal beliefs and experiences, memory, attention, values, and awareness of where they are and what is going on around them (orientation in time and space) will all be assessed.

Interviews provide most of the information required for the core assessment (case history), although some may come from the referral letter and from other parties such as social workers or relatives. Lindsay and Powell suggest that this should cover all of the items.

Table 2.11. Information needed for the Core Assessment

Reason for referral, including client's description of problem(s) and immediate reason for seeking help

- History of difficulties
- Medical, occupational, educational, sexual and marital history
- Current situation (job/home) and difficulties resulting from problem
- Effect of problem on biological functioning
- Effect of problem on others
- Abnormal moods, thoughts, sensory experiences
- Current appearance, behaviour and cognitive functioning
- Attitude towards problem
- Current drug use
- Family history of psychological problems

Interviews also contribute to the functional analysis of behaviour, (which identifies the reinforcements maintaining behaviour), and to the assessment of social functioning at work, at home, in relationships and in leisure activities.

Evaluation

Interviews are obviously the major source for a lot of useful information, but their reliability and validity are both questionable. The client may not be totally honest, may be embarrassed, or may simply make errors when recalling past events. The very nature of some syndromes, such as depression, where self-esteem is affected, means that clients are unlikely to recall personal experiences accurately. The clinician may be biased, or may affect the client's behaviour in a variety of ways, and the client may also affect the clinician. Paurohit, for example, have shown that the race, sex, age and appearance of the interviewer may influence the client's responses. Clinicians may also vary in their interpretation of information, and they may make errors when recording what was said, especially if they do not make detailed notes at the time. First impressions may affect the way that subsequent information is interpreted. Even when the same questions are asked of the same clients, it has been shown that different clinicians will obtain different information and form different conclusions.

Observations

In some cases it is desirable to see behaviours as they occur, rather than discuss them in an interview. The clinical observation allows this to be done, either in the natural setting or in a controlled environment. The interaction of a child with other family members, for example, may be recorded in the home, or in a mock living room in the clinic using a one-way mirror. Barkley used this approach with hyperactive children and their mothers. If the observation is to take place in the home, a participant observer may be employed; this is the use of someone with whom the child is familiar to carry out the observation. Teachers, for example, can be asked to give ratings of behaviour in the classroom using the Conners' Teacher Rating Scale. The advantage of this is that the child may behave more naturally. Typically, a relatively small number of behaviours (known as 'target behaviours') will be selected for observation, for reasons of practicality. Their frequency of occurrence and/or severity will be recorded over a specified period of time, as in the example in Table 2.12. Standardised scales, such as the Family Interaction Coding Scale, may be used for recording purposes.

It is important to look at not only the frequency of occurrence but at the sequences and patterns of behaviours to see what immediately causes them. This is the key feature of **functional analysis**, carried out by behavioural psychologists, to identify the reinforcements maintaining the client's undesirable behaviours. This can be carried out using the STAR system as a guide, and involves identifying:

Table 2.12. Behavioural Checklist for Performance Anxiety (after Pramod 1966)

Behaviour	Time period (minutes)								
	1	2	3	4	5	6	7	8	9
Face pale									
Muscles tense									
Swallows									
Voice shakes									
Stammers									
Lack of eye contact									

S: the setting conditions or environments in which the behaviour occurs;

T : the triggers or specific events that prompt the behaviour;
A : the antecedent events that occur before the behaviour;
R : the results of the behaviour for the client.

In some cases, where behaviours are infrequent, where the clinician cannot spend a long time with the client, or where thought processes (which cannot be monitored by outside observers) are involved, clients may be asked to *self-monitor*. For example, bulimics may be asked to record the feelings and situations that lead to the urge to binge, or obsessionals to record the frequency of their obsessive thoughts. This is useful to establish the antecedents that trigger behaviours.

Another type of observation occurs when measures are taken of physiological and neurological behaviours. Physiological measures such as changes in heart rate, blood pressure or muscle tension can be used to indicate the level of a client's anxiety. A plethysmograph can be used to record blood flow in the vagina or penis, as a measure of sexual arousal when assessing sexual disorders. In the case of neurological behaviours, instruments such as the electro-encephalogram or a scanner such as PET (Positron Emission Tomograph) can be used to record the electrical activity of the brain. The aim is to detect the presence and extent of brain damage or malfunction. Baxter, for example, measured the brain activity of obsessive-compulsive patients during various activities, compared with that of controls. They found that the patients showed greater activity in the caudate nuclei than did the controls. Andreasen used scanners to explore the size of the ventricles (fluid-filled spaces) in the brains of schizophrenics, compared to those of normal controls. The research showed that the ventricles were larger in the schizo-phrenics, particularly on the left side of the brain.

Evaluation

The observational method is particularly useful with children or other clients (such as schizophrenics) who are unwilling or unable to co-operate with interviews or tests. Some researchers have found observations to be better indicators of recovery after treatment than interviews and tests. However, observation is restricted in its application, since only observable, frequent behaviours can be studied; maladaptive thought processes cannot.

It is also limited in reliability and validity. The most important reliability issue is that of inter-observer reliability—do different observers give the same results? What one observer interprets as aggression, for example, another may not. It is generally found that initially they may not agree, although careful training and the use of checklists and clear definitions of the behaviours can improve this. Self-monitoring may have particular problems with respect to reliability. It can be improved by motivating clients using rewards, by training, and by informing them that their monitoring is being checked. *Reactivity* is the term used to describe change in behaviour that can result from observation (particularly self-observation). It is generally found that 'good' behaviour increases, and 'bad' behaviour decreases, indicating a therapeutic effect.

Validity may be limited by the change in behaviour of the client when he or she is aware of being watched the audience effect and also by the situation chosen for the observation (ecological validity). A child may misbehave at home, for example, but not at school. Zeigob showed that when mothers knew that they were being observed, they behaved more positively towards their children.

Physiological and neurophysiological observations are also subject to difficulties, although they are very precise when used properly. The equipment required is expensive and not always readily available. A great deal of training is usually required before it can be used with any accuracy. It often requires that recordings are taken in the artificial environment of the laboratory, and only limited behaviours can be carried out at the same time. The equipment itself may be frightening, and may change behaviour. It is not always easy to link any observed changes with the client's emotional state; for example, blood pressure may change as a result of many factors and feelings and not simply as a result of anxiety.

Psychometric Tests

Psychometric tests are specially devised instruments (often paper and pencil tests) that take a small sample of the client's behaviour in order to make inferences about broader aspects of their functioning. There are many different types for different purposes. For example, the Halstead-Reitan test battery and Bender-Gestalt test have been devised to assess different areas of neurological functioning. The Significant Others Scale (SOS) devised by Power provides ratings of how much social support clients expect from others in different situations. There are also specific tests for screening clients for psychiatric distress, such as the General Health Questionnaire or GHQ. Long-term difficulties can be assessed using the Symptom Check-List-90-Revised (SCL-90-R), devised by Derogatis. This consists of 90 questions designed to measure nine dimensions of psychopathology, including obsessive-compulsive problems, depression, paranoia, phobia, anxiety etc. Here we will look at intelligence and aptitude tests, personality questionnaires and projective tests.

Intelligence tests aim to provide a measure of general cognitive ability, often in the form of an intelligence quotient (IQ). There are many different tests available. Some, such as the Stanford-Binet and the Wechsler Adult Intelligence Scale (WAIS), are administered to individuals, and these are more likely to be used as clinical instruments. The WAIS has 11 subtests, including digit span, block design and vocabulary tests. There are other Wechsler tests for preschool children (the WPPSI) and for older children (the WISC). Other intelligence tests, such as the AH series (AH2, AH3 etc) are designed to be administered to people in a group situation. Many of the tests, but not all, are timed. Aptitude tests, such as the British Ability Scales, are similar but more specific, in that they focus on one particular ability, such as mechanical or spatial for example. Performance can then be compared with that of others of the same age. Many clinicians prefer a rapid, nonverbal screening test such as Raven's Progressive Matrices.

Evaluation

Most of the tests in current use have been carefully constructed and standardised on large samples of the population. They have high reliability in that the results obtained by the same person on different occasions will be similar, and high internal consistency. Test administrators, however, must always be on guard for illness and motivational and emotional problems that may affect a particular client's performance on the test. They also show good concurrent validity, relating well to school performance for example. However, their predictive validity is not always as good, probably because performance on either the test or the other measure can be affected by factors such as motivation. Construct validity can also be debated, as there is no agreed theory about what intelligence is. In connection with this, some psychologists have argued that the intelligence tests in current use focus on only a narrow spectrum of skills, ignoring 'streetwise intelligence' and interpersonal intelligence, for example. Finally, intelligence tests have been criticized for not being culture-fair, in the sense that individuals from minority groups or deprived backgrounds may be less familiar with the types of language or items used in the test, and may therefore not perform as well as other groups. Since the tests play an important role in the assessment of mental retardation and brain damage, as well as in the educational and occupational spheres, it is important to recognize this.

Personality questionnaires (or inventories) are self-report scales that require the client to respond to a series of statements by indicating whether or not each one applies to them. There are many different tests, all aimed at measuring different aspects of personality. Other tests measure affect or emotion (such as the Beck Depression Inventory), cognition or social skills. The Beck scale, for example, consists of 21 items with four responses to each, such as: I can work as well as I used to; it takes extra effort to get started doing something; I have to push myself to do anything; I can't work at all. One of the best known inventories is the Minnesota Multiphasic Personality Inventory. The current version contains 567 items such as 'I go to a party every week', 'I often feel hopeless about the future' and 'I am easily embarrassed' (each scored 'true', 'false' or 'cannot say'). It provides an assessment on 10 basic clinical scales as well as functioning at work, tendency to abuse drugs and vulnerability to eating disorders. The scales include schizophrenia, paranoia, depression, mania, introversion, hypochondria, hysteria, and fears and obsessions. On each scale, scores can range from 0-120. The normal score is 50 and a score above 70 is considered indicative of deviance. There are also scales that aim to detect lying, careless or defensive responding, or response sets such as a tendency to give negative answers. Tests such as the MMPI can be used together with more specific tests such as the State-Trait Anxiety Inventory where needed. The latter test asks people to rate how tense they feel, for example, both in general (trait) and at that time (state). This information will be supplemented with that obtained from interviews and observations.

Evaluation

Personality inventories have the advantage of being quick to administer compared with other methods of assessment. They are also quick to score (most can be computer-scored nowadays), objective, and provide an easy way of comparing responses of the client with the average in the population. Well-designed personality tests should also have good reliability and validity. For example, the Beck Depression inventory has a reasonable reliability correlation of 0.73 and accords with ratings of severity of depression given by psychiatrists. MMPI scales also relate well to clinical diagnoses.

The problem, as already indicated, is that their purpose is obvious to the client, who may then be able to fake responses. This type of problem, and the problem of response sets, can be solved to some extent by the use of specially designed test items to identify when this is happening. A more difficult problem is that in many cases clients may not have sufficient self-knowledge to give useful information about themselves. They may also respond in socially desirable ways—especially to items such as 'I go to a party every week'. Furthermore, not all characteristics are in fact stable over time; this makes it difficult to tell if the change observed is real or due to the test being unreliable. These tests may also not be culturally fair. In Puerto Rico it would not be considered abnormal to respond 'true' to the statement (included in the MMPI) 'evil spirits possess me at times'.

Projective techniques provide a different approach to the assessment of personality. Rather than requiring the client to choose a response from a set of options, projective techniques present clients with unstructured material to respond to as they see fit. The responses are then analysed with the aid of a test manual according to the nature of the images described and the style of the responses (*e.g.* whether the client responds to the whole design or just part of it). Computer-generated interpretations are now available for certain Rorschach scores, making interpretation more objective. Another test is the Thematic Apperception Test or TAT, which consists of a series of ambiguous pictures. In this case, the client is asked to make up a story about what is happening in each picture. Clients may also be asked to complete sentences, or to draw figures; this latter is particularly useful with children.

Evaluation

The Rorschach and the TAT are among the 10 most popular psychological tests. However, they present problems when it comes to interpretation. In reliability studies, different clinicians have been found to give different scores to the same responses, and although there are now standardised procedures for scoring the tests, they are not widely accepted. Trained clinicians using modern standardised versions can achieve high interrater reliability. However, Smith and Dumont found that 14% of the clinicians they sampled, who had no training in the use of projective tests, nevertheless used them to make diagnostic and aetiological inferences. Eighty-seven per cent of those who did so produced inferences that had no scientific basis.

Some support is available for the validity of projective tests. Compared with questionnaires, projective tests allow the client freedom of expression. They also have the advantage that faking of responses is difficult. Erdberg and Exner found the predicted increase in inanimate movement responses (*e.g.* seeing flames flickering), which are indicators of anxiety, in those awaiting surgery. However, the tests may also lack validity, for two reasons. First, the results do not always agree with independent judgements about the client made in other ways; second, some may be biased against minority groups, because the materials used may not be appropriate (*e.g.* the TAT does not have any pictures of minority group members).

Conclusion

There are clearly a variety of different ways in which the clinician can obtain the information needed in order to make informed decisions about the client. These methods differ in their utility according to the nature of the client, and also vary in terms of the key criteria of reliability and validity. The model of mental disorder adopted by the clinician will also affect the choice of method; a behavioural model would suggest an observational approach, for example, and a psychodynamic model an interview. Choice and utilisation of method, as well as putting information together and making a decision about the client, involve the clinician in an interpretative process that can easily lead to errors. Progress exercise

(i) Which methods of assessment – interviews, observations or psychometric tests - would you use to assess the following areas of a client's functioning?:

Case history; cognitive functioning; neuropsychological functioning; personality/mood; behaviour; social functioning.

Give examples of assessment instruments where you can.

(ii) Draw up a chart to show the advantages and disadvantages of the different methods of assessment outlined above.

Evaluation of Classification and Diagnosis

In previous sections we have explained the potential value of classification and diagnosis. Here we will be considering the scientific status of the existing systems and procedures, and the difficulties that may arise whenever classification systems are used. The first section, then, is a specific critique, whereas the second makes more general points.

Criticisms of the existing systems of classification

Blashfield and Draguns suggest that four criteria can be used for evaluation: coverage; reliability; **descriptive validity; predictive validity**. To these, we can add **aetiological validity**. We will consider each of these in turn.

Coverage. This refers to the idea that the categories included in the system should cover all of those who are in need of help. Early versions of DSM had good coverage, because the categories were so vague. The later versions have stricter criteria for each category, but needed to have more categories overall. DSM IV defines disorders in terms of observable symptoms that are more precisely described than in previous systems. This makes the categories more homogeneous but reduces coverage. Perhaps because of this, it also has several residual categories (such as 'psychotic disorder not otherwise specified'), often referred to as 'wastebasket categories' for cases that do not fit the system. For some categories, such as dissociative disorders, most patients receive 'not otherwise specified' (NOS) diagnoses. This indicates that the fit between clients and system is not particularly good. There are also codes (rather than categories) available for disorders that do not fit into the system, such as problems related to an unwanted pregnancy. DSM has V codes and ICD has Z codes.

Reliability. In order for the classification system to be seen as reliable, different clinicians should assign a given client to the same category. In general, agreement between clinicians about what a client's main difficulties are and how they are maintained has been found to be poor, even when they are given the same data about the client. Overlap between categories, and the fact that cases that fit the criteria exactly are rare, does not make the task any easier.

Studies on Agreement Between Clinicians

However, specific studies carried out on DSM have shown that it is increasing in reliability. For example, Beck asked four clinicians to diagnose 153 patients independently, using DSM I, and found that only 54% of their diagnoses were the same. Kendell found that if very specific categories were used for classification, reliability was as low as 32% in some cases. Since then, successive versions of DSM have attempted to clarify the categories and provide more specific, objective criteria for inclusion. In 1985, Lipton and Simon were still able to show that 75% of 131 cases were given different diagnoses by clinicians in one American hospital (*i.e.* agreement was 25%). However, looking at a different behaviour, Di Nardo reported around 70% agreement using DSM III and IIIR. The APA claim that version IV is more reliable than this, as a result of redrafting criteria for the categories that earlier research had shown to be particularly unreliable.

Other studies have explored the differences in reliability of different categories. Davison and Neale reported that the correlation between clinicians ranged from 0.92 for psychosexual disorders down to 0.54 for somatoform disorders, so there is clearly still a difference in reliability between categories. Nathan and Langenbucher reported that the reliability of a few categories (conduct disorder and substance abuse) had increased, but there had been no improvements in personality disorder (Axis II), and Axis I sleep, childhood and some schizophrenic disorders. Holmes found increased reliability using decision trees and computer programs to eliminate subjective bias on the part of clinicians.

Some researchers have argued that the lack of reliability just outlined may not be as bad as it seems. Falek and Moser, for example, made the point that medical diagnoses may not be any more reliable than those for mental disorders, reporting only a 66% agreement for the cause of death on death certificates (signed by two different doctors). This, however, is hardly reassuring, and Klein consider that further research is still required before DSM can be assumed to be acceptably reliable.

Cultural Variation

Another point to bear in mind here is cultural variation. For example, it has been shown that a diagnosis of schizophrenia was more likely to be given in Soviet Russia and in America than in the UK. Copeland found that within the UK the age and location of clinicians affected the diagnosis, with older, Glasgow-trained clinicians giving higher ratings for abnormal behaviour than younger, London-trained ones. This highlights the need for continuing training. Training clinicians in the use of specific criteria and standardised interviews has been found to improve agreement.

The system also seems to be applied in different ways to people from non-Western cultures. For example, schizophrenia seems to be overdiagnosed in West Indian and Asian immigrants to Britain. There are several reasons why this might be the case including the possibility that the difference accurately represents a different prevalence of schizophrenia in those ethnic groups. However, Garb found that when the amount and severity of symptoms were controlled, the difference was still observed, with African-American and Hispanic clients being more likely than whites to be diagnosed as schizophrenic. This indicates a diagnostic bias in this case.

Gender Differences

It has also been found that females are more likely than males to be diagnosed with histrionic and dependent personality disorders and depression, and males are more likely to be diagnosed with antisocial personality disorder and obsessive-compulsive disorder. This is found with both male and female clinicians. It may occur because some behaviours that are part of the traditional gender role for males or females are mentioned in the diagnostic criteria — for example, submissiveness and dependency are traditionally female behaviours, but are mentioned as important features of dependent personality disorder. Thus sexism in the categories themselves may be responsible for the observed differences in prevalence. Now we will move on to look at issues of validity; remember, however, that if the system is not reliable it cannot be valid.

Descriptive Validity

This depends on the categories themselves being homogeneous, and the symptoms being different from those of other categories. DSM IV operates in terms of 'prototypes'; it acknowledges that some features of disorders will be the same in different cases, but that others will vary. Hence it has a list of criteria for each disorder, of which a certain number must be evident, while others may or may not be present. Given this, it is not surprising that the categories are not homogeneous. Schizophrenics, for example, differ so widely that it is difficult to see what they have in common, and DSM has several subgroups for the category.

Individuals with different diagnoses may also show similar symptoms—depression may be seen in some anxiety disorders and in manic depression, for example. In fact, most patients do show comorbidity, meaning that they have several disorders at once. If disorders are prone to occur together, it raises questions about whether they are in fact separate disorders. Disorders most likely to be associated with comorbidity include depression, substance abuse, anxiety and personality disorders.

One way of trying to assess this type of validity is by comparing DSM categories against clinical judgement in field trials, and many of these were carried out prior to the publication of DSM IV. Spitzer asked large numbers of clinicians to rate clients on various criteria to see if they could agree on what was important. As a result, a proposed new category of self-defeating personality disorder was rejected, as it could not be clearly distinguished from the existing categories. However, Pope sampled 367 American psychiatrists, asking if they thought that Dissociative Identity Disorder should be included as a category in DSM IV. Only about a quarter felt that there was scientific evidence for its validity. However, this reference to clinical judgement as a criterion is a very limited form of validity - how do we know that clinical judgement is valid in the first place?

It is sufficient to note that for descriptive validity to be established it is more important to show that the category is distinct from others in terms of symptoms, causes and treatments.

Predictive Validity

This depends on the categories having predictive value in terms of the future course of the disorder, and has yet to be investigated fully. Heather pointed out that there is only a 50% chance of predicting which treatment will be given from the diagnosis. In some cases, there is evidence of predictive validity. For example, many schizophrenics improve when given neuroleptic drugs, whereas other types of client do not. Depressive clients respond well to electroconvulsive shock therapy; schizophrenics do not.

Aetiological Validity

This requires that all patients who have the same diagnosis should have developed the disorder for the same reason(s). This is clearly not the case. For example, schizophrenia would appear to have a genetic basis in some cases; in others, however, there is no evidence of a family history of the problem. Such differences may be the result of inadequacies in the diagnostic system. It is also possible that this type of validity is unattainable, simply because there are generally multiple causes for disorders.

DSM may also fail to be valid cross-culturally; Littlewood argues that Axis V of DSM IV makes ethnocentric (*i.e.* white Western) assumptions about the nature of family life, work and education. Lewis-Fernandez has criticised the fourth revision of DSM for ignoring the recommendations of the National Institute of Mental Health Committeee on Culture and Diagnosis as regards dissociative disorders, for example. Of the 36 recommendations aimed at taking cultural diversity into account, only 42% were included in the final version, and 'critique of the universality of DSM IV diagnoses was not tolerated'. The implication of this is that they are considered to be applicable world-wide.

Rosenhan's Study

Finally, in a very well-known study called 'On being sane in insane places', Rosenhan presented evidence that relates to the issue of validity.

The study was asking whether clinicians could reliably distinguish the sane from the insane. Remember that if they cannot do this, the system cannot be valid either, since reliability is a prerequisite for validity.

Briefly, Rosenhan's researchers presented themselves to admissions officers at psychiatric hospitals, claiming to hear voices but otherwise behaving as they normally would. They were admitted (mostly with a diagnosis of schizophrenia) and behaved normally once inside the hospital. Staff, however, interpreted their normal behaviours in ways consistent with the diagnosis. Writing notes, for example, was seen as pathological behaviour, and pacing the corridors as nervousness rather than boredom. It took the hospitals concerned 7-52 days to discharge the pseudopatients.

In a parallel study, staff were warned that 'fake' patients might try to gain admission to the hospital, and were asked to assess whether or not new patients were likely to be fakes (in fact there were no fake patients). Around 20% of new patients were assessed as fakes by at least one member of staff. This study shows that, in 1973 at any rate, staff could be deceived, and did find it difficult to discriminate between normal and mentally disordered individuals in a psychiatric hospital. However, as Kety has pointed out, using a fake blood capsule to simulate vomiting blood would hardly be a fair test of medical ability to diagnose the source of the blood. Similarly, faking the symptoms of mental disorder is not a fair test of clinicians' ability to diagnose that condition. However, the study does still demonstrate the clinicians' inability to assess the accurate information that was presented subsequently.

Compared with the data available on DSM IV, there are very few for ICD 10. However, it is thought that ICD 10 is an improvement on its predecessors and probably quite similar to DSM IV, although DSM is more specific in categories and symptomatology, and therefore probably more reliable. Sartorius reported from field trials that interrater reliability was particularly high for schizophrenia and substance abuse, but less good for personality disorders.

Practical Issues Regarding Classification

Clinical Bias

As implied in the definition of reliability, whatever the system in use for classification, it has to contend with the biases and limitations of the clinicians using it. At the outset, they may have different styles of interviewing and information-gathering, as noted earlier. Clinicians have been shown to pay more attention to data gathered earlier in the process than to later data and McCoy found that they put more weight on information from some sources (such as parents, rather than children, for example). Clinicians may expect people that they see to be abnormal, and overemphasise information that supports this idea. They also have personal biases relating to age, race, socio-economic status and gender. Political use of diagnosis as a form of social control may also influence decision-making processes.

Medical Basis

Many psychologists are also unhappy about the assumption inherent in the classification systems that mental disorders may prove to be biologically based and are therefore to be treated medically. This includes those who subscribe to the humanistic, psychodynamic, cognitive-behavioural, systemic and constructionist models. Szasz took this point further in his argument that there is no such thing as mental illness, because illness can only affect the body, not the mind. In practice, many clinicians have objected that DSM does not provide practical guidance about treatment. Lindsay and Powell further point out that DSM ignores functional analysis, which is an important part of many behavioural interventions used by psychologists.

Categories or Dimensions

The use of categories, rather than dimensions, has also been criticised on the basis that attempting to create clear-cut categories may be attempting to tidy up human behaviour too much. In practice, people are much too complex for this to be feasible. Most behaviours are in fact normally distributed in the population (*i.e.* are dimensional) rather than being bimodal (*i.e.* in categories such as normal/ abnormal). The argument for dimensions is still ongoing, but of course it has to face the problem of deciding on the appropriate dimensions to use. It may not prove to be appropriate for all disorders either, since some may be dimensional (*e.g.* mental retardation) while others appear to be categorical (*e.g.* dyslexia).

Individuals or Systems

A final point is that the current classification systems rely on the individual as the unit of analysis. The client is often seen and assessed in isolation from social influences. Some clinicians, especially those who adopt a family systems approach, regard this as inappropriate because the behaviour forms part of a complex pattern of interaction between individuals, and cannot be understood in isolation.

Ethical Issues Regarding Classification

In some instances, the use of classification and diagnosis can be seen to be harmful; this may be the case whether it is used correctly or incorrectly.

Legal Aspects

The first issue to consider is the legal consequences of the procedure. Although it is less common than it used to be now that care in the community is the norm, it is still possible under the Mental Health Act for individuals to be compulsorily detained in a psychiatric hospital. Commitment orders can be from 3 days to 6 months, and can include a provision for treatment (although only emergency treatment can be given without the patient's consent). Sectioned individuals also lose some rights (such as voting rights), and they are excluded from jury service and from holding gun licences.

As regards criminal law, in Britain individuals classified as suffering from a mental disorder can be judged incompetent to stand trial for criminal offences under the Criminal procedure (insanity and unfitness to plead) Act. This is an uncommon plea, and does not relate to ability to give evidence in court. They have to prove that they are incapable of doing at least one of the following:

- instructing counsel;
- appreciating the significance of their plea;
- challenging a juror;
- examining a witness;
- understanding and following evidence.

Even if sane at the time of the trial, they can put forward an insanity defence if they can convince the court that they were insane at the time of the crime. This goes back to the McNaughten (or M'Naghten) rules of 1843, which excuse the individual from responsibility if he can show that he did not know the act was wrong or was unaware of its nature. Again, this is rarely applied, as few people are disordered enough to qualify. A plea of diminished responsibility can also be presented in murder cases, under the Homicide Act. It allows the sentence to be reduced or a hospital order made.

Clearly, there can be a great deal to gain by doing this, although Szasz has noted the case of Joe Skulski, who was judged unfit to plead but ended up spending more time in a psychiatric hospital than he would have spent in prison had he been found guilty of the offence. On the other hand, Peter Sutcliffe (the 'Yorkshire Ripper') had such pleas rejected and was sent to prison for his crimes, where he has been brutalised by the other inmates. In Britain most mentally disordered offenders do stand trial. If found guilty, psychiatric evidence is offered in mitigation pleas to alter the sentencing given; they may be sent to a secure psychiatric hospital rather than a prison.

Labelling Aspects

Another ethical issue relates to the use of psychiatric diagnoses to persecute minority groups, as suggested by Szasz. Soviet Russia, as mentioned earlier, used psychiatric labelling in order to marginalise those who objected to the political regime. Cochrane and Sashidharan argue that the systems in use at present assume that the white, Western norms of behaviour should be followed by all, and that those who depart from these norms require treatment. As Scheff states: 'Far from being culture-free symptoms are themselves offenses against implicit understandings of particular cultures'. On the other hand, Lopez and Hernandez have suggested that clinicians may overreact and take too much account of subcultural norms.

Laypersons and professionals alike may favour diagnoses on the grounds that they provide an explanation for behaviour that is otherwise difficult to understand (*e.g.* referring to a murderer as a 'psychopath'), but this is clearly not the case; they are only shorthand descriptions. Similarly, it has been argued that the diagnosis can be unhelpful for the client, in that the responsibility for behaviour is then taken away— it is the disorder that makes them behave in that way, and the doctors or psychiatrists have responsibility for treatment. There may even be a tendency to adopt the role suggested by the diagnosis, which could prevent recovery as it would then become a self-fulfilling prophecy.

Finally, such diagnostic labels may themselves have negative effects on the way that mentally disordered persons are viewed and treated by others. This was demonstrated in the study by Rosenhan discussed earlier. The labelling theory of deviance has been applied to mental disorder by Scheff, who considers that once labelled, people are then rewarded when they behave in ways that fit in with stereotypes associated with the label, and punished when they do not. Thus only disordered behaviour is reinforced. Langer and Abelson found that clinicians watching a video of a person labelled as a job applicant rated him as better adjusted than did those who saw the same video with the person labelled as a patient. The stigma associated with such labels may also lead to the individual losing employment, home and social support. With potential consequences such as these, it is doubly important that the system in use is thoroughly researched and appropriately used, and that the benefits outweigh the costs to the individual.

3

Abnormalities of Psychomotor Functions

Introduction

The term sensorimotor, therefore, pertains to "neural activity, in which both the afferent and efferent segments of the neural arc are involved, or pertaining to the structure contained in such activity." The term ideomotor, on the other hand pertains to "the sequence of movements upon ideas."

This method of conceptualizing certain kinds of behaviour is obsolescent, but it has nevertheless a certain usefulness in bringing together for the purposes of this chapter a large variety of very different tasks. For instance, the classic example of a psychomotor task is the cancellation test, in which the subject is required to cancel certain letters only in a long series. In this situation, the motor act of cancellation follows the perception of the correct stimulus. Now it is clear that a large number of psychological tests can be defined in sensorimotor or ideomotor terms. In the reaction-time (R.T.) test, for instance, which superficially seems very different from a cancellation test, the subject is required to perform a motor act when, and only when, a given stimulus is present. Both of these tests are descriptively similar in that a sensation is followed by a response of a particular kind. On the other hand the best-known example of an ideomotor test is a simple fluency test in which the subject is required to say as many words as possible, beginning, for example, with the letter C.

In this case, although there is a general set, there is no specific external stimulus for each separate response hence the term ideomotor.

It is clear, therefore, from these examples, that psychomotor tests are not in any way concerned as such with motor *ability*. The interest does not lie in the subject's skill in lifting his finger off the key in an R.T. experiment. It is, in fact, implicitly assumed in many psychomotor studies that all subjects are equal in their ability as far as the motor act itself is concerned. Psychomotor tests are simply a means of measuring the *speed* and *accuracy* of central functioning. Interest lies in what goes on *between* the objective onset of the stimulus (*e.g.* the light in an R.T. experiment) and the objectively observed motor response (*e.g.* lifting the finger). One major difficulty of course lies in the fact that a number of sequences take place between stimulus and observed response and differences, for example, between subjects in R.T. experiments may be related to differences within one or more of these sequences. Even where records of complex psychomotor responses have been analysed, it has been assumed that these responses do not indicate impairment of the motor system itself (such as might follow injury to the motor cortex) but rather some kind of central disorganization which is *reflected* in the motor response.

It is clear that there will be a boundary where the change from a motor response which is used to reflect individual differences in speed and accuracy of central functions to a motor response which can be said to involve individual differences in the skill required to make the response itself will be difficult to detect. For example, it would be easy to analyse finger or manual dexterity in a way similar to that outlined above, *i.e.* as a constant interchange of stimulus-response mechanisms.

Hence the tests included in this chapter are somewhat arbitrary. After an examination of various possibilities it was decided to divide the tests into sections according to the type of response required. Three levels were found necessary to satisfy this criterion, the tests being allocated as follows:

(a) Simple motor response mechanisms

1. Simple and complex R.T.
2. Cancellation
3. Tapping
4. Davis-type tests

(b) Complex motor response mechanisms

1. Luria-type test
2. Mirror-drawing
3. Manual and finger dexterity
4. Rail-walking

(c) Continuous motor response tasks

1. Static ataxia
2. Body sway (suggestibility)
3. Steadiness
4. Perseveration
5. Fluency
6. Persistence
7. Continuous work

The present chapter will be organized into two sections, one attempting to summarize the facts concerning psychomotor functions, in so far as these have been clearly demonstrated, the other attempting to relate these facts in an orderly way and evaluate the various theories which have been put forward to account for the facts. Before this can be done, however, some of the general difficulties met with in the analysis will be briefly mentioned. These problems should be borne in mind when reading the chapter.

One of the major problems which has occupied workers in this field has been the puzzling question of the specificity or generality of the ability required to perform psychomotor tasks. The earlier studies in the field suggested that the ability to do one type of motor task was relatively independent of the ability to do any other. Many functional analyses have since been carried out and the results are quite clear. For example, the analysis of thirty-eight psychomotor tests by Fleishman resulted in a matrix of almost uniformly positive, but largely low correlations. Consequently although the existence of a general factor of psychomotor ability cannot be doubted, its importance has been generally rejected and a solution resulting in independent group factors preferred. Thus, Fleishman analysed his correlation matrix into ten independent group factors. The most interesting feature of this table lies in the narrow abilities which are defined by each of the factors. The wrist-finger factor, for instance, is defined primarily by two simple tapping tests. The R.T. factor, on the other hand, is defined by visual and auditory R.T. only.

Table 3.1. Some Psychomotor Factors Identified by Factor Analysis

1. Wrist-finger speed
2. Finger dexterity
3. Rate of arm movement
4. Aiming
5. Arm-hand steadiness
6. Reaction-time
7. Manual dexterity
8. Psychomotor speed
9. Psychomotor co-ordination
10. Spatial relations

The intercorrelation of these four tests shows clearly that proficiency in R.T. bears little relationship to proficiency in tapping a surprising finding in view of the apparent simplicity of the two tasks which appear to be measures of uncomplicated motor speed. Yet this finding has been repeated many times.

Table 3.2. Intercorrelations of Four Psychomotor Tests

	2	3	4
1. Visual R.T.	0·56	0·30	0·24
2. Auditory R.T.		0·20	0·17
3. Medium tapping			0·72
4. Large tapping			–

The factors isolated by Fleishman should not be regarded as definitive. The factors obtained by such analyses are dependent on the nature of the tests used, which have differed widely from study to study. Thus, Seashore, factor-analysed a group of 21 tests and isolated five factors which they designated:

1. Speed of single reaction.
2. Finger, hand and forearm speed in restricted oscillatory movement.
3. Forearm and hand speed in oscillatory movements of moderate extent.
4. Steadiness or precision.
5. Skill in manipulating spatial relations.

The first factor was defined by four R.T. tests, horizontal tapping and rotation of speed drill, in contrast with Fleishman who found tapping and R.T. to be quite different abilities. The majority of factorial studies carried out have little direct bearing on this chapter, since in most instances they were carried out on highly selected groups for special purposes (for this reason also the group factors have been stressed more than the general factor). However, it is a fact that few investigations into psychomotor function in abnormal subjects have made any use of factorial methods or even of those results from factorial studies which are of general importance. One immediate difficulty, of course, would seem to lie in the very use of psychomotor tests in abnormals. If the correlations between tests are on the whole much lower than those found with intelligence tests then it would seem to be difficult to put forward any general theory to account for differences in psychomotor performance in abnormals as compared with normals; since poor performance on one test might be accompanied by good performance on another, if the correlation is low.

This leads to the second major problem. While intercorrelations between psychomotor tests tend to be low, though positive in normal groups, in abnormal groups the correlations tend to be very much higher, *i.e.* an abnormal who is poor on one test will tend to be poor on all other psychomotor tests. This difference can be seen clearly in data provided by Shapiro and Nelson. The explanation of this curious and important fact has usually been given in terms of the small spread of scores shown by normal subjects, *i.e.* it is argued that the tests are much easier for normals than for abnormals. That this is not the correct explanation is shown quite clearly by the data provided by Fleishman in the study already referred to. He gives means and S.D.s for his normal group of subjects for all thirty-eight tests; on nearly all of these tests the distribution of scores is quite satisfactory for the purposes of correlation. Furthermore, the reliability of Fleishman's tests is quite satisfactory, most of them being above 0·70. Although, therefore, it is true that abnormal groups usually show a wider range of scores than do normal groups, the differences would not appear to be such as to account for the difference in correlations between the tests.

Table 3.3. Number of Significant Correlations between Error-free Speed Tests (Total Number of Correlations in Each Sample = 45)

Sample	5 per cent level r = 0·44 to 0·55	1 per cent level r > 0·56
Normals	3	1
Schizophrenics	8	19
Manic-depressives	3	22
Organics	8	12
Neurotics	9	13

A further problem consists of the scattered and uncoordinated nature of many of the studies published on psychomotor functions in abnormals. The use of different kinds of tests to measure the same attribute (*e.g.* reaction-time), the use of criterion groups of abnormal subjects chosen in quite different ways (though bearing the same title) and the purely empirical nature of much of the research has led to results both confusing and discouraging. For this reason, stress has been laid in this chapter on those studies which have been most carefully performed and whose results are relatively unequivocal. In most cases, early and perhaps pioneering studies are neglected in favour of later, better controlled studies. In view of the known unreliability of diagnosis, reference in general will be made only to differences between neurotics (and within neurotics, between dysthymics and hysterics), psychotics and normals.

A much neglected problem is that of the role of learning in psychomotor tests. In general, it has been assumed that practice or learning has little or no effect on performance, since the tasks involved (*e.g.* simple R.T., tapping, cancellation, etc.) are so simple that the subject works at his maximum right from the start. That this is not the case has most clearly been demonstrated quite recently by King.

In so far as differences in learning are known to exist they will not be treated in this chapter; it should be remembered, however, that differences in learning may account for some of the puzzling findings with abnormal groups. This leads naturally to the problem of the relationship between skilled and unskilled motor tasks. Fleishman, for instance, uses many tests which undoubtedly could be termed skilled tasks, *i.e.* tasks which involve a very considerable amount of learning. On the other hand, he includes a number of tasks (*e.g.* simple R.T., tapping) where the learning involved must be *relatively* small. Yet he calls all of these tests psychomotor tests. Fortunately, the problem is solved by the fact that very few tests involving *motor skills* have been given to abnormal groups. These include manual and finger dexterity and mirror-drawing, which will be included in this chapter. The choice of measures to be discussed is, however, somewhat arbitrary.

Simple Motor Response Mechanisms

Reaction-time (R.T.). The R.T. experiment has perhaps been more frequently used in the study of psychomotor function in abnormal subjects than any of the other tests we shall study; also a vast array of information is available for comparative studies on normal subjects.The early experiments on abnormal subjects were of the most simple kind, involving the measurement of simple reaction-time to an auditory or visual stimulus and were carried out on miscellaneous, small groups of psychiatric patients. Later work has been more concerned to test the validity of certain theories concerning responsiveness in abnormal (usually schizophrenic) patients. The methodology adopted by the different investigators has been very variable. Some of the factors which have been controlled include:

i. Simple R.T. versus complex R.T.
ii. Short interval versus long interval between stimuli.
iii. Regular interval versus irregular interval between stimuli.
iv. Warning signal versus no warning signal.
v. Auditory versus visual stimulus.
vi. Auditory versus visual warning signal.
vii. Type of response required—

a. simple lift R.T.;
b. simple jump R.T.;
c. simple disjunctive lift R.T.;
d. simple disjunctive jump R.T.;
e. reaction by pressing;
f. reaction by lifting and pressing in own time;
g. movement in own time from one key to another.

viii. Musculature involved—

a. hand—left or right;
b. foot—left or right;
c. other limbs.

ix. Groups used. These include—

a. normals;
b. schizophrenics (acute and chronic);
c. manic-depressives (in manic or depressed state);
d. organics;
e. neurotics;
f. pseudoneurotic schizophrenics.

Broadly speaking, however, the technique developed by Shakow and his colleagues is that now used by most investigators—principally with the aim of testing the hypothesis set up by Shakow. His technique was as follows. The stimulus to which the response was required (usually a sound, but sometimes a light) would be presented at regular or irregular intervals after a warning sound. When the regular interval was used, there would be ten trials for each interval of 1, 2, 4, 7·5, 15 and 25 seconds, each set of trials for a given interval being completed before the next interval was started. There was a 5-second interval between each trial and a rest of one minute after each series of ten trials. In effect, the subject knew how soon after the warning bell, the stimulus would appear. In the irregular method, however, the interval between the warning bell and the stimulus was varied at random (but in such a way that each interval was presented an equal number of times) so that the subject did not know whether the stimulus would follow the warning after one second or after 7·5 seconds or after 25 seconds, etc. In this part each of the intervals was presented a total of twelve times in random order and there was a rest pause of 3 minutes after thirty-six trials. This technique has been used on a number of occasions, both with and without drugs, and with normal and abnormal subjects. Practically all investigators use simple R.T. to sound or light, presumably because choice R.T. is considered too difficult for many patients. Other investigators, have used simple R.T. with a standard interval (5 seconds) with no warning, or delayed R.T. with a long interval (10 seconds) but with warning. A few investigators have investigated the practice effect of repeated trials on R.T. It is obvious that the number of different ways of investigating R.T. in abnormals is legion. The results obtained by these methods present a rather confused picture, but the following results would seem to be relatively clear-cut:

i. Undifferentiated schizophrenic groups are significantly slower than depressives and neurotics;
ii. Chronic schizophrenics are significantly slower than acute schizophrenics, depressives and neurotics and normals. Chronic psychotics are poorer than acute psychotics on a complex R.T. test.
iii. Acute schizophrenics are *not* significantly slower than depressives, but are significantly slower than neurotics.
iv. Neurotics are significantly faster than depressives, chronic and acute schizophrenics, and are not significantly slower than normals matched for age.
v. Depressives are not significantly different from normals if the groups are roughly matched for age.

These results are not very clear-cut. It is not easy to divide the various groups into psychotic and neurotic, since both Hall and Stride, and Huston and Senf employed psychotic depressives who apparently behave quite differently from schizophrenics, while the latter can be split into acute and chronic. Again the results with regard to neurotics are equivocal, but the differences which exist would seem to be much less than for groups of psychotics. The one clear-cut result would seem to be that patients diagnosed as chronic schizophrenics have consistently been found to be significantly slower than all other psychiatric groups, and than normals. Sex differences assumed some importance in the study by Hall and Stride, but were found to be minimal in most other studies, especially the large scale one of King. With regard to age differences, Hall and Stride found that in the neurotic and depressive groups, subjects under 40 tended to be significantly faster than subjects over 40, while King found that subjects showed significant slowing with age but that old schizophrenics tended to be faster than young ones. Research, however, has not been confined to the investigation of group differences only.

Table 3.4. Change in R.T. under Varying Preparatory Intervals for Regular and Irregular Procedure in Normals and Schizophrenics

Interval (seconds)	Regular procedure mean	Irregular procedure mean
	A. 25 SCHIZOPHRENICS	
	Milliseconds	*Milliseconds*
1	668.7	722.5
2	544.4	665.6
4	531.0	619.5
7·5	648.5	583.0
15	639.3	587.9
25	653.5	560.8
	B. 10 NORMAL CONTROLS	
1	262.7	315.2
2	239.2	290.7
4	261.1	296.6
7·5	275.5	303.6
15	278.1	296.0
25	312.3	305.3

Certain other aspects of R.T. have been investigated, with the following main results:

> Schizophrenics show more inter- and intra individual variability in their R.T. responses than do normals and this increased variability is apparent both under normal testing conditions and under the influence of drugs.
>
> When the regular procedure is compared with the irregular procedure, schizophrenic patients show a curious reversal of behaviour. For short intervals of time the irregular procedure leads to a longer R.T. than does the regular procedure (for the same intervals). With longer intervals, the pattern is reversed,

> the change in behaviour apparently taking place somewhere between the intervals of 4 seconds and 7·5 seconds. The validity of this finding seems undoubted. In Rodnick and Shakow's data there is some suggestion that the same phenomenon may occur *later* (in terms of intervals) in normals.

Huston and Senf found that the Set Index was not significantly affected by the degree of co operation, duration of illness and change of affect with drugs. These findings do not agree with those of King. Although he found no relationship between R.T. and *duration* of illness, he did find a clear relationship between R.T. and *severity* of illness.

Cancellation

The cancellation test is a classic example of a psychomotor task. It is clearly analogous to a choice R.T. test in that the subject has to adopt a set and respond to the correct stimulus when it appears at irregular intervals by making a simple motor response. Although this test was extensively used by earlier workers in its many different forms surprisingly little systematic use has been made of it in abnormal psychology. Mohr and Gundlach found no differences between asthenics and pyknics when intelligence was partialled out, a finding confirmed by Klineberg, Asch and Block. More recently, Bonnet investigated changes in speed and accuracy on a cancellation test in psychotic patients who were given five to twenty repetitions of the test over a period of eight months.

Tapping

Even such a simple test as tapping may be administered in a number of forms. Some investigators, for instance, have been interested in the simple speed of tapping on a single plate; others have studied oscillatory tapping alternately on two plates; others, again, have measured the spread or scatter of the taps. Again, preferred speed has been studied in contrast with maximum speed; while ability to repeat or copy a certain rhythm has been investigated. Even with such a simple function, the results obtained on abnormal subjects are inconsistent:

i. It is largely agreed that *speed* or *rate* of tapping does not discriminate between normals and neurotics. King found that his neurotics were significantly slower than his normals, but his neurotic group was small (N = 23) and the mean difference very small.

While H. J. Eysenck found that two measures of *scatter* discriminated significantly between normals and neurotics on the one hand (neurotics showing more scatter) and between dysthymics and hysterics on the other (dysthymics showing more scatter), these results were not repeated by S. B. G. Eysenck who found no difference in scatter between normals and neurotics.

ii. Shakow and Huston found that psychotics were significantly *slower* in tapping rate than normals (with schizophrenics slower than manic-depressives within the psychotic group). This finding was confirmed by King for *chronic* schizophrenics who were slower than both normals and neurotics. S. B. G. Eysenck found that while individual left- or right-hand speed scores did not differentiate between normals, neurotics and psychotics, the latter were slower than either of the other two groups on a combined score. The only contrary evidence here is that of Wulfeck who found no differences between normals, schizophrenics, depressives and neurotics.

iii. S. B. G. Eysenck found that psychotics did not differ in amount of scatter from normals or neurotics.

We may conclude that rate of tapping does not discriminate between normals and neurotics but that there is a suggestion that scatter may do so. On the other hand, rate of tapping does discriminate between psychotic and other abnormal or normal groups, whereas scatter does not.

Control Movements (Davis)

Davis carried out a series of experiments on the causes of pilot error. In some experiments he used a simulated cockpit in which instruments on a panel respond realistically to movements of the controls; in other experiments, he used an apparatus in which a pointer could be moved to a given position to the right or left of it.

He observed two types of errors; errors of *overaction* and errors of *inertia*. Subjects who were overactive "obtained large scores on control movements ... responses to instrument deviations were excessive, the extent and gradient of the movements being greatly increased and over-correcting frequent. Numerous restless movements were observed ... subjects felt excited and under strain, tense and irritable and sometimes frankly anxious." Subjects who were inert, on the other hand, made "errors which were large and of long duration, whereas activity, represented by scores of control movements, was relatively little. The individual responses were less hurried and less disturbed by restless movements than were those of the pilots showing the overactivity reaction, but they were often more extensive than at the beginning of the test. Subjects reported that their interest had flagged and that their concentration had failed. A feeling of strain had now given way to one of mild boredom, tedium or tiredness. "Davis went on to show that if responses in the test are classified into three categories (normal, overactive, inert), then only 33 per cent of neurotic pilots showed a normal reaction, compared with 75 per cent of normals. Further, pilots suffering from anxiety states showed a strong tendency to make overactive responses; whereas pilots suffering from hysteria tended to display inert responses.

Table 3.5. Test Results of Normal and Neurotic Pilots

	Normal		Overactive		Inert		Total
	N	% age	N	% age	N	% age	
Normal pilots	268	75	59	17	28	8	355
Neurotic pilots	13	33	11	28	15	38	39
Acute anxiety state	6	43	7	20	1	7	14
Hysteria	1	12.5	1	12.5	6	75	8
Other	6	35	3	18	8	47	17

In another experiment 355 fit pilots were classified by two psychiatrists with regard to predisposition to neurosis as: nil, slight, moderate; and further classified on the Cockpit test as normal, over active, inert. The results indicate a significant association between grade of predisposition and test class, the percentage of normal responses decreasing with increasing predisposition to neurosis. Fit pilots who were rated as obsessional tended to fall into the overactive class. In an experiment using a simple pointer apparatus instead of the Cockpit, healthy, acutely anxious and hysteric pilots were given "extent" scores (ranging from 3-8) on the test. The results showed clearly that the acutely anxious pilots tended to make more extensive responses than did normals; the hysterics showing the opposite tendency. Further, the response time of the hysterics was significantly *longer* than that of the normals, the latter being similar in this respect to the acutely anxious.

Table 3.6. Association of Neuroticism and Test Score

Predisposition	Type of response			
	Normal	Overactive	Inert	Per cent normal
Nil	130	13	12	84
Slight	113	32	9	73
Moderate	25	14	7	54
Per cent moderate	9	24	25	

Table 3.7. Degree of Error of Normal, Anxious and Hysteric Pilots

	Distribution of cases (Extent scores in arbitrary unit)						
	3	4	5	6	7	8	Total
Healthy pilots	1	3	21	29	14	1	69
Acutely anxious	1	1	2	3	6	2	15
Hysterics	4	5	2	1	0	0	12

Davis's experiments may be summarized in the following way:

1. Neurotics tend to make more errors of judgement compared with normals.
2. Within the neurotic group, dysthymics tend to make errors of overactivity, hysterics errors of inertia.
3. Similar tendencies are found within normal groups.

Davis also noted that "the errors in the instrument readings increased in size towards the end of the test and there were few large errors in place of many small ones." Similarly, the number of errors in resetting the "fuel contents" indicator fell from the first to the third period but then increased significantly. These phenomena, which Davis called "late effects" indicate that, in general, errors of inertia tend to predominate over errors of overactivity *in all subjects* provided the test is continued for a long enough period.

Complex Motor Response Mechanisms

The Luria Technique. This technique is a development by Luria of the original work of Nunberg who combined the Word Association test with measurements of hand movement at the time of and between verbal responses. The underlying rationale is that the internal conflict thought to occur when the subject is required to respond to an emotionally disturbing stimulus will be reflected in motor movements which, being overt, can be recorded. Many studies have been published which support this general hypothesis. A large number of variables have been recorded which may be classified generally as follows:

1. Reaction-time measures:
   (a) time of verbal response;
   (b) time of manual response;
   (c) variability of time of response.
2. R-hand response (usually voluntary, made at time of verbal response):
   (a) regularity and duration of response;
   (b) Height;
   (c) number of disturbances.
   (d) number of double depressions;
   (e) number of depressions omitted;
   (f) three longest—three shortest responses.
3. L-hand response (usually involuntary, both at time of R-hand response and between R-hand responses):
   (a) height, length, number of changes in direction, number of items producing L-hand response;
   (b) number of reversals;
   (c) maximum distance from base line.
4. Length of base line, *i.e.* actual length of the kymographic record.

Little attention has been paid to the degree of relationship between these variables. Malmo Albino, Krause and Sharp give figures which indicate low positive correlations between L- and R-hand disturbance, but indicate no relationship between amount of motor disturbance and speed of response (R.T.). Clarke showed that it was important to partial out differences in intelligence between psychiatric groups before group differences could be examined. The results obtained on psychiatric groups may be summarized as follows:

i. R-hand voluntary response is significantly more disturbed in neurotics than in normals.

ii. L-hand involuntary response is significantly more disturbed in neurotics than in normals, provided the apparatus used is sufficiently sensitive.

iii. Both local and general motor disturbance is greater in neurotics than in normals.

These conclusions are further supported by the work of Morgan and Ojeman who found significant differences between groups rated as having low, intermediate and high degrees of conflict.

iv. There is some evidence that the motor disorganization shown by dysthymics is different from that shown by hysterics related introversion-extraversion to amount of L-hand disturbance and concluded that introverts tended to respond more than extraverts with the L-hand (*i.e.* showed more involuntary disturbance). Ebaugh's study indicated that anxiety cases showed more *general* disturbance than hysterics; and possibly more *local* disturbance.

v. Results obtained with psychotics indicate that they show at least as much disorganization as neurotics, if not more. Shuey distinguished four types of motor reaction with the R hand (small, large, mixed, chaotic) and attempted to relate these to specific psychotic groups (manic depressive, paranoid, catatonic) without much success.

The above general findings have been confirmed by the recent well-controlled study of S. B. G. Eysenck. Using one hundred and twenty-three controls, fifty-five psychotics and fifty-five neurotics and a number of response categories, she obtained the results shown in Table 3.8. From these data she concluded that R-hand disturbance differentiates better than L-hand disturbance, and that psychotics show even greater disorganization than do neurotics.

Table 3.8. Differences between Normals, Neurotics and Psychotics on the Luria Test

Variables	Controls (N = 123)	Neurotics (N = 55)	Psychotics (N = 55)	*F*	*p*
	M	M	M		
Motor R.T.					
No. of delays	22.7	27.0	29.1	16.61	0.001
Σ total delays	112.2	233.3	294.5	20.13	0.001
R-hand disturbances					
No. double depressions	2.0	4.7	5.9	11.71	0.001
No. omitted depressions	0.1	0.3	1.8	9.79	0.001
Σ 3 longest – Σ 3 shortest R.T	14.2	16.7	18.6	5.21	0.01
L-hand disturbances					
No. reversals	8.2	8.4	13.5	4.18	0.01
Max. distance from base line	1.5	1.9	2.2	3.69	0.05
Length of baseline	297.9	406.9	503.2	21.74	0.001

Mirror Drawing

Results obtained on the mirror-drawing test which has been extensively used with normal and abnormal groups are not so clear-cut as those obtained on the Luria test. Earlier studies suggested that speed and error scores in this test discriminate between "stable" and "unstable" individuals; that there is a negative correlation between mirror-drawing ability and inadequacy of social adjustment; that psychotics and delinquents are significantly slower than normals; and that anxiety cases are significantly slower than normals.

Two carefully controlled studies throw light on these suggestions (in both cases a diamond-shaped figure was used compared with the more common star-shape). Using the groups of normals, neurotics and psychotics already referred to, S. B. G. Eysenck found that psychotics were significantly poorer than either neurotics or normals on five speed measures (first time, longest time, shortest time, average time, and first minus third time). The neurotics were also slower than the normals, but the main differences were much smaller. These results are in agreement with those of Eysenck who found highly significant differences on time taken between normals and psychotics.

We may conclude that the mirror-drawing test discriminates at a high level between normals and psychotics and possibly between normals and neurotics. No reliable information is available concerning errors.

Manual and Finger Dexterity

Relatively little work on abnormal subjects has been reported with this type of test. Lubin found a correlation with the normal-neurotic dichotomy of about + 0·60, while O'Connor, testing high grade mental defectives obtained a neurotic factor saturation of 0·43 on manual and finger dexterity tests.

S. B. G. Eysenck found that parts M, N, O and P of the USES battery all discriminated significantly between psychotics and normals, while neurotics fell in between, but were significantly poorer than normals. These results support those by Eysenck who compared normals with neurotics, the neurotics being significantly poorer on all four parts of the test. A comparison of the two studies. Tizard and O'Connor also found that manual and finger dexterity tests had significant loadings on a factor of neuroticism.

Table 3.9. A Comparison of two Studies on Manual and Finger Dexterity Tests

	S. B. G. Eysenck		Eysenck	
	Controls	Neurotics	Controls	Neurotics
	M	M	M	M
Part M	75.45	72.62	77.29	71.87
Part N	88.60	86.75	83.06	75.58
Part O	27.76	25.29	26.22	23.60
Part P	25.65	23.95	25.56	22.90
Total	217.36	208.61	212.13	193.95

Rail-walking Test

This test, which was devised by Heath usually employs two 9 ft long rails, one 4 in. and one 2 in. wide, and one 6 ft long rail, 1 in wide. The test is given in an unlimed form, the subject being required to walk along it in his stockinged feet. It has been extensively standardized and has a high reliability. Heath discovered an adjustment syndrome, characterized by poor motor co-ordination among other things, and the possible relationship of this lack of motor co-ordination to neuroticism was confirmed by the work of Tizard and Tizard and O'Connor. Using it along with a number of other tests, they found that it had a significant loading on the neuroticism factor which resulted from their factorial analysis. Unfortunately little work has since been carried out with this test on psychiatric groups.

Continuous Motor Response Tests

In this test the subject is told simply to stand still and relax, with the eyes closed and the hands hanging down the side, feet together. The test lasts for 30 seconds, usually, and maximum sway either forward or backward is the score. Data for one hundred and twenty normal controls and 1,230 neurotics show that 81 per cent of normals swayed less than 1 in., compared with only 32 per cent of neurotics; no normals swayed more than 2 in., while 31 per cent of neurotics did so. In another study, four times as many neurotics swayed more than 1 in. when compared with normals.

Body Sway (Suggestibility)

Two main problems have confronted workers on suggestibility. The first of these concerns the question whether or not suggestibility tests have anything in common (*i.e.* define one or more factors). The second concerns the relationship between suggestibility and abnormality.

(a) Types of Suggestibility

Early investigations produced conflicting reports. Thus Aveling and Hargreaves and others believed they had demonstrated the existence of general and group factors of suggestibility whereas Estabrooks reported zero or very low correlations. Still other writers believed in the existence of group factors of suggestibility Hull, for example, distinguished "prestige" and "non-prestige" suggestion. A considerable amount of light was thrown on this problem by the researches of Eysenck. In one study, for example he used eight tests of suggestibility and intercorrelated the resultant scores, with results shown in Table 3.10. Two clear-cut independent factors emerged.

Table 3.10. Factor Analysis of 8 Tests of Suggestibility

Test	Loadings	
	Factor I	Factor II
1. Weights (personal)	+ 0.509	- 0.371
2. Lines (personal)	+ 0.772	- 0.002
3. Weights (impersonal)	+ 0.558	+ 0.048
4. Lines (impersonal)	+ 0.386	+ 0.016
5. Pendulum	+ 0.094	+ 0.386
6. Body sway	- 0.041	+ 0.623
7. Levitation up	- 0.194	+ 0.370
8. Levitation down	- 0.100	+ 0.546

i. **Primary Suggestibility.** This factor is revealed by tests of the ideomotor type, *i.e.* psychomotor tests in which a motor movement is executed by the subject following the repeated suggestion by the experimenter that such a movement will take place, without conscious participation in the movement on the subject's part. The test which most satisfactorily defines this factor is Hull's Body Sway Test which has been extensively used for this purpose. The factor is also defined by the Chevreul Pendulum Test, the Arm Levitation Test and the Press-Release Test.

ii. **Secondary Suggestibility.** This factor is defined by tests other than motor tests and need not be considered further.

The main characteristics of primary suggestibility are as follows:

1. It is distributed in the experimental population as a U-curve (this U-curve being, however, an artefact of the method of measurement.
2. It correlates in a significantly non-linear way with intelligence (subjects of average I.Q. being most suggestible).
3. It may manifest itself in a positive or negative response.
4. It is a highly reliable phenomenon.

It is clear, therefore, that primary suggestibility is an important trait in that it can be clearly differentiated from other traits, can be measured by a group of objective tests and is a reliable phenomenon.

Its relationship to personality differences is, therefore, of great interest.

(b) Suggestibility and Personality

Early studies considered that suggestibility is related to neuroticism but that it bears a special relationship to hysteria in that in this disorder an increased and exaggerated state of suggestibility can usually be found. However, Eysenck's researches showed conclusively that:

1. There is a close relationship between primary suggestibility and neurosis. In one study one hundred and ten neurotics were compared with one hundred and ten normals (paired for Matrices I.Q.) on the Body Sway and Static Ataxia test. It was found that on the Body Sway test 63 per cent of male and 42 per cent of female neurotics were suggestible compared with 7 per cent of male and 8 per cent of female normals; sixteen neurotics fell outright, whereas no normal did. The correlation between primary suggestibility and neuroticism was 0·66. The study of Messer found a correlation between amount of sway and tendency to give neurotic responses on the Bernreuter Inventory in normal subjects.
2. Later researches showed clearly that there is a strong correlation between amount of sway and amount of neuroticism. It shows the average amount of suggestibility (on a Body Sway test) for six groups of neurotic patients, a total of nine hundred and sixty males and three hundred and ninety females. It is clear that sway increases steadily with increase in severity of illness.
3. Contrary to the earlier suggestions in the literature, there is some evidence that while neurotics as a group are more suggestible than normals, dysthymics are most suggestible of all. Eysenck reports that correlations between anxiety as a symptom and suggestibility are 0·26 for men and 0·33 for women, while for conversion hysteria the correlations are 0·12 for men and - 0·08 for women. Figures for hysterical personality and anxious personality are similar.
4. There is some evidence that suggestible patients are of two kinds in relation to tests of primary suggestibility. On the one hand there are suggestible subjects who constitute an active,

alert group; on the other there are suggestible subjects who constitute a passive, lethargic group. The similarity of these two groups to the overactive *v.* inert dichotomy found by Davis will be readily apparent.

5. There is some evidence that catatonic schizophrenics are negatively suggestible; paranoid schizophrenics positively suggestible; while manics are non-suggestible.

Finger Tremor

In this type of test, the intention is to measure the amount of involuntary movement which appears when the finger, hand, arm or body as a whole is held as motionless as possible. Static Ataxia and Body Sway have already been discussed. With regard to Finger Tremor, it has been found that schizophrenics have significantly greater finger tremor than normal, as have defectives. Kellogg investigated the effects of emotional excitement upon muscular steadiness and found that those subjects who reported emotional upset were less steady than those who did not.

Perseveration

(a) Dimensional Analysis of Tests of Perseveration

Perseveration has been defined in somewhat different ways by various authors. Cameron and Caunt define it as "the tendency for an activity to persist after the subject has decided to change that activity, this persistence in the primary activity being shown by a transitory interference with the new activity which follows it." Jasper defined perseveration as "the tendency of a set of neurons, once excited, to persist in the state of excitation autonomously, showing resistance to any change in this state." Both of these authors stress the involuntary nature of perseverative activity. Other authors have preferred to stress the behavioural acts which may be said to define perseveration. Thus, Kleemeier and Dudek define flexibility (the obverse of perseveration) "simply as the ability (*a*) to shift from one task to another or (*b*) to break through an established set in order to perform a task," *i.e.* their definition makes no assumptions concerning brain processes (*cf.* Jasper above). Scheier and Ferguson, similarly, define rigidity and flexibility in terms of negative transfer effects. The concept of perseveration derives originally from clinical observations, which were first systematized by Gross in terms of primary and secondary function. Primary function was defined by Gross as the *intensity* of any stimulus. The intensity of the primary function would determine how long it would perseverate after the stimulus had been removed. The *duration* of the response was called the secondary function. An intense primary response would be followed by a long secondary response, a weak primary response by a short secondary response. Gross then proceeded to relate type of function to type of personality, again basing his ideas on clinical experience. A person showing strong primary and long secondary responses would be deep-narrow (*i.e.* would suffer from a restriction of conscious awareness) or *introverted*; a person showing weak primary and short secondary responses would be broad-shallow (*i.e.* suffer from wide conscious awareness) or *extraverted*. The deep-narrow person would tend to perseverate and have difficulty in switching from one task to another; the broad-shallow person would tend to flit from one subject to another and hence show little perseveration. Most of the work carried out subsequently on perseveration derives directly or indirectly from the original work of Gross. Secondary function could manifest itself in at least four ways—

i. the perseveration of a response after the stimulus has ceased, *e.g.* the length of time an after- image persists after the stimulus has been withdrawn.

ii. the spontaneous reappearance of a response in consciousness after the original stimulus and response have both ceased. For example, a subject responding to successive stimuli A, B, C, D, etc., might respond with response A, to A; B, to B; C, to C, and then A, to D.

iii. the extent to which the perseveration of a response to stimulus A *interferes with* (delays or prevents) the response to stimulus B, *e.g.* the extent to which writing S interferes with writing Z immediately afterwards.

iv. the extent to which an ingrained (through repetition) response-habit interferes with a new response, although the interfering response may not itself be performed, *e.g.* mirror-writing.

The complicated nature and differing interpretations of perseveration tests may be shown by brief consideration of one of the simplest of such tests: the S-t tests. In this test, three steps are usually taken:

i. writing S as quickly as possible for 1 minute;
ii. writing t test as quickly as possible for 1 minute;
iii. writing SS, etc., as quickly as possible for 2 minutes.

Such a test has been scored in a number of ways, each method intended as a measure of perseveration:

a. The score (i - ii) may be regarded as a measure of the interference of the ingrained habit of writing S on a new, unfamiliar habit (such a measure may of course be obtained without (i) above being given at all).
b. The score (i + ii) - iii may be regarded as a measure of the interference of writing S immediately before i and vice versa, compared with writing either S or t alone without interference.

Alternatively, the test may be given in the form:

i. writing S
ii. writing t
iii. writing S

in which case (i – iii) would indicate the amount of interference of (ii) on (iii) Cattell attempted to elucidate the nature of perseveration by giving many different kinds of "p" tests and intercorrelating the scores. Stephenson had pointed out three kinds of "p" tests:

i. alternation tests;
ii. creative effort tests;
iii. direct "p" tests.

Using a large number of such tests Cattell intercorrelated the results obtained on fifty-two adults. As a result of this and later work he distinguished:

i. *Inertia of mental processes*, shown in "alternation tests" in which the subject has to switch to and fro between two interfering, alternate ways of performing tasks, the tasks being otherwise equivalent.

   AAAA, etc.

   BBBB, etc.

   AB AB AB AB, etc.

Here the X and Y activities must follow in rapid temporal succession, producing interference by their momentum, inertia or after-effect.

ii. *Disposition rigidity* or inertia of structural disposition. This shows itself in "creative effort" tests in which the score is measured as the difference between performing a task in some old, accustomed fashion and performing it in some new fashion, *e.g.*

SSSSS

Here immediate temporal contiguity of the X and Y tasks is not essential, *i.e.* there is no question of inertia of functioning process. Cattell argued that most of the published studies showed no evidence for the first type of perseveration; those which appeared to, did so because of the scoring technique when this was corrected, no "p" factor was present. He concluded that there was a general factor proved only for motor "creative effort" tests and that this factor was best called "disposition rigidity." He reported a study of his own in which six tests involving solely the "creative effort" principle and confined largely to motor performance tests were given to one hundred women students. From the resultant analysis, a general disposition rigidity factor emerged which accounted satisfactorily for the variance.

The conclusions at which Cattell arrived remained unchallenged for some time as they seemed to account adequately for most of the published findings. Thus Jasper, using sensory and motor tests on normal subjects had found no evidence for an overall factor of perseveration but concluded that there was some evidence for the existence of a narrow group factor of motor perseveration. Jones, using sensory, motor and ideational tests on manics and depressives, had found evidence in the test intercorrelations of a "general" factor covering ideational and motor tests in the melancholics but not in the manics. Pinard had found evidence of a group factor covering tests of both the alternation and creative effort type (all motor tests). Rethlingshafer in a factor analysis of twenty-nine variables on normal college adults of high I.Q. found (among others) a factor she named perseveration which had significant loadings on six tests (time the subject worked at a task; length of time hand grip is maintained; preferred motor tapping rate; effect of a slower intervening rate on preferred rate of tapping; and answers to questions on the Maller-Elkin Attention test).

Notcutt gave a number of tests purporting to measure the four supposed kinds of perseveration (sensory; motor creative effort; motor alternation; associative, *i.e.* tendency for ideas to occur involuntarily). Of the eighty correlations between individual tests, thirty-nine were positive and forty-one negative, the mean $r = 0{\cdot}005 \pm 0{\cdot}011$, *i.e.* the results were precisely what would be expected by chance fluctuations in the scores. With regard to the four types, he concluded that there was no evidence for a factor of sensory perseveration; that the evidence for a creative factor was inconclusive; that the alternation tests had a mean *r* of 0·181 (if one test was omitted), indicating a genuine though very small common factor; and that there was no evidence for associative perseveration. Nor did he find any correlation between the two motor groups of tests.The situation was further reviewed by Walker who concluded that the evidence for a general "p" factor was in all studies either decidedly negative or, at best, only weakly positive. They further pointed out that the tests used, by their very nature, made it impossible to distinguish (even if a general factor did exist) whether perseveration was due to mental inertia (as in the alternation-type test) or disposition rigidity (as in the creative-effort tests) since the latter usually entered into the former.In spite of Cattell's efforts to elucidate the field, therefore, the evidence for either a general, or unrelated group factors, of perseveration remained extremely tenuous. However, a new light was thrown on the matter by Kleemeier and Dudek who carried out an obvious (but until then unthought-of) study. They used simple psychomotor tests which previous studies had shown would result by factorial analysis in numerical speed, perceptual speed and verbal factors. Within each set one task involved shifting. If these latter tests appeared on an independent axis in a factor analysis, there would be evidence for a factor of flexibility. Thirteen paper and pencil tests were used on two hundred and five college students. Four factors accounted satisfactorily for the variance. These were factors of perceptual speed, verbal, single-digit number, and two-digit number. The flexibility tests did not group themselves along an independent axis but could be accounted for in terms of the other factors. They concluded that "no factor of flexibility need be postulated to account for differences in performance on these simple alternation tasks."While the study of Kleemeier and Dudek does not entirely solve the "riddle of perseveration" (they did not, for example, include any of the classical "p" tests) it does suggest that the classical "p" tests may be measuring factors other than perseveration and that a factor of perseveration, even if it genuinely exists, may contribute little to the total variance of the test. This conclusion was, of course, implicit in the previous findings which, even when positive, indicated a relatively unimportant factor and was supported by a recent careful study by Rim. He used twenty-one tests of perseveration on both normal and neurotic subjects, and derived three factors of perseveration. With intelligence controlled, these factors were defined as:

i. Disposition-rigidity, operating in motor and perceptual tasks—the rigidity of old-established habits in the presence of new demands.
ii. Creative-effort rigidity—carrying out a new task never done before.
iii. Cognitive or ideational rigidity—this was defined by tests similar to those used by Kleemeier and Dudek.

The interesting point about Rim's study is that the amount of variance accounted for by the three factors of perseveration was as follows:

Factor I— 5.8 per cent
Factor II— 7.8 per cent
Factor III— 8.8 per cent.

These three factors together accounted for only about 23 per cent of the total variance of the tests, other factors and specifics presumably accounting for the remainder. It would seem reasonable to suppose, therefore, that a combination of the approach of Kleemeier and Dudek on the one hand, and of Rim on the other would yield fruitful results. This was carried out, more or less, by Scheier and Ferguson who included tests of reasoning ability, cognitive rigidity, motor speed and motor rigidity in a battery given to sixty students. They identified three factors:

Factor A—a reasoning factor, involved in all tests to some extent.

Factor B—a motor speed factor with high loadings on the motor speed *and motor rigidity tests.*

Factor C—a non-motor rigidity factor.

However, they also concluded that "the motor rigidity tests used ... have a factorial composition which is very largely reasoning and motor speed."

It seems reasonable to conclude from the evidence reviewed above that the most recent careful work confirms the existence of two forms of motor perseveration alternation "p" and creative effort "p"; that these two factors nevertheless account for only a small proportion of the total variance attributable to the tests which are the best measures of perseveration; and that when suitable reference tests are included in a battery of perseveration tests, the amount of variance attributable to the factors of motor perseveration is negligible when compared with that attributable to other factors, especially the factor of motor (perceptual-motor) speed.

(b) Perseveration and Personality

Many attempts have been made to relate the supposed factors of perseveration with personality factors. Early studies suggested that low "p" scores were characteristic of manics. High "p" scores, on the other hand, were said to characterize depressives; schizophrenics; stutterers; "emotionality" and various traits such as "youngest child in the family, being brought up indulgently, being more ailing as a child, being socially isolated, poorer prognosis with therapy".

In a series of studies Kendig found high "p" scores to be associated with induced failure in the task and with acceptance of the task as a test, rather than as a casual affair.

Jasper found effectively zero correlations between perseveration scores and introversion-extraversion scores (as measured by Conklin's E-1 Interest test); however, as he also found a significant correlation between introversion and depression it seems likely that this scale was measuring neuroticism rather than introversion.

In his first study Pinard appeared to relate extreme "p" scores to different types of neurosis. Thus, in a study on children, he found that 75 per cent of the most difficult and unreliable children were either over- or under-perseverators while the opposite was true of the self-controlled children, *i.e.* they showed moderate perseveration. The extremely perseverative children were the real rebels, irritable, bad tempered and moody; the non-perseverators were "petty," nagging and whining. These results were confirmed for adult neurotics, 75 per cent of the most difficult and unreliable patients being over- or under- perseverators. Thus, neurotics seemed to be abnormal perseverators, but to fall into two clear-cut and opposite groups.

In a later study he attempted to relate perseveration to introversion. Patients were interviewed and rated themselves on a scale covering all points related to introversion by previous investigators. He found that "the extreme perseverators and non-perseverators have in common lack of self control and perseverance to a marked degree and they are unreliable, obstinate, 'touchy' and difficult. They differ from each other in that the extreme perseverator tends to be effeminate, 'nervous,' sensitive, sentimental, serious, shy and solitary, whereas the extreme nonperseverator tends to be suspicious, inconsiderate, critical, impatient of criticism, tactless, silent and anxious and in a state of general tension with ups and downs in mood." Pinard's diagram summarizing his findings resembles Eysenck's dimensional system very closely.

Notcutt found a correlation of only - 0·03 between alternation "p" scores and introversion, using normal subjects, but this is not surprising since he found no clear-cut factor of perseveration.

Cattell found a negative correlation between "w" and "p" in neurotics, supporting the earlier finding by Brogden whose first factor was identified as one of perseveration and was said by Brogden to bear "a considerable resemblance to Webb's 'w' factor." This would suggest a relationship between perseveration and neuroticism (since Eysenck has shown that Webb's "w" factor is the normal pole of a normal-neuroticism dimension).

However, Cattell also found that "p"-scores were negatively correlated with his own E-factor (Dominance-Submission) which seems to be similar to Eysenck's I-E factor. In a further study on two hundred men and one hundred women, the correlation between dominance and rigidity was - 0·44. Furthermore, he found, like Pinard, that the relation of "p"-score to dominance was curvilinear—

He concludes that "the factor of rigidity is simply a relative inability to mould old habits, in one performance, to new ones this means slowness of learning under the usual conditions of repetition of training we shall assume that rigidity means a general slowness of learning." This *schema* also fits closely Eysenck's recent formulations characterizing the *introverted* neurotic as a rapid learner or over socialized and the *extraverted* neurotic as a slow learner, or under-socialized. Cattell's final position, however, is far from clear.It is clear from the definitions of primary and secondary function and their relationship to the deep narrow and broad-shallow personality types that it would be predicted that high perseveration would be characteristic of introversion and low perseveration characteristic of extraversion in Eysenck's dimensional system; and that such a pattern would be expected to be found in normal subjects as well, since it is characteristic of introverts and extraverts, rather than neurotics. The findings of Cattell and Pinard in particular appear to support this hypothesis, especially in their suggestion of a curvilinear relationship indicating distinct groups of high and low perseverators. However, the careful study by Rim failed to reveal any evidence of a non-linear relationship between perseveration and neuroticism; failed to reveal any significant differences among neurotic subgroups which included hysterics and psychopaths, anxiety states and obsessives, and a mixed group of neurotics; and failed to reveal any correlation between perseveration and neuroticism on the one hand, or between perseveration and introversion-extraversion on the other. Similarly Petrie found no differences between hysterics and dysthymics on four tests of perseveration.We must, therefore, conclude that factors of perseveration are of little importance in defining differences either between neurotics and normals or between extraverts and introverts. This is not surprising in view of the small amount of variance of the tests used to measure perseveration accounted for by the factors.

Fluency

Fluency tests constitute a classic example of the ideomotor type of psychomotor test, *i.e.* a verbal response following upon an "idea." The principal findings with respect to tests of fluency may be summarized as follows:

i. The major variance of a battery of fluency tests can be accounted for by a general factor, which Rogers identifies as "g" plus Vernon's "v: ed" factor (verbal-educational).
ii. Two orthogonal factors (in addition to the general factor) have been identified by Rogers. The first factor is one of *oral* fluency;

the second, a factor of *written* fluency. In independent studies, Rogers found that these three factors were extraordinarily stable, both as regards the tests which define them and the factor loadings of these tests.

iii. Two further factors have been suggested by Rim. One factor in his study defined three tests of oral verbal fluency where relatively *less constriction* is given in the instructions, viz. "towns," "trees" and "animals." This factor is the same as Rogers' factor of oral fluency. Rim's second factor defined three tests of oral verbal fluency where *more constriction* was given in the instructions, viz. "first letter A," "suffix -ion," and "anagrams." This factor is similar to a factor found by Rogers which he defined as "dealing with words in which one or more formal restrictions were placed on the response." The factor, however, cuts across the previous factors of oral and written fluency, since Rogers's study showed it was defined by both oral and written tests. These results agree with earlier studies by Carroll, Gewirtz and others.

iv. Psychotics are significantly less fluent than either normals or neurotics. S. B. G. Eysenck found psychotics significantly poorer than either neurotics or normals (using three tests of relatively *less* constriction); while Eysenck found similar results in a comparison of psychotics and normals only.

v. The evidence for neurotic's being less fluent than normals is of doubtful significance. S. B. G. Eysenck found that they were, but to a much less degree than psychotics; while Rim could find no differences between normals and neurotics on six tests of fluency.

vi. Earlier suggestions that fluency may be related to differences in introversion-extraversion have not been confirmed. Petrie found no differences in fluency between hysterics and dysthymics, nor did Himmelweit and Rim. Petrie, however, did find that hysterics tend to make more *errors* than dysthymics under appropriately controlled test conditions.

While the existence of various factors of fluency has clearly been demonstrated, therefore, it must be concluded that they have not been very useful in the analysis of differences in behaviour of different psychiatric groups.

Persistence

(a) Dimensional Analysis of Persistence Tests

Like perseveration, persistence tests have been subjected to a great deal of experimentation in an effort to discover whether a unitary factor of persistence can be demonstrated or not. Much of the work has been unsatisfactory and inconclusive but on the whole appears to point to the existence of a general factor. However, the position was clarified considerably by the work of MacArthur. He intercorrelated twenty-two measures of persistence from which the influence of intellectual differences had been partialled out; 75 per cent of the correlations were positive, with 29 per cent significant. A factor analysis using simple structure revealed four factors: (1) a general persistence factor; (2) a bipolar factor contrasting individual with group (prestige) persistence; (3) a bipolar factor contrasting reputation for persistence with objective evidence of persistence; (4) a factor of persistence in a group of physical tests holding foot over chair (leg persistence), maintained hand-grip (dynamometer), time of holding breath, and arm extension.This last factor is relevant to the present chapter since it is measurable by tests of a psychomotor nature, particularly leg persistence and maintained hand-grip. The existence of such a factor has been demonstrated by other writers in addition to MacArthur. Thornton described a factor of "ability and/ or willingness to withstand discomfort in order to achieve a goal" with high loadings on "time holding breath," "time standing shock," "time standing pressure," "maintained hand-grip." Likewise Rethlingshafer described a factor of "willingness and/or ability to endure discomfort." As Eysenck points out the group factors of persistence demonstrated by MacArthur "are subject to measurement with a degree of validity probably not much below general persistence itself."

(b) Persistence and Personality

1. Leg Persistence. This test has been most commonly employed in studies with abnormals. The test is a very simple one, the subject usually being required to hold the leg outstretched one inch above the seat of a chair for as long as he can. The results obtained are conflicting and may be summarized as follows:

i. Careful studies have shown that neurotics are not differentiated from normals in terms of persistence. Thus Eysenck compared several groups of neurotics with normals; although all the neurotics had *lower* mean scores than the normal group, the differences were not significant. Similarly, S. B. G. Eysenck compared neurotics with normals and found no difference, as did Himmelweit and Petrie with neurotic and normal children. Ryans concludes from his review of the literature that non-persistent subjects "may show more pronounced leanings towards neuroticism and introversion than persistent persons" (introversion here is probably to be equated with neuroticism). However, this conclusion cannot be said to apply to motor persistence.

ii. Several studies also suggest that there are no significant differences between hysterics and dysthymics on leg persistence. Petrie on the other hand, found that dysthymics persevered over twice as long as hysterics.

iii. Eysenck found no differences between normals and psychotics in leg persistence.

2. Dynamometer Persistence. In this test, strength of grip is usually measured first and the subject then required to squeeze for as long as possible at half or two-thirds the maximum strength.

The major findings with this test are as follows:

i. S. B. G. Eysenck reported that neurotics showed significantly less persistence than normals. As, however, the neurotics showed a much weaker initial maximum grip, it is possible that this affected their subsequent persistence. Similar results for normal v. neurotic children were reported by Himmelweit and Petrie.

ii. No comparisons are available for dysthymics and hysterics separately.

iii. S. B. G. Eysenck also reported that psychotics showed significantly less persistence than normals (with the same reservations as to initial strength of grip). The psychotics did not differ from the neurotics in persistence.

Work Decrement

The "curve of work" (*i.e.* the changes occurring in performance under conditions of prolonged performance of mental or physical work) has mediated a large amount of research on normal subjects. The work studied may be either physical in nature (*e.g.* ergographic) or "mental" (*e.g.* continual addition, naming colours, etc.). Among the major trends noted in the objective work curve are (*a*) warm up effect; (*b*) practice effect; (*c*) spurts and rhythms; (*d*) general (work) decrement; (*e*) blocking. The two latter phenomena are of particular importance. Work decrement refers to the decline in amount of work done per unit time during a period of continuous practice. Blocking refers to temporary complete stoppages of work under the same conditions of practice. Such blockages and work decrements have been observed in both physical and mental work but are more easily observed in the former since the phenomena appear to be directly related to the lack of rest pauses. Such rest pauses are naturally more common in "continuous" physical work than in "continuous" mental work. However, under appropriate conditions of forced continuous mental work (such as naming colours) the involuntary blockages can be readily observed.

Both phenomena have been considered to be functions of fatigue induced by continuous work. Blockings could be obviated by enforcing rest pauses at about the same rate; while they could be increased by making the material more homogeneous. Thus, where conditions of work were most homogeneous, the average blocks per minute were 2·1; where they were least homogeneous, only 1·4 per minute.

The phenomena involved in the work curve have, of course, long attracted the attention of psychologists. However, little attention has been paid to the possibilities such phenomena offered in the investigation of abnormal subjects. Apart from the early work of Kraepelin and Hoch little information was available until very recently. Kraepelin had found that the performance of schizophrenics on a simple ten-minute addition test was characterized by rapid deterioration; if a rest was introduced after five minutes, performance increased markedly on the sixth minute, but then deteriorated rapidly again in the remaining four minutes. Hoch, on the other hand, reported that manic-depressives increased in strength of performance on the ergograph in the early stages of performance before showing the usual fatigue effects.

Since these early studies, little work has been done in this field. Mailloux and Newburger presented patients with a task involving four coloured lights with corresponding keys. Depression of the appropriate key extinguished a light and served to activate another. Thus continuous work was carried on for ten minutes. Patients were classified into six groups according to speed and type of response activity. Compared with the normal rate of seventy- two responses per minute, psychotics averaged a response rate of only 52·5, only one psychotic exceeding the normal mean. Psychotics averaged five blocks per minute compared with three for the normal group, Mailloux and Newburger found no relationship between work curve and blocking on the one hand and type of psychosis on the other.

More recently, using a very similar method, Venables and Tizard and O'Connor have repeated the study of Mailloux and Newburger. Venables and Tizard found an initial rise in performance (probably due to practice effects) followed by a fall, a further rise after rest and subsequent deterioration in schizophrenics. Long-stay schizophrenics performed consistently below short stay schizophrenics at all stages of performance. A group of endogenous depressives were intermediate between the two schizophrenic groups but showed no deterioration in performance, either before or after the rest pauses. It seems clear, therefore, that schizophrenics do show blockings and rapid work decrement compared with normals. This conclusion is supported by a recent study of Baruk. No information is available concerning the performance of neurotics.

The bewildering and often contradictory results brought together above do not mediate any obvious theories concerning the behaviour on psychomotor tests of neurotics and psychotics as compared with normals. For reasons which will be discussed below this is not surprising. However, some tentative suggestions will be made concerning possible reasons for those differences which are generally clear-cut.Four relatively definite statements may be made concerning the psychomotor behaviour of abnormals and normals.

1. Compared with normal subjects, neurotics show no significant disorganization on *simple* psychomotor tasks (and may actually be better than normals). They do, however, show marked disorganization compared with normals on *complex* psychomotor tasks. This disorganization is not a function of lower intelligence or poorer special abilities.
2. Within the total neurotic subgroup, there is evidence that introverted neurotics (*i.e.* dysthymics) show a different kind of motor disorganization compared with extraverted neurotics (*i.e.* hysterics); this difference is found also in normal extraverts and introverts.
3. Compared with normal subjects, psychotics show significant disorganization on both *simple* and *complex* psychomotor tasks.
4. There is some evidence that psychomotor tests which discriminate best between neurotics and normals are different from those which discriminate best between psychotics and normals, *i.e.* that psychosis and neurosis represent different dimensions.

In the following discussion, four important points should be borne in mind:

1. The differences outlined above refer to differences in *performance*, not to differences in *learning*. This distinction has become an important matter in theories of behaviour in recent years. The frequent failure to control for differences in learning ability before measuring differences in level of performance (*i.e.* when learning has been maximized) is extremely unfortunate and has undoubtedly contributed to much of the confusion prevailing in this field.
2. The method adopted above of summarizing the main findings in terms of type of response required (*e.g.* reaction-time, tapping, etc.) was dictated by the prevailing method of experimenting on two groups by comparing their performance on a single task. This method is particularly inappropriate in this field, since psychomotor tests are often short and correspondingly unreliable. It is extremely dangerous,

therefore, to draw conclusions from studies using a single test. Psychomotor tests should be used as one strand among others in the investigation and testing of theories concerning abnormalities of behaviour. They can rarely be used satisfactorily on their own.

3. A major difficulty in interpreting the results of diverse studies in relation to a given theory is that the analysis of results of earlier studies may be quite inappropriate. A good example of this is the interpretation of the work of Davis outlined above. Davis showed that introverted neurotics gave a characteristically different kind of manual response as compared with extraverted neurotics. Now it would seem reasonable to suppose that similar results would be expected from the Luria test. Unfortunately, although much valuable work has been done on the Luria and although it is clear that neurotics do show motor disorganization in this test, it is difficult from the earlier studies to determine whether introverted and extraverted neurotics showed different kinds of responses comparable to those found by Davis, since no precise analysis of this kind has been carried out. Thus it is possible only to point out that such differences would be expected if the Luria results were analysed in a particular way.
4. Very similar to this difficulty is the problem of negative results. The often repeated dictum that one negative result invalidates a theory is only a half truth. It is true only if the experiment is sufficiently precisely controlled that a negative result will have an unequivocal interpretation. Now this is seldom true in the field of psychology. Let us suppose our theory predicts that extraverted neurotics will have a slower rate of tapping than introverted neurotics due to the more rapid growth of reactive inhibition in the former group.

The analysis of the results in terms of number of taps per unit time may show no significant differences between the groups. This does not necessarily mean that the hypothesis has to be abandoned. The failure to find significant differences may be in the method of analysis adopted. A study by Boder is relevant. He showed that even such a simple activity as tapping has at least four components (movement up, upper reversal, movement down and bottom reversal). By means of oscillograph recordings he found that between both progressions there is a definite stop, which, in finger tapping, lasts from twice to four times as long as the progressions. He found that concomitant activities led to reduced speed, alterations in pattern of tapping, *differences in duration of arrested movement*, and reduction in tapping excursion. Now it is possible that taking an overall tapping rate as score on this test obscures significant differences in duration of arrested movement since extraverted neurotics may well "catch up" on other aspects of performance. In other words the prediction is relevant only to one aspect of performance and failure to isolate that aspect may lead to negative results in relation to the theory. This point should be remembered in all instances where negative results are obtained, especially where the theory is supported by other evidence.

Psychomotor Performance of Neurotics

The following postulates help to account for the observed differences between neurotics and normals in psychomotor tasks and mediate new predictions which support the general theory:

1. Performance in the test situation may be conceptualized as dependent upon the interaction of drive strength and task complexity.
2. Neurotics are characterized by high drive.
3. High drive may also be defined in terms of the strength of a stimulus. Thus a strong stimulus will have high drive value; a weak stimulus low drive value.
4. Where the response required is simple, it will be facilitated by high drive.
5. Where the response required has to be chosen from among others (*i.e.* discrimination is involved), it will be impeded in its appearance by high drive.

The above postulates would mediate the following predictions:

a. Neurotics will show psychomotor disorganization compared with normal subjects on complex but not simple tasks.

b. An increase in the strength of the stimulus will lead to an increased amplitude and speed of response in normal subjects. This prediction has been abundantly verified particularly in the field of reaction-time studies. Thus Johnson in an early study showed that increasing the strength of the stimulus led to a faster R.T., as did Chocholle; Steinman and Veniar found that faster reactions to a constant stimulus ratio were obtained at the stronger of two levels of visual intensity. Higher muscular tension levels, increased motivation and mild electric shock all facilitate speed of simple reaction-time. Above a certain intensity, however, a stimulus ceases to facilitate response and begins to inhibit it. This was shown by Johnson and by Pascal who found that when a loud disturbing noise was given with the ready signal for reaction-time, some subjects showed complete disruption of performance. This result would be expected from the Yerkes-Dodson law since it specifies *optimal* levels of intensity for most adequate performance.

Henry also showed that mild electric shock significantly speeded up speed of snatching a ball and speed of treadle pressing.

c. An increase in induced anxiety in normals (usually by means of some stressful situation) will facilitate amplitude and speed of simple responses. Thus, Ross found that speed of tapping increased significantly with an increase in anxiety just before the subject engaged in a boxing match. An important study relevant here is that by Castaneda which links anxiety as drive and stimulus intensity as drive. His subjects were high and low-anxiety high-school boys and girls; the stimulus a buzzer with two intensities; the response, squeezing a dynamometer; and the scores recorded, amplitude and speed of reaction. On the theory that differences in intensity produce differences in relevant drive and differences in anxiety produce differences in irrelevant drive he predicted that (1) speed of reaction of anxious subjects should be faster than that of non-anxious subjects; and (2) the increase in speed of reaction attributed to increased stimulus intensity should be relatively greater for non-anxious subjects, thus reducing the difference between anxious and non-anxious subjects. With regard to amplitude Castaneda found that anxious subjects did indeed show significantly higher amplitude at weak intensities and that there was a greater increase with the more intense stimulus in non-anxious as compared with anxious (though the latter finding held only for boys). With regard to speed of reaction, Castaneda found no difference at the weaker intensity between anxious and non anxious subjects and contrary to prediction found a greater increase in speed at the higher intensity for the anxious subjects.

d. Whereas increasing stimulus strength, inducing anxiety or stress in normals appears on the whole to facilitate response amplitude and speed in normals where the response required is simple in nature, it is predicted from the theory that the same factors would disrupt performance where the response required had to be selected from a range of possible choices or where the response itself is of a complex nature. There is a reasonable amount of evidence indicating the correctness of this prediction. Thus, a study by Grice indicates a significant increase in discrimination response time under conditions of induced anxiety or stress and this is supported by the work of Patrick.

Several studies on induced conflict (stress) indicate that "the probability of blockage as a reaction to conflict increases with the approach of the strengths of the conflicting responses to equality" and this conclusion is supported by several other studies.

Similarly, it has been shown that complex motor reactions deteriorate markedly under stress in normal subjects. This holds for steadiness; the work curve and.more cómplex tasks.

Thus we may reasonably conclude with Davis that in normal subjects "under conditions in which anticipatory tension was increased, skilled responses were more extensive, more precipitate, more disturbed by restless movements and less accurate than single conditions (simple stimuli) in which anticipatory tension was normal." The above results and those reported in the body of the chapter do seem to support the hypothesis that neurotics are characterized by a high state of drive which facilitates the correct response in a simple situation but impedes the correct response in a complex situation.

Psychomotor Performance of Introverts and Extraverts

Little can be said about this aspect of performance in psychomotor tasks, except to repeat that it seems to be clearly established that the *type* of motor response on a given task will differ for extraverts as compared with introverts where the appropriate experimental conditions are set. Within the neurotic disorganization apparent on complex tasks, hysterics will tend to react differently as compared with dysthymics. The main evidence for this proposition derives from the work of Davis, which has been discussed above in detail, but similar differences could no doubt be obtained on tests such as those of the Luria, under appropriate conditions.

4

Heredity and Psychological Abnormality

Introduction

We are not speaking here of social heredity, in the sense in which a kingdom or a family business may be said to be hereditary. Our concern is the differences between individuals which arise from differences in their genetical make-up; and in this sense the hereditary are distinguished from the environmental causes of variation. Genetical and environmental factors interact with one another, and can never be completely disentangled. But by appropriate techniques it is possible to estimate how much of the total variance observed in a group of individuals, sharing a common environment, is contributed by genetical causes, though we are not thereby entitled to assume that the contribution would be the same if either the genetic constitution of the group, or the environment, were significantly changed.

Principles of Heredity

Before trying to deal with the extent to which psychological abnormalities may be said to be genetical, we must describe briefly the physical basis of heredity and what we know of the genes and their mode of action. In so far as psychological differences between individuals are genetically caused, they must be due to such differences between genes, *i.e.* to differences of a physical kind.

Nature of the Gene and its Effect on Development

The basic units of heredity are the genes. Chemically, they are thought probably to take the form of very large and elaborately constructed molecules of desoxyribonucleic acid (DNA). It may give some idea of the complexity of these molecules. Unless altered by mutation, the genes are transmitted from one generation to the next unchanged. They are capable of building up from the materials with which they are supplied other genes identical with themselves, so that one cell of the body can grow and divide into two, mother and daughter cells having the same genetical constitution. Mutation is a rare and rather haphazard event, which can be artificially brought about by the use of chemicals which will penetrate the nucleus of the cell without destroying it or by physical agents such as radiation. Apart from such experiments it is not likely to occur spontaneously much more frequently than once in every fifty thousand generations for any one gene. Such a change, when it does occur, will be a chemical one and consist in such an event as a rearrangement of a group of atoms, or the loss of a side-chain from a molecule. Differences so caused may be trifling or critical in their effects.

The genes exert their effects through their control of biochemical reactions, by speeding up some chemical reactions and retarding others, or by inhibiting some reaction until the chemical environment is such as to trigger it off. Their action resembles that of enzymes in that, though involved in chemical changes, they maintain their own identity. They control the development of the individual from the earliest stage of the fertilized ovum up to adult life and into old age. The variation due to some genetic differences may be seen very early, *e.g.* into a male or female constitution, but in other cases much later; and there is no point in life at which one can say that all latent genetic potentialities must have been manifested.

As a simple example of a genetic difference we may take the condition known as phenylketonuria which can be attributed to a single abnormal gene. Whereas the normal gene permits of normal body chemistry, the abnormal gene fails to provide an enzyme which converts the amino-acid phenylalanine into tyrosine, a foodstuff of vital importance to the brain. If the individual has one normal and one abnormal gene, he can still deal with the phenylalanine and can be mentally normal; if he has two abnormal genes, he cannot carry out the essential chemical processes, and the phenylalanine is excreted in the urine as phenylpyruvic acid and can be identified by a simple colour reaction. The metabolic deficiency prevents normal development of the brain, and the abnormal individual is mentally defective.

We must think of these genetic-biochemical relationships as being ones of great complexity, involving many stages. H. J. Muller puts it:

> Whatever may be the nature of the primary chemical products of genes within the cell, these products must be of thousands of different kinds, corresponding with the thousands of different genes, and these products must interact with one another in innumerable ways to form secondary products, tertiary products and those ever further removed from the genes. It is usually only after a most intricate web of these inter-actions has been followed through that those end-products are at last found which we become aware of as the characteristics of the organism. Because of the great indirectness of the route connecting the genes with these end results, it is evident that any given characteristic must be a resultant of the action of many genes, some playing a major role in its development but many more playing only a minor role.

Although the genes are transmitted as independent units, we must think of the genetic constitution as also largely acting as a whole. We shall find that the cumulative effects of the minor end results of many genes will be just as important in some fields as the major effects of single genes in other fields.

Once a major gene has produced its distinctive difference, this is not the end of the matter; for the specific abnormality so caused will become involved in a tangled web of secondary and tertiary consequences. Grüneberg has shown how, in the experimental animal though not in man, such complex problems of causation may be sorted out by tracking back through ever earlier stages in the development of the embryo. In the case of one particular gene in the rat, the abnormality caused is quite simply an anomaly in the development of cartilage; the more distant effects, however, are of an extremely various kind, so that apparently clinically distinct diseases, liable to lead to death in quite different ways, can be traced back to this one cause.

Just as the effects of one gene may be many, so also the converse is true and the same end results can be brought about by different genes. There is a well known form of blindness which is caused by a disease of the retina of the eye, *retinitis pigmentosa*. This condition can be watched by the oculist, with the aid of the ophthalmoscope, from its very earliest stages; and the actual pathological processes involved can be seen in all their detail. Nevertheless there are several different genes which can bring about this condition; and by an examination of the eye alone it is impossible to say which of the genes is the one responsible.

The effect of the genes is not limited to early development. Both growth and regression in all stages from the embryonic to senile decay are under genetic control. Many genetically determined conditions baldness in men, for example do not usually become DNA is found in the chromosomes, and (with minor exceptions) only in the chromosomes, of all living cells. A single molecule probably consists of at least a thousand turns of the helix shown above. The section shows how the groups of atoms are arranged in two intertwining spiral chains. Each chain consists of phosphate and sugar groups. Attached to the latter are various chemical "bases" which link one chain with the other. The varying sequence of the bases along the molecule may provide a kind of code by which hereditary characteristics are transmitted from one generation to the next.

In many of these the "pedigree of causes" will be more complex than in phenylketonuria, and allow, therefore, greater scope for variability in manifestation. *Diabetes mellitus* is a disease which is often genetically determined. It is due fundamentally to a deficiency of a circulating enzyme, insulin. It shows part of the network of consequences which can be set in motion by the failure to secrete sufficient insulin. Some of the end results are due to the impaired ability to burn sugar, others to the efforts of the organism to compensate for this. The course taken by the abnormality is influenced by secondary factors, some of them attributable to other genes, others the products of non-genetical factors, such as medical treatment, including the administration of insulin.

For an understanding of the way in which a genetical difference may manifest itself in an observable characteristic of the individual we depend on research and knowledge in many fields, such as embryology, biochemistry and physiology. Even in the best studied instances, our knowledge of the dynamic chain will be full of gaps. The application of genetics to the study of abnormal psychology is no different in principle from its applications in biology or medicine. We may, indeed, suppose that the route from the gene to the end result will be more complex and indirect than ever; but we may still be able to show that certain effects can be put down to genetical causes. though we can claim no detailed knowledge of the hypothetical genes involved or their mode of operation.

From what has been said it can be seen that it is the genes which are inherited, and not abnormalities or diseases themselves. The genes can only act in an environmental framework; and their effects will be influenced to a greater or lesser degree by the nature of that environment. One of the aims of genetical research is to discover how much of the total variance occurring in a given population can be attributed to genetical and to environmental differences between individuals. To understand how genetical variation can occur, we have to observe the way in which the genes are distributed in their descent from parent to child.

Location of the Genes on the Chromosomes

The totality of the genes are organized into chromosomes, which are contained within the nucleus of the cell. Every species of living thing, with the exception of the most primitive, has its own characteristic number of chromosomes, there normally being twenty three pairs in man. Every cell in the body has its full complement of chromosomes, except for the sex cells, ova and spermatozoa which contain only half the normal number, one from each pair. The genes are too small to be seen individually it has been estimated that in man each cell contains between 40,000 and 80,000 genes but the human chromosomes can be seen when suitably stained. The chromosomes exist in pairs, each member of which is homologous to the other; the genes of which they consist are also homologous and paired, each member of a pair being either chemically identical with its partner, or differing from it in some small though possibly important way. The genes are arranged along the length of the chromosomes, which are threadlike structures, often condensed in appearance because they are spirally twisted. The order in which the genes are arranged along the chromosome is largely held fixed, so that gene pairs lie opposite one another in the chromosome pairs. In experimental animals, the gene can be identified both by its position along the length of a particular chromosome, and also by its effects, so that chromosome maps can be drawn. A particular gene can be shown to be capable of taking, in some instances, one of two or more alternative forms; and each of these forms will be likely to have a slightly different effect in development. Thus one of the genes which determines a man's blood group can take one of three forms, A, B and O. This gives the possibility of six different types of constitution – AA, AB, AO, BB, BO, and OO. The serologist can test for the presence or absence of an A or B gene, and so can distinguish some of these blood types from one another; but he has no way of testing for the presence of the O gene, so that some genetic types cannot be absolutely identified by serology alone.

These blood factors are representative of genes which cause no abnormality, and which are individually very common. Most of the severe conditions which have a simple genetical explanation are due to rare genes, *i.e.* the gene which is compatible with normality is extremely common, while its alternative form or allele is rare. Genetically man is extremely diverse, perhaps more so than any other species. To take a limited but practical illustration, Bertinshaw tested the bloods of four hundred and seventy-five Londoners with eight groups of antisera, and were able to identify two hundred and ninety-six different combinations of blood groups. With the exception of identical twins, each individual is genetically unique. The existence of so much genetical diversity is a good reason to expect a genetical contribution to many modes of variation in which we are interested.

Formation of the Sex Cells: Fertilization

In the ordinary process of bodily growth and multiplication of cells, each chromosome builds up a duplicate of itself before the cell divides, so that each daughter-cell contains twenty-three pairs of chromosomes like the mother-cell. When the daughter-cell is to be a sex-cell (ovum or spermatozoon) the chromosomes do not build up duplicates but simply separate, so that the daughter-cell contains twenty-three single chromosomes. When spermatozoon unites with ovum in the process of fertilization the twenty-three pairs are re-established. The new individual therefore comes to have half his chromosomes from his father and half from his mother; but of the chromosomes he obtained from his father, the proportion derived from his father's father and from his father's mother need not be equal at all. The process of selection within pairs of chromosomes is entirely random. In this way a great deal of mixing up of chromosomes, and therefore of genes, goes on from generation to generation; but the mixing is much more intimate than this method alone would permit. Pairs of chromosomes may exchange parts with one another by a process called crossing-over, so that the pair of chromosomes $A_1B_1C_1D_1$ and $A_2B_2C_2D_2$ may give rise to the new chromosomes $A_1B_1C_2D_2$ and $A_2B_2C_1D_1$. The exchange of genes occurs in whole blocks at a time; and in this way a single chromosome passed from father to child may contain genes from both the two paternal grandparents.

Dominant, Recessive and Intermediate Genes

In discussing the blood groups it was indicated that the serologist cannot distinguish between individuals of the AA and AO constitution, because both give, equally strongly, the reaction typical of A gene carriers. If the A gene is present, the O gene appears to have no effect. Under these circumstances A is said to be dominant and O to be recessive. If AA produced a stronger reaction than AO, one could call the A gene intermediate. Not only is A dominant to O, but so also is B, so that the serologist is equally unable to distinguish between BB and BO individuals. However A and B are not dominant or recessive to one another, and the AB individual gives both the A and the B serological reactions.

From knowing what happens in the formation of the sex-cells and at fertilization, we can easily see what the offspring will be when individuals of the various types mate together. O is by far the commonest of the three genes, with A the next, while B is relatively rare. The commonest constitutions are therefore OO and AO. The first, having two genes of the same kind, is said to be homozygous for O, while the second is heterozygous. If an AO man mates with an OO woman, the child will be able to get either an A or an O gene from the father, only an O gene from the mother. The children of such a mating will tend to be AO and OO with an equal frequency. Suppose the dominant gene in which we are interested is not the normal A gene, but a gene which causes some abnormality or defect. Then, as this gene, *D* let us call it, will be rare compared with its normal allele *d*, the great majority of people will be of the *dd* constitution and normal, while there will be some people of the *Dd* constitution and abnormal. The *DD* constitution will be so very rare that it can be neglected (perhaps even incapable of surviving). A mating between normal and abnormal persons will be a mating of *Dd* with *dd*, and half the children can be expected to be *Dd* and to show the same abnormality while the other half will be *dd* and normal. In this way the abnormality will appear to go down the generations from parent to child in a simple and direct way.

Let us take the case of two AO parents. As their child could take either an A or an O gene from either parent, he would have one chance in four of being AA, one chance of being AO, one of being OA and one of being OO. One quarter of the expected children would, in fact, be of a different blood type, the O or not-A type, from both of their parents and from the rest of their brothers and sisters. Now let us suppose that the recessive gene, *d*, in which we are interested is one which causes abnormality, while the dominant gene *D* is now compatible with normality. Then two heterozygotes, or carriers, of the *Dd* type, though normal themselves, will have children one quarter of whom can be expected to be *dd* and abnormal. If such an abnormal person mates it will probably be with a person who is homozygous for the normal gene, of the type *DD*; all the children of this mating will be *Dd* and normal in appearance (though they carry the abnormal gene). In this case the abnormality, being due to a recessive gene, appears out of the blue in a family tree, is not apparently handed on from parent to child, but may easily strike more than one member of a sibship. An understanding of the simple principles enables one to work out the results of any particular mating for oneself.

Intermediate genes, neither dominant nor recessive, will frequently be found in cases where an effect can be shown to greater or lesser degree, instead of in an all-or-none way. Quantitative genetic variation is almost the rule when we are concerned with normal and not pathological events.

Sex-linked Inheritance: Colour-blindness

One of the twenty-three pairs of chromosomes is anomalous in that the two members of the pair are not the same size and hence not strictly homologous. These are the sex chromosomes, of which the X chromosome is of full size, while the Y-chromosome is hardly more than a fragment containing very little genetic material in proportion. In the case of man, it is the female which is the homogametic sex, having two X-chromosomes, while the male is heterogametic and has one X- and one Y-chromosome. It will be seen that the female can only produce ova of one kind, with one X-chromosome, whereas the man can produce two kinds of spermatozoa, with an X- or with a Y-chromosome, which will in turn, after union with an ovum, produce respectively a female or a male.

As the X-chromosome is so much bigger than the Y-chromosome, the greater part of it in the male has no matching partner.

X = abnormal sex-linked recessive gene

XX = normal female

XY = normal male

XX = carrier female (unaffected)

XY = affected male

XX = affected female (rare)

Any gene, dominant or recessive, on this part of the X-chromosome, will have its full effect in the male, but if recessive will be liable to be suppressed in the female. Conditions so determined tend to show a very characteristic pedigree, with transmission occurring through the female, but manifestation being practically confined to males. An affected male, mating with a normal female, will have nothing but normal children. His sons will have taken a Y-chromosome from him, without the abnormal gene; his daughters will have taken an X-chromosome carrying the abnormal gene, but will also have inherited from their mother a normal X-chromosome, with the normal dominant allele. If one of these heterozygous daughters marries a normal male, as one may readily see, all her daughters will be normal, though some of them will be heterozygous, whereas some of her sons will be abnormal. Those of them who inherit their grandmother's X-chromosome will be normal, those who inherit the grandfather's X chromosome will get with it an abnormal gene which can now show its effect. For a female to show the abnormality, she must be the daughter of an affected father and a heterozygous mother.

Red-green colour-blindness is a relatively common perceptual anomaly, in which the affected person has difficulty in distinguishing red and green. Its dependence on a recessive sex-linked, or X-borne, gene is well established. In this country the gene frequency is over one in twenty, so that rather more than five per cent of males are colour-blind, while colour-blind females are rare. Clearly the frequency of the character in the female will be the square of the frequency in the male, *i.e.* something over one in four hundred. If p is the frequency of the abnormal gene, and q the frequency of the normal allele, then persons homozygous for the abnormal gene will have a frequency of p^2, persons homozygous for the normal gene a frequency of q^2, while heterozygotes will have a frequency of $2pq$.So far theory. According to Stern the actual figures observed are fairly close to those expected. There is, however, some discrepancy, in the sense that there are rather more "colour-blind" women than there should be theoretically. First, the gene, or genes, involved is not absolutely recessive but can be regarded as weakly intermediate. Some heterozygous women have "poor colour aptitude," which can be mistaken for colour-blindness. Secondly, there are four main subtypes of partial colour-blindness: deuteranopia and protanopia which are dichromatic types, and deuteranomaly and protanomaly which are trichromatic types. Although all four subtypes are inherited in a recessive sex-linked way, two loci might be involved, each with the possibility of three alleles:

1. Gene for normal colour vision, which is dominant to the gene for deuteranomaly, which in turn is dominant to the gene for deuteranopia.
2. Gene for normal colour vision, which is dominant to the gene for protanomaly, which in turn is dominant to the gene for protanopia.

Total colour-blindness, or the ability to see no colours, distinguishing only shades of white and grey, is much rarer. It can be genetically determined by a recessive gene on the homologous part of the X- and Y-chromosomes. Such so-called partially sex-linked genes are much less easily recognized as having a connexion with the sex chromosomes.

Sex-linked inheritance contributes little to the total of psychiatric abnormality. It was once suggested that a sex-linked dominant gene played a part in the causation of manic-depressive disorder, because this diagnosis is made more frequently in women than men. Clearly, women with two X-chromosomes would have twice the chance of receiving the gene that a man with one X-chromosome would have. However, it is easily seen that the fathers and mothers of affected females would have equal chances of being gene- carriers, whereas one would expect only the mothers of affected males to be gene-carriers. In fact, no such differential incidence is found, and other explanations have to be sought, *e.g.*, in the difference between the male and the female constitution in the broad sense.

Examples of Dominant Inheritance

Although it is probable that there are as many single genes of large effect causing psychiatric illness as other conditions such as metabolic disorders and eye disease, it is not surprising that so far very few have been identified. Nevertheless we have one excellent example in *Huntington's chorea*. This disease received its name from the fact that it was first satisfactorily described by an American country doctor of that name, whose father and grandfather, doctors before him in the same district of Long Island, had observed its appearance in generation after generation of certain local families. These families could be traced back to immigrants in a ship which had docked in Boston Bay some centuries before, and who had sailed from Bures in Suffolk.

In persons who carry the gene, nerve cells in the cortex and the basal ganglia of the brain are liable to die off prematurely. The first symptoms are usually shown in middle life, and the mean age of onset is 35. Men and women are equally liable. The characteristic symptoms are spontaneous jerky movements of the head, trunk and limbs, progressive personality changes, and progressive intellectual deterioration to severe dementia and eventual death, perhaps fifteen years after the onset. The personality changes are often the earliest signs of anything being wrong, and include such changes as increased irritability and aggressiveness, slovenliness, unreliability, lack of control and delinquency. Admission to a mental hospital is likely to become necessary in time. The condition is a rare one: Minski and Guttman found sixteen cases in 23,000 inmates in London mental hospitals. However, for every case in hospital, there may be as many as four at home. It was recently estimated that there may be 2,000 cases in England and Wales and perhaps twice as many persons destined to develop the disease.

As the condition is dominant and rare, affected persons will be heterozygous. They may pass on to their children either the chromosome with the normal gene, or the chromosome with the Huntington gene. One can expect, therefore, that 50 per cent of the children of a Huntington patient will develop the condition in time. A gene-carrier, however, may marry and have a family, and die of some other cause before the disease has had time to develop; in such a case, if some of his children develop the disease, the condition will have skipped a generation. Most gene carriers do, in fact, have their families before they fall ill, so that the gene is not eliminated at all quickly from the population by the processes of natural selection. This sort of thing is rather the rule with dominant genes; the abnormalities they cause are often late in onset, or not very severe, or very variable in their gravity. Dominant genes which caused early death, before procreation could occur, would extinguish themselves on their appearance; and every new case would be due to a fresh mutation. The genetic nature of the abnormality would then be very difficult toExtracts from a larger pedigree. None of the offspring of the normal members of the family have had Huntington's chorea. Spouses, all of whom were normal, are not shown, nor are children who died in infancy. The ages given for the unaffected members are those at death or when last heard of. It will be noted that many of the youngest generation still run considerable risk of being affected.

With a condition of late onset as severe as Huntington's chorea the early detection of genetic carriers becomes important. Not only would this be helpful, especially for the genetic counsellor, in deciding which members of a family were and which were not liable to develop the disease, and to pass on the potentiality to children;

but it could also lead to a better understanding of the pathology of the condition. No reliable indications have been found in Huntington's chorea. Minski and Guttmann have suggested that future choreic cases tend to resemble physically the ancestors in the family who had had the disease, rather than those who had not. They also thought it possible that subtle differences in muscular coordination and control might be found in heterozygotes. Leese, Pond and Shields studied a family in which it seemed possible that members who later became affected would show a definite type of abnormality in the EEG some years before other signs were detectable.

Huntington's chorea can be classified among the presenile dementias. Another example of this group of conditions is *Pick's disease*. This is of rather later onset, and is clinically less well defined and less easily diagnosed; but there is evidence that it too is determined by a dominant gene. Its manifestation rate is not as high as that of the Huntington gene, and modifying genes must play a more important part. Sjögren has calculated that 19 per cent of the parents and 7 per cent of the sibs of patients with Pick's disease were similarly affected, instead of the 50 per cent in each case required by theory. This would mean that the majority of gene-carriers were protected against developing the disease. Sanders, has claimed (with doubtful reliability) that carriers can be detected by means of the Rorschach test some years before the onset of definite symptoms.

Another presenile dementia is *Alzheimer's disease*, pathologically quite distinct from Pick's disease although clinically often difficult to distinguish. Sjögren thinks that multifactorial inheritance is more likely than dominant inheritance in this case. The pathological changes are identical with those of ordinary senile dementia, though they are occurring unduly early; and the genetical basis may be the presence of a number of genes each favouring to some degree an early senility.

No gene, whose only effect is to cause deterioration and death at an age well after the normal cessation of procreation, will be eliminated from the population by processes of natural selection. It is accordingly probable that the changes of normal senility are primarily gene-determined. However, among the various forms that senile dementia may take, it is quite possible that further specific conditions, like Pick's disease, still remain to be discovered.

Epiloia (tuberose sclerosis) is a rare disease, affecting about one in every 30,000 of the general population; it causes multiple benign tumours of the brain, kidney, skin and other tissues and generally mental deficiency and epilepsy. It shows itself in childhood, and as a rule the individual is too abnormal to have the chance of reproduction. Sometimes, however, if the brain is not severely involved, institutional life is not required, and procreation can occur. Nevertheless, because of the restricted fertility the dominant gene which is the cause of the condition is rapidly eliminated from the population, the balance being maintained by fresh mutation; it is estimated that about one case in four is due to a mutation.

Of the commoner mental illnesses, the genetic basis of *manic-depressive psychosis* has been regarded as probably unifactorial and dominant. The gene would ordinarily show itself by causing a tendency to spontaneous variations of mood, probably only in some cases and at some times severe enough to need psychiatric treatment; in fact, the manifestation rate would be more like 30 per cent than 100 per cent, indicating the significance of aetiological factors other than the hypothetical specific gene. The main evidence to support this theory is the high incidence of severe disorders of a similar kind in parents, siblings, and children of manic-depressives.

Leonhard, has investigated the families of patients with *atypical psychoses*. In many such families there appears to be a dominant form of inheritance, the same atypical features being shown in the mental illnesses of parents and children. Again, in some families schizophrenia appears to be related to a dominant gene of weak and variable manifestation. The schizophrenic illnesses observed by Book in an isolated community in the north of Sweden were attributed by him to a gene which manifested itself fully in the homozygote, but also in 20 per cent of heterozygotes.

Although the genetics of affective and schizophrenic psychoses are obscure, it seems likely that a fair proportion of mental illness may be due to specific dominant genes with low penetrance.

The above risk figures, based largely on Stenstedt, are in most instances calculated after inclusion of some relatives with affective but not certainly manic-depressive disorders. Weinberg's abridged method of age-correction has generally been used. With the use of other methods higher figures would be obtained.

Table 4.1. Expectancy (Per Cent) of Manic-depressive Disorders among Relatives of Manic Depressive Probands

Investigator	Parents	Sibs	Children
Banse	10.8	18.1	–
Roll and Entres	13.0	–	10.7
Slater	15.5	–	15.2
Stromgren	7.5	10.7	–
Sjogren	7.0	3.6	–
Kallmann	23.4	23.0	
		26.3	–
Stenstedt	7.4	12.3	9.4

Other psychological abnormalities which have been attributed to dominant inheritance include *specific dyslexia* (congenital word blindness) and *tune deafness*. In the first condition, despite normal intelligence there is a marked difficulty in learning to read and write. Hallgren, found that only twelve out of one hundred and sixteen unselected cases were isolated ones in the family, and that about 50 per cent of siblings having one affected parent were similarly handicapped.

Kalmus, devised a battery of tests which discriminated persons who were unable to recognize commonly known melodies or to sing in tune. The trait showed bimodal distribution, and clear-cut differences were frequently shown between members of the same family, in such a way as to suggest that the variation might be caused by a single dominant gene. Kalmus suggested that the intrusion of such a gene into families of composers like Bach may have contributed to causes which disrupted long-standing musical traditions.

Examples of Recessive Inheritance

Rather less than 1 per cent of certified mental defectives suffer from *phenylketonuria* (PKU). As has been said earlier in this chapter, this condition is attributable to an inborn metabolic error. Individuals who carry two abnormal PKU genes are entirely unable to metabolize phenylalanine. These homozygotes are nearly always of very low intelligence, seldom being above imbecile level; and they very rarely propagate. It follows that practically all phenylketonurics will be derived from the mating of two heterozygotes, and in such sibships one in four will be expected to show the trait. Investigations by Folling, the Norwegian biochemist who discovered the condition by Jervis in the U.S.A. and by Munro in Great Britain bear this out. After sometimes Jervis analysed all family data then available from these and other investigations Among two hundred and sixty-six sibships, four hundred and thirty-three persons out of a total of 1,527 were affected, or a little over 28 per cent. When allowance is made by appropriate methods for the fact that only families including at least one affected member are represented, figures closer to the expected 25 per cent are obtained.

In rare recessive conditions like this, one may expect an excess of cousin-marriage in the parents of affected persons. If p is the gene frequency, p^2 is the frequency of the homozygote, which may be roughly equated with the observed frequency of the abnormality. It has accordingly been calculated that in the case of PKU $p = 1/245$. The frequency of the heterozygote $= 2p(1 - p) = 1/123$; so we see that heterozygotes may be by no means uncommon even in the case of very rare conditions caused by a recessive gene. If one is a gene-bearer one runs no risk of producing a child with PKU unless one mates with another heterozygote; mating at random the chance of doing this would be 1/123, but only 1/8 if one were to mate with a first cousin. Hence it happens that there will be more cousin-marriage among the parents of persons suffering from rare recessive abnormalities than in the general population, and that the rarer the gene the higher the cousin-marriage rate will be. In Munro's series of forty-seven families, the parents were first cousins in five cases (10 per cent), against an expectation of 0·5 per cent for the general population. In the U.S.A. where p is estimated at the higher figure of 1/173, Jervis found that about 5 per cent of the parents of PKU patients were first cousins.

Unlike pathological dominant genes, recessive genes are quite widely spread in the population, being carried by heterozygotes who suffer no ill-effects; in this way they are protected against elimination by natural selection. Muller has opined that we all carry somewhere about eight pathogenic recessive genes. Recessive conditions, because of this immunity to selective processes, tend to be graver than dominant abnormalities, of earlier onset and less variable in their manifestations, and possibly also less open to environmental modification of their effects. This latter quality, however, depends very much on the degree of understanding of their mode of operation. There is evidence to suggest, for instance, that PKU subjects may be partly protected against excessive retardation of intellectual development by controlling their consumption of phenylalanine.

Note the presence of the defect in collateral branches of the family but not among direct ascendants. In one instance the parents were first cousins. It is quite probable that the contribution of rare recessive genes, *in toto*, to the lower grades of mental deficiency is a significant one. This is most likely in the case of patients who show neurological abnormalities in addition to low intelligence. In his survey of all cases of mental deficiency in the Royal Eastern Counties Institution, Colchester, Penrose classified one hundred and twenty-eight patients as showing disease of the nervous system; of these eight, or 6·2 per cent had consanguineous parents. Even among the non-neurological patients there was an increased consanguinity rate of 3·1 per cent, suggesting that undifferentiated cases of defect include a proportion due to recessive genetic abnormalities. It is interesting that, until the discovery of the characteristic colour reaction in the urine, cases of PKU were indistinguishable from other defectives.

Other recessive conditions in mental deficiency include *familial amaurotic idiocy*, both of the infantile and of the juvenile type, "true" *microcephaly*, and some cases of spastic paraplegia. These and other conditions are described by Penrose.

Recessive defects are less well-known in the field of the *psychoses*. *Wilson's disease*, which is an error of metabolism causing the depositions of copper in the tissues, sometimes causes mental illness; and it is due to a recessive gene. One form of epilepsy, *myoclonic epilepsy*, is due to a recessive; and there is a strong belief that some, at least, of the illnesses called schizophrenic are also recessively determined. The problem of the genetics of schizophrenia is discussed later.

In the field of *sense perception*, recessive genes make their own contribution to the total abnormality in a population. Many cases of deaf-mutism are caused in this way. A study of the offspring of cousins revealed a relatively high proportion of persons who were blind or partially blind. The inability to taste phenylthiocarbamide (PTC), a substance which most people find distinctly bitter, can hardly be regarded as an abnormality, since about 30 per cent of British and white American people fail to taste the standard solution; but it is an example of a relatively objective and clear-cut variation in perception which behaves as a recessive trait. It is not the total inability to taste PTC which is due to a single pair of genes, but rather the taste threshold. When a group of people is tested with a series of solutions of PTC of different strengths, the lowest strength at which they taste a bitter being recorded, the resulting distribution is a bimodal one. Analysis of the family data suggests that those who fall within the non-tasting part of the curve are homozygous for a recessive gene though the genetics may be more complex than was at first thought, and there is some overlap between tasters and non-tasters.

Intermediate Inheritance

When PKU was first discovered, it was not possible to distinguish between the heterozygote and the normal homozygote, and the gene could be classified as recessive. However, this distinction is now possible; if the heterozygote is given a considerable amount of phenylalanine the percentage concentration of this substance in the blood rises to a higher level than in the normal homozygote, and is maintained at a raised level for a much longer time. It would therefore be more strictly correct to regard the gene as intermediate between dominance and recessivity. The same can be said if, in the case of a dominant gene, it is found possible to distinguish between the homozygous carrier of two abnormal genes and the heterozygote; in this case dominance would have to be reclassified as incomplete dominance, and the gene be better regarded as intermediate than dominant. Book, Schut and Reed have suggested that the gene for recessive microcephaly might express itself in heterozygous form as moderate intellectual impairment, and Penrose has reported an excess of psychopaths among the relatives of microcephalics. Though microcephaly itself is a rare condition the gene frequency was estimated as between 1/162 and 1/230. Book *et al.*, conclude that if this is the case borderline intellectual development in 0·5 to 1 per cent of the population might be due to the intermediate expression of the gene for genetic microcephaly. The evidence, however, is scanty so far and other interpretations are possible.

Sometimes it is found that the heterozygote possesses advantages over both types of homozygote. This is the case in the condition known as *sickle-cell anaemia*. The abnormal gene causes the production of a different haemoglobin from that produced by the normal gene. In persons homozygous for the abnormal gene, all the haemoglobin is of the abnormal kind, and the individual suffers from a severe anaemia and with difficulty survives childhood. The heterozygote has a mixture of normal and abnormal haemoglobins, and suffers only from a slight tendency to get anaemic if circumstances are such as to encourage such a tendency. On the other hand he has a biological advantage in being relatively much more resistant, than persons with only the normal haemoglobin are, to malignant types of malaria. Thus it is that in, for example, certain parts of Africa where malaria is common, the gene for the sickle-cell trait (as it is called in the heterozygote) is common too, despite its disastrous effects in the homozygote.

There is no certain case of intermediate inheritance in the field of psychological abnormality. Nevertheless it is possible that one or more of the genes involved in the causation of schizophrenia may be of this kind. It is often held that, if a recessive gene causes schizophrenia in the homozygote, in the heterozygote it may cause only a slight deviation of personality the "schizoid" personality. If schizoid persons are, as it is often thought, cool, reserved, self-sufficient, then one can imagine circumstances in which they might have a considerable biological advantage over others. The high frequency of schizophrenia and of schizoid personality which Book (1953) found in his north Swedish population could be regarded as related to the advantage conferred by schizoid traits in such a remote and hostile environment, in which opportunities for social life are reduced to a minimum. This idea approaches very near indeed to pure speculation. Nevertheless it bears thinking of when we try to explain why schizophrenia, which is biologically so disadvantageous, should also be so common.

Principles of Polygenic Inheritance

So far, largely for reasons of simplicity of exposition, we have dealt with conditions which are due to single pairs of genes. We now turn to multifactorial or polygenic inheritance. The genes we have discussed so far show themselves by causing some single massive difference, by which they are, so to speak, labelled. But their effects do not end there. For instance, there is a recessive gene which in double dose causes the carrier to be an albino. But albinos differ from normal individuals not only in being unable to produce normal pigments in the hair, the skin and elsewhere, but also in being, on the average, smaller in stature, less fertile, less intelligent and shorter lived than others. There is no doubt that such fundamental biological variables as size, vitality and fertility are influenced, to some degree, by very great numbers of genes; these variables then show quantitative variation, and one is likely to find curves of distribution of the "normal" or Gaussian kind, as is the case for instance with intelligence on the Binet scale. It is probable that the great majority of the genes which influence such graded characters do not have any single massive effect of their own; and to them the name of genes of small effect, or polygenes, is given. They are subject to the same laws of segregation as all other genes; but the description of the effects of segregation will be different. Thus Mendel bred races of tall and short peas, the difference depending on a single gene, and got tall and short progeny. In mankind, matings of tall and short parents will have a tendency to produce children of intermediate size, while two parents both of middle height are quite capable of producing both tall and short children. When we leave pathology for normal physiology and psychology, most of the characteristics in which we are interested are of a quantitatively variable kind, and, in so far as they are subject to genetical influence, regulated by multifactorial and not unifactorial inheritance.

Let us suppose that a particular characteristic, say that of height, is determined by three gene pairs, A and a, B and b, C and c. We will suppose that the capital letters tend to cause tallness, the lower-case letters shortness, that there is neither dominance nor recessivity, that all genes are equally common, and that mating is taking place at random. Then the tallest individual we can find, with the constitution AABBCC, will be relatively uncommon; for every one of him there will be six individuals one degree less tall: aABBCC, AaBBCC, AAbBCC, AABbCC, AABBcC, AABBCc. There will be fifteen combinations of four capitals with two lower-case letters, and in fact the population, graded by height, will be distributed according to the terms of the expansion of $(\frac{1}{2} + \frac{1}{2})^6 = (1 + 6 + 15 + 20 + 15 + 6 + 1)/64$. It is readily seen that the commonest group will be the middle group, with average height. It will also be seen that if we generalize, and write the expansion of $(p + q)^n$, in which $p + q = 1$, as n gets bigger and bigger we get a closer and closer approximation to the normal curve, which is skewed over the middle part of the curve very little, when n is big, even if p is bigger than q.

We may, in fact, say that where we find distributions of a normal kind we shall think of multifactorial inheritance, but not in cases where the distribution is not normal. The ability to taste PTC is, indeed, a graded character; but its distribution is not normal but bimodal with relatively little overlap in the middle part of the curve. Multifactorial inheritance will not do, therefore, in that case. However, even if the distribution is normal, this is no proof of a genetic and polygenic determination. A multiplicity of environmental or non-genetical factors, capable of operating additively, could conceivably result in the same sort of distribution; and a combination of polygenic and environmental factors could very easily do so. The proof of a genetical basis will depend on other observations.

Such a further observation, which may be made with a character showing normal distribution, is the demonstration of a regression equation linking the deviation from average values shown by a series of subjects with the deviation shown by their relatives.

Estimate based on Binet test of three hundred and one defective and two hundred and sixty-one normal children. Jaederholm's data, from Pearson. Scores are shown in terms of standard deviations.

As an example, we may take the case of intelligence. As is well known, the Binet I.Q. is normally distributed, with mean at 100 and with a standard deviation of about 16 points. If we measure the intelligence of a series of schoolchildren, and also those of their sibs, it will be found that the correlated data are fairly well described by a linear equation: the I.Q. of the sib will tend to deviate from the mean in the same direction as that of the original subject or proband, though not so far. Similar regression equations will link I.Q.s of children with those of their parents, or those of parents with their children. In each case the "regression" is towards the mean. If we put the data in the form of correlation coefficients, they are of the order + 0·5 or rather more. This corresponds rather exactly with expectation on the genetical hypothesis, which involves the fact that pairs of sibs, or parent- child pairs, will have half their genetical equipment in common. Such a finding is very difficult indeed to explain on any environmental causation. The strength of the argument is to some extent reduced by the fact that, in fact, people do not mate at random but preferentially with others of like intelligence to their own, and that there is a high positive correlation coefficient between the I.Q.s of spouses (as also of betrothed couples, and even friends). The existence of this homogamy would cause by itself some degree of positive correlation between sibs, but not enough to explain all that is found.

One need not be restricted to the closer blood relationships. A correlation coefficient of + 0.25 would be expected between probands and their grandparents, grandchildren, uncles, aunts, nephews and nieces; for first cousins the correlation should be + 0.125. These were in fact the order of the resemblances found between relatives in various physical measurements by Karl Pearson and the biometricians in the early years of the century, and were thought by them to be a disproof of Mendelism. The interpretation of the findings, on a Mendeliar basis in terms of multifactorial inheritance, had to wait until the work of Fisher on stature. It was twenty years after that before the concept of polygenic inheritance was applied to intelligence, although its normal distribution was known.

Low Intelligence

Jaederholm made a survey of the intelligence of the great majority of all children in Sweden who were excluded from the ordinary schools on account of mental deficiency, together with a sample of normal schoolchildren. He used a modification of the Binet test. The results were analysed by Karl Pearson. He showed that the distribution of scores corresponded reasonably well with the normal curve. The fit was three times better if the defective group was included along with the normal group. Not more than one-third of the defective group fell outside it, and there was a good deal of overlap between the scores of the brighter of the so-called defective children and those of the dullest children attending the ordinary schools.

Roberts made a special study of the siblings of the 8 per cent of the children with the lowest I.Q.s Their mean score was 77·4, that of their sibs 88·1, and the regression coefficient was 0·53. At the other end of the scale, Terman's "superior children," with I.Q.s over 140, had offspring with mean I.Q. of 128. As has been said, these regressions are expected on the basis of polygenic inheritance, and are not compatible with single factor inheritance. However, when we come to persons of extremely low intelligence, idiots and imbeciles with I.Q. of 45 or less, comparable regressions are no longer observed. On Robert's small series, the I.Q.s of sibs of the imbeciles ranged from 88 to 117 with a mean of 99·9. This suggests that the occurrence of such grave defects is not accounted for by normal variation and polygenic inheritance. a conclusion which also follows from the fact that the curve of distribution deviates from normality at its negative extreme. What is suggested is the operation of special factors, such as injury, disease and, if genetical in nature, single dominant or recessive genes. A small part may also be played by incompatibilities of blood group between mother and unborn child such as may occur with respect to the Rhesus factor, or chromosomal anomalies as is now suspected in Mongolism. However, this whole class is not a numerous one, and not to be compared, as a social problem, with the very much larger numbers of the feeble-minded.

Table 4.2. Normality of Lower Part of the Frequency Curve of Standford-binet I.Q.s
(Based on a complete sample of 3,361 children)

Range of I.Q.	Expected No.	Observed No.
Above 73.78	3,193.0	3,195.2
73.78 - 67.57	100.8	94.9
67.57 - 44.97	66.5	58.4
Below	0.7	12.5

Personality as a Graded Character

The genetical background of intellectual abnormality can thus be regarded as determined polygenically for the greater part. The same is probably largely true on general grounds for the genetical background of personality abnormality. The situation, however, is more complex than in the case of intelligence. Personality is more difficult to assess or measure, it is a much less unitary character than intelligence and its manifestation throughout life is subject to quite wide fluctuations depending on a variety of circumstances. However, it is generally found helpful to regard personality traits as graded characters, and the same is true of major factors in personality, such as extraversion and neuroticism. When a group of persons is rated or measured on any personality scale it is generally found that, as in the case of intelligence, the scores tend to fall into the shape of the normal distribution curve. In so far as this distribution is reliable and is genetically determined it is likely to be due to the combined influence of many genes. In our opinion, that is certainly a likely hypothesis in the cases of neuroticism and extraversion, as described in this book, though there are certain points that will need clarification. Thus Eysenck finds it profitable to see the factor of neuroticism, as a psychological measure, as unitary in nature. The psychiatric geneticist would think rather of a predisposition determined by polygenic factors of somewhat heterogeneous kinds, though their effects, measured along a single dimension, could well fit in with Eysenck's findings.

In the psychotic dimension, matters are different again. A continuously graded factor of psychoticism would not account, by itself, for the specificities of inheritance in schizophrenic and manic-depressive families; but it might describe the non-specific variation in the susceptibility to these illnesses. Hypothetical specific schizophrenic and manic-depressive genes must both be supposed to have reduced rates of manifestation, and whether they are manifested or not could well depend on the intensity of a "psychoticism" factor. Such a conception would have consequences which could be tested by appropriate investigations.

Methods and Aims of Genetical Analysis

It is now the place to give an account of the research methods which may be used in psychiatric genetics, including those which help us to understand the mode of inheritance, such as family and population studies, and those which help to distinguish between the effects of heredity and environment, such as the study of foster-children and twins. A beginning must be made with work on animal behaviour.

Animal Studies

Although human beings are in some ways very favourable subjects for genetical study, there are ways in which they present particular difficulties. One cannot plan human breeding experiments; the size of the human family is small; and there is a time interval of some thirty years between one generation and the next. There are, therefore, advantages in pursuing psychological studies on laboratory-bred mammals such as rats and mice. This field of work has been dignified by the title of "psychogenetics."

A suitable technique is to select some characteristic of behaviour in which individual differences are shown and can, preferably, be measured. High scorers and low scorers are then separated and inbred with a view to producing distinct strains. If this is successful members of the two strains may then be cross-mated, and the capacities of their offspring measured. If genetical factors play a part, the two strains, with very different patterns of behaviour, can be built up; and the result of cross-mating is to reproduce individuals of intermediate performance.

Calvin S. Hall, one of the leading American investigators in this field, has summarized the work that has been done on selective breeding up till 1951. His review shows that heredity is an important factor, not only in variations in maze-learning ability, but also in the choice of hypothesis (visual and spatial) adopted in maze-learning, in the preference for a high or low cage temperature, in the amount of voluntary activity displayed, in the speed of reaction, in wildness or tameness, in aggressivity, in emotionality, and in susceptibility to audiogenic seizures, which occur in some rats when the experimenter jingles a bunch of keys. This last trait was found to be inherited as a dominant in one strain and as a recessive in another.

In studies of aggression, black mice have been found to be more aggressive than albinos. One investigator tested the hypothesis that this difference might be caused by early environment, in that the mice might learn their behaviour from cues presented by their mother at an age when they were particularly susceptible. He did this by having some of his black mice reared by albinos, and some of his albino mice reared by black mothers. However, the young ones resembled their biological mothers, and not their foster-mothers or foster-sibs, in aggressiveness. This experiment supported the hypothesis that there are innate differences in aggressiveness in mice.

In a study of Hall's own, emotionality was measured by the extent to which rats tended to defaecate or urinate when placed in a strange environment. Rats scoring high, on this definition, were bred together, as were the low-scorers. The emotional strain became increasingly emotional up to the ninth generation. Selection for non-emotionality yielded less systematic results, though the maximum effect was obtained in a single generation. When the emotional and non-emotional strains were eventually crossed, the offspring had a mean score and S.D. close to that of the heterogeneous parent population, from which they had been bred, but with an excess of low-scorers. Hall inferred that non-emotionality is dominant over emotionality. The emotional rats had significantly heavier thyroids (both sexes), adrenals (males only) and pituitary glands (females only).

Broadhurst, working in the animal laboratory at Bethlem Royal Hospital, repeated parts of Hall's investigation, using more refined methods including brother-sister matings. He too was able to breed emotional and non-emotional strains from an originally mixed population. A cross-fostering experiment showed that maternal influence had no significant effect. There is thus strong evidence that emotionality in the rat, as measured by defaecation under stress, is under genetical control. Broadhurst has so far found it easier to select for non-emotionality than for emotionality. He has not investigated the mode of inheritance, but has gone on to use his pure strains to study the effect of emotionality on drive. The mode of investigation shows the value of making genetics the servant of psychology.

Hall looks forward to the time when the science of psychogenetics will make a real contribution towards our understanding of the *modus operandi* of the genes and of the environmental modifiability of innate behaviour patterns. "An understanding of psychogenetics," he concludes, "is a prerequisite of a dynamic psychology." A very similar viewpoint is adopted by Williams and his collaborators. They and Mardones have succeeded in breeding strains of rats which are, and are not, liable to alcoholic addiction; on the basis of this work Williams develops the concept of genetotrophic diseases, in which the genetical deviation is merely the starting point of a chain of effects, into which environmental factors, such as nutritional ones, also enter.

Problems of Human Genetics

The peculiar difficulties of genetical investigations in man have led to the elaboration of special techniques, particularly in the development and refinement of statistical methods. In the hands of mathematical geneticists, such as Sir Ronald Fisher, these have been brought to a level of power and refinement in advance of the observational knowledge to which only they can be applied. Special adjustments have to be made, in the analysis of data, for the fact that the likelihood of making some observations on an individual is affected by the age he has reached, for the fact that nearly all simple and practical methods of selection involve some kind of bias, and for other sources of error, some of which will emerge in what follows.

In genetical investigations on human families, much of the information required is likely to concern people who are dead or otherwise inaccessible, or who have little motive to co-operate. The readiness of contacts to provide information is affected by the theme of the investigation and by the climate of opinion. Owing to an increased liberality of opinion, such investigations in psychiatry are now a good deal easier than they used to be; but it is much easier to carry out research into pairs of twins than, say, into the children of parents both of whom have been mentally ill. It is, as a rule, easy to make a good contact with twins, owing to the fact that the public at large regards twinship as a matter of fascinating interest; it is easier to persuade a pair of twins to come to a psychological laboratory than a complete family.

Where medical records are involved, insurmountable obstacles may arise, especially when members of a past generation are inquired about. Old, and sometimes even current, records from mental hospitals may be bare in the extreme, and insufficient for a reliable diagnosis. As has been said, sampling nearly always gives rise to problems. The investigator may have to make a choice between the carefully conducted personal study of a small group, with a possible sampling bias, and an unselected series which will include cases about which there is inadequate information. It is nearly always useless, at any rate in this country, to take investigation further than first-degree relatives; but even within this limited family group the obtaining of adequate information about personality and psychological abnormality will be very time- consuming. Parents cannot be equated with sibs or children, for not only do they belong to an earlier generation, but also they have been selected for health by the fact of having attained parenthood.

In studying the genetics of mental abnormality, psychological tests, desirable though they are on theoretical grounds, are often of no great value. Mental illnesses, both neurotic and psychotic, take a fluctuating course, and the state at any one time may be but a poor guide to the nature of a deviation which is best seen over a whole lifetime.

Psychiatric diagnoses, though extremely important for genetical studies, contain unfortunately a large subjective element; the very standards on which they are based vary to some extent from school to school. Efforts, not very successful ones, have been made to get away from diagnosis to single symptoms, to avoid this source of confusion or disagreement. A rather better method of by-passing the subjectivity of diagnosis was used by Leonhard and Schulz in an investigation into the families of schizophrenics: Leonhard diagnosed and classified the probands, and Schulz carried out the family investigations, each without any knowledge of the judgements of the other.

Family Investigation

Pedigree Studies

The first attempts to study human heredity were by means of the inspection of single family histories that happened to catch the interest of the physician. In this form the family method was open to some rather obvious objections. Families that are obtained in this way are likely to be the unusual and heavily loaded ones; selected on account of their curiosity value, they are highly unrepresentative and tend to give an exaggerated view of the frequency with which abnormalities occur in the families of affected persons. However, when carried out systematically, on representative material and perhaps in combination with other methods, family studies remain the basic tool of the genetical research worker. They can take various forms and have various aims.

Empirische Erbprognose

By investigating all the parents, siblings and sometimes other more remote relatives of a complete and representative series of patients with a given clear-cut diagnosis one can obtain a reliable idea of what the facts are concerning the family incidence of the same and similar disorders. In some conditions mostly rare ones inspection or analysis of the pedigrees obtained in this way will reveal a simple mode of Mendelian inheritance. This was the case, as we have seen, with Huntington's chorea and phenylketonuria. With the commoner psychiatric abnormalities, such as schizophrenia, hereditary mechanisms are likely to be more complex and environmental factors to play a greater part. For these conditions family studies of the type described are nevertheless useful, even though the genetics of the condition may not be clear-cut. Empirical risk figures can be calculated which show the chances of different degrees of relative being similarly affected. The method, known as *empirische Erbprognose*, was first developed by the school of Rüdin in Munich during the 1920s and it has been used fairly extensively so far as the psychoses are concerned, in Germany, Scandinavia and other parts of the world. Not only do the results of adequately planned investigations of this kind often give valuable information on the probable mode of inheritance and the degree to which those persons who are presumed to be carrying the abnormal gene or genes responsible are likely to manifest the psychosis in question; but also the empirical risk figures are of particular value in estimating the genetic prognosis for other members of the family and their potential offspring. Thus the chance of a child of an epileptic developing epilepsy is about 5 per cent, the chance of the child of a manic-depressive developing a recognizable manic-depressive state is about 15 per cent, and the risk for the child of a schizophrenic has been estimated at figures from 9 per cent for some forms of the illness to 20 per cent for others. Estimates have similarly been obtained for siblings, nephews and nieces, and grandchildren in these and other a number of heredity counselling clinics have grown up, which rely heavily on the results of family investigations of this kind. The risks for relatives must of course be compared with those for the population in general, which are higher than might have been thought.

Because of the particular value of twins to genetical research, Kallmann in the United States has combined the twin and family methods, starting with a large series of patients who happened to be twins, and investigating their co-twins and other relatives.

Table 4.3. Risk of Schizophrenia for Relatives of Schizophrenics

Class	Percentage risk of schizophrenia
Children of two non-schizophrenic parents (general population)	0.9
Relatives of adult schizophrenic index cases—	
Not consanguineous	
Step-sibs	1.8
Spouse	2.1
First cousins	2.6
Nephews and nieces	3.9
Grandchildren	4.3
Half-sibs	7.1
Parents	9.2
Full-sibs	14.2
Dizygotic co-twins	14.5
Dizygotic co-twins of same sex	17.6
Children with one schizophrenic parent	16.4
Children with two schizophrenic parents	68.1
Monozygotic co-twins	86.2
Monozygotic co-twins living apart for at least five years	77.6
Monozygotic co-twins not so separated	91.5

It will be seen that the expectation of schizophrenia increases with closeness of blood relationship to the proband, rather than with environmental similarity, though the latter has some effect, as is shown in the figures for step-sibs and for identical twins living together or apart.

Although in practice most family investigations of abnormalities start from hospital populations, others originate in surveys of schoolchildren or army conscripts. In some studies it has been possible to ascertain all cases of a specific abnormality in a defined area, and to start family investigations from there.

Among the earliest positive results of systematic family research was the elimination of some old and hoary misconceptions, such as the theory of anticipation. According to this, familial disorders tended to occur earlier and earlier in life in succeeding generations, until, mental deficiency taking the place of mental disorder, the morbid strain was eliminated. This has been shown to be a statistical artefact, caused by the fact that the most accessible information in a family study will be about the later disorders of the older generations, and the earlier disorders of the younger generations. With this exploded theory went also the idea that the defectiveness of a human strain might show itself indifferently in a great number of forms, schizophrenia, epilepsy, psychopathy, criminality, prostitution, vagrancy, mental defect, etc., all arising from a single genetical cause. *Empirische Erbprognose* taught the lesson that different forms of psychiatric abnormality must be distinguished; and thereby it has become one of the foundation stones on which a scientific diagnostic classification will have to be based.

Genetical Analysis and Psychiatric Classification

It is a fashionable tendency in psychiatry to consider that there is no real difference between the "psychoses" and "neuroses," both these words being mere terms of convenience. This view is not supported by the results of family investigations. Such studies, in the hands of many workers, consistently confirm the existence of a real difference between conditions like schizophrenia or manic-depressive disorder, on the one side, and anxiety states, hysteria, etc., on the other. The difference between these two classes of conditions is not one of gravity but of specificity. Thus investigations of the relatives of schizophrenics have shown that they are more than normally liable to schizophrenia, but have no excessive risk of becoming manic-depressive or epileptic. On the neurotic side, the relatives of anxiety neurotics are more than normally liable to anxiety neurosis, but also are more than normally liable to hysterical illnesses, reactive depressions, and other neuroses. On the genetical hypothesis we are able to account for this class difference by supposing that in the aetiology of schizophrenia and manic-depressive disorder single genes of large specific effect are involved, whereas in the aetiology of anxiety states and hysteria, any genetical factors involved are probably polygenic and not very specific in their effects. This fits in well with the observation that neurotic modes of behaviour are within the compass of all of us, and can be regarded as non-pathological, whereas schizophrenic behaviour is beyond the normal range. If large numbers of individuals are subjected to physiological and psychological stress, such as occurs in war-time, the incidence of neuroses increases *pari passu* with the increase of stress, while the incidence of schizophrenia remains practically constant.

As a matter of historical fact, the classification most frequently used in genetical investigations in psychiatry has been derived from Kraepelin. This does not mean that psychiatric genetics is permanently wedded to it. Great improvements can be expected, and genetics can be expected to make its contribution. Kraepelin regarded the condition he called "paranoia" as being a syndrome in its own right; but his pupil Kolle, who investigated the families of the patients whom Kraepelin himself had diagnosed as cases of paranoia, found that, from the familial genetical point of view, they did not distinguish themselves from paranoid schizophrenics. This investigation gave the death blow to paranoia as a specific disease, and thereby solved a problem of classification which was beyond the reach of the unaided clinician.

Offspring of Two Psychotic Parents

By investigating the children of particular matings, light may be thrown both on the mode of inheritance of a predisposition and on its genetical homogeneity. An excellent example of what may be done in this way is provided by the work of Elsässer. He collected, from his own material and from the work of others, one hundred and thirty-four pairs of husbands and wives, both of whom had suffered from an endogenous psychosis. Most of these were either typical cases of schizophrenia or fairly typical manic depressives, but as many as 29 per cent were sufficiently atypical, not to be readily classified in either of the two main diagnostic groups; they included paranoid involutional psychoses, confusional psychoses, etc., and Elsässer thinks that there were so many of them because psychotic parents are not a random selection of psychotic patients in general. There were four hundred and twenty-four children who passed the age of sixteen from these unions, and of these eighty eight certainly and twenty-three probably had had psychotic illnesses by the time of the investigation. In his calculations Elsässer counts each of the doubtful cases as a half. Of course, a considerable part of the total number of children observed had lived through only a fraction of the life-span during which they would be liable to an endogenous psychosis (approximately fourteen to forty-five in the case of schizophrenia). When allowance is made for this, Elsässer could say that he had observed three hundred and twenty-nine life-expectancies for schizophrenia, two hundred and five for manic-depressive psychosis. Set against these denominators, the risks these children faced of developing schizophrenia or manic-depressive illness were two to three times as great as those facing children of one psychotic and one normal parent. This fact alone fits well with a genetical hypothesis of causation.

Elsasser calculated risks separately for the different combinations of psychotic parents. There were thirty-four families where both parents were schizophrenic; they produced twenty certain and eight probable schizophrenics in a corrected total of 61·3, equivalent to a percentage of 39·2. Not one of the children was manic-depressive.

There were only twenty unions where both parents were manic-depressive; they produced nine certain and one probable manic-depressive children and four other psychotics. One of these last, the daughter of two manic-depressives with not quite typical illnesses beginning in each case after the age of fifty, was a schizophrenic. The risk for psychosis was 44.4 per cent. The offspring of matings of schizophrenics with manic-depressives produced equal numbers of both major psychoses; the risk for psychosis was 31.2 per cent.

Table 4.4. The Children of Two Psychotic Parents. Data of Elsässer, Schulz and Kahn

			Non-psychotic children			Psychotic children (doubtful cases shown as 1)					
Number of Parental pairs	Parental mating	Number of children over 16	Normal	With psychiatric abnormality (mostly minor) or uncertain information	Total	Schizophrenia	Manic-depressive psychosis	Atypical psychosis	Endogenous psychosis. nature	Total persons	Corrected risk for endogenous psychosis (per cent)
34	Schizophrenia × Schizophrenia	96	38	30	68	20 8/2	—	—	—	28	39·2
20	Manic-dep. × Manic-dep	47	28	5	33	1	9½	2	1	14	44·4
19	Schizophrenia × Manic-dep.	68	35	14	49	6 2/2	6 2/2	1	2	19	31·2
23	Atypical × Schizophrenia	91	53	23	76	8	1½	3	½	15	21·3
21	Atypical x Manic-dep.	55	32	12	44	—	4 2/2	4½	—	11	28·8
17	Atypical × Atypical	67	27	16	43	5	5½	10½		24	41·3
134		424	213	100	313	88 certain + 23 doubtful = 111					

The matings in which one or both parents had an atypical psychosis also resulted in a risk for the offspring of about the same magnitude. While analysis suggested that these atypical psychoses in the parents were in some instances, genetically, schizophrenic or manic-depressive, it also indicated that in others they were breeding true and appeared to be genetical entities in their own right. This is in keeping with the findings of Leonhard.

It seems clear from these results that, if there is a genetical relationship between schizophrenia and manic-depressive psychosis, it cannot be a close one. It is interesting also that the illnesses of the children were not of any exceptional severity; if a child received two abnormal dominant genes, one from each parent, he might well show something of that kind, or perhaps a lethal or semilethal condition. There was one child of two schizophrenics who was born with supernumerary fingers and toes and died when a few days old — but this was probably coincidental.

Probably the most important finding is that not more than 40 per cent of the children of two schizophrenics were similarly affected, and that only some 16 per cent of their non-psychotic sibs could be described as schizoid personalities. If all schizophrenic illnesses depended on a single recessive gene, then all the children of two schizophrenics would themselves be homozygotes, and accordingly liable to the disease. On this theory, the fall from the expected 100 per cent to 40 per cent is difficult to explain; it becomes easier to suppose either that schizophrenia is heterogeneous, and that a variety of different specific genes are responsible from case to case, or that dominant inheritance with diminished penetrance plays a role. It is interesting, however, that in the only family where both parents had a deteriorating schizophrenia of hebephrenic or catatonic type with early onset, five out of the six children who survived infancy were schizophrenic and the sixth was an odd personality. It would seem likely that in this family, at least, parents and children were all homozygous for the same gene. This family was not used in Elsässer's statistics as, unlike the other families, it had been selected through knowledge of the abnormal children.

Another highly important point is that of the non psychotic children of these marriages 70 per cent were completely normal and only 5 per cent were regarded by Elsasser as psychopathic. On this ground any attempt to explain the high incidence of psychosis in the children as the result of the psychological effects of being brought up by a pair of psychotic or psychotic- to-be parents becomes very unconvincing; if the environment was as pathogenic as that, how were these normal children so completely spared?

Offspring of Consanguineous Matings

The heterozygous carrier of a rare recessive gene is much more likely to mate with another heterozygote if he marries a blood relative, such as a cousin, than if he marries at random. If he does, he will greatly increase his chances of producing a homozygous and abnormal child. The present authors, with their colleague W. L. B. Nixon, investigated a series of three hundred and fifty-five mental hospital patients who were notified as the children of related parents, and compared them with a control series of equal size. There were significantly more schizophrenics in the proband than in the control series, ninety against sixty-three, the distribution of other diagnoses showing no significant difference. The existence of a so much higher incidence in the one series than in the other is what would be expected on the hypothesis of a recessive gene, but on this hypothesis alone one would have expected a greater difference. Taking into account the figures obtained, the best estimates available of the frequency of cousin marriage and the frequency of schizophrenia, the authors calculate that not more than one-sixth of the totality of schizophrenia could be attributed to a recessive gene. This is of course a provisional view, and would have to be modified if later workers found different incidences.

Linkage

If two genes are carried on the same chromosome, they are said to be linked, and the way in which each is handed on from parent to child will not be independent. Let us suppose that *X* has both the gene for Huntington's chorea and also the dominant gene for polydactyly, and that these two genes are linked. Now if *X* got both these genes from one parent, they will have come to him on the same chromosome, and any child he has will be liable to get from him either both of them or both of their normal alleles. If, however, *X* got one gene from his mother and the other from his father, then they will be on opposite members of the chromosome pair, and his children will be liable to get one or the other, but not both or neither. There is a certain amount of recombination of parts of chromosomes by "crossing over," so that the above rule is not absolute; the degree to which it approaches truth depends on how near the two genes are to one another on the chromosome. Family studies show whether or not two genes are linked, and if so how closely; so that by their aid it should theoretically be possible to build up a chromosome map. Very complete chromosome maps have been drawn up for experimental animals like *Drosophila,* but in man so far a beginning has only been made with the XY chromosome pair. If it were possible to link rare pathological genes with common normal blood-group genes, a new and powerful technique of genetical analysis of the pathological condition would become available.

Detection of Carriers

Sometimes carriers can be detected more directly by means of family studies. Suggestive findings have been made, for example, in diabetes, where relatives are often found to have a low glucose tolerance; these persons may be potential diabetics. In the families of some patients with cystinuria the stone formation can be shown to be due to homozygosity for a gene which can be detected in its heterozygous form. By the technique of paper chromatography the expected proportion of relatives was found by Harris and Warren to have a raised excretion of cystine. The application of biochemical and other techniques to the relatives of psychiatric patients is perhaps a promising but no doubt complex field for future research and one which might have therapeutic possibilities. Already it has become possible to identify the carriers of phenylketonuria. The relatives of epileptics frequently show abnormalities in their electro-encephalogram which suggest genetical interpretations, though not simple ones. Psychological tests could also be applied to relatives of psychiatric patients with a similar purpose in view.

Assortative Mating

A simplifying assumption which is very frequently made in theoretical genetics is that mating occurs at random. This is far from being even approximately true, and in man is even less true than in other species. In point of fact, the choice of a mate is limited in a great number of ways, so that the population can be, in a rough way, divided into separate inbreeding segments, or "isolates," along a number of dimensions. Thus there are geographical, economic, occupational, religious and many other divisions, within which most matings occur. In general, like tends to mate with like, Briton to marry Briton, worker to marry worker rather than the Boss's daughter, clerk to marry clerk, Catholic to marry Catholic. This tendency to homogamy is seen also in psychological traits, both normal and pathological. It has already been mentioned that intelligent people tend to marry others of more than mean I.Q., and the stupid to marry those less than average. It is well known that deaf persons often marry one another, as do persons with other disabilities. If a number of genetically influenced conditions occur in one family, the most likely explanation is often neither genetical linkage, nor variability of manifestation, but assortative mating. In Huntington families one commonly finds other defects, such as eye conditions, tuberculosis, etc., which have probably entered the one family by selective mating. A study of assortative mating in respect of temperamental traits has shown the same tendency. Slater and Woodside investigated controlled series of normal and neurotic soldiers and their wives. The wives of the neurotics were themselves more neurotic and came from more neurotic families than those of the normal soldiers, and the dynamic factors involved could be partially clarified.

Homogamy in respect of genetically-determined traits has interesting consequences in increasing the variance shown by a population and in aiding the appearance of pure lines; homozygotes are favoured at the expense of heterozygotes. In itself homogamy is neither eugenic nor dysgenic, but makes the population more susceptible to change from selective influences of either kind. From the social point of view, it helps in the production of specialists of all kinds; we should probably have far fewer capable musicians if musical people did not tend to marry one another.

Fertility

The study of fertility is obviously another one of considerable genetical importance. It has a bearing on population genetics and is of relevance to the future health of the community. The possible consequences for the future of the negative correlation between intelligence and family size is one which has attracted a good deal of attention. A number of studies have shown that, both in the population as a whole and within single occupational groups, the more intelligent have fewer children than the less intelligent. A negative correlation of about 0.2 has been found by most investigators. On the assumption that intelligence is to a considerable extent inherited one would expect a gradual decline in the national intelligence. Summarizing the evidence Burt calculated that this would amount to 1.5 – 2 points in I.Q. per generation. If such a trend were to continue to the end of the present century, the proportion of persons with I.Q.s over one hundred and thirty in the population would fall to less than half the existing figure and that of the feeble-minded would be more than doubled. An opportunity occurred to test the prediction that the I.Q. was falling. Fifteen years earlier all the eleven-year-old age group in Scottish schools had been tested with a group intelligence test. When the same age group was tested again with the same test by a team of workers under Sir Godfrey Thomson, instead of the feared fall in mean score there had been a slight rise. The association between family size and intelligence, however, was as marked as before. There seems to be general agreement that improved environmental conditions and increased test sophistication has contributed to the rise, but it is still an open question whether the improvement due to environment masks a decline in genetical quality. The decline, if real, would stop if the association between higher intelligence and lower fertility ceased to operate. There can be no doubt that the association is susceptible to cultural and psychological influences, and that secular changes occur. In Sweden, family limitation began many years ago in the best educated sections but has now permeated the entire population; the differential fertility, which was once very marked and alarming, is now practically zero. If the well educated are open to suggestions of the desirability of family limitation, they are also open to the suggestion that the one- or two-child family is disadvantageous, psychologically for the children and perhaps also eugenically for the population. Recent studies of the fertility of university graduates and other favoured classes show a tendency to produce more rather than fewer children.

In the field of psychological abnormalities, the usual finding is one of lessened fertility. Thus many studies of schizophrenic families consistently show reduced fertility, and the work of Slater and

Woodside already mentioned showed reduced rather than increased fertility among neurotics and psychopaths.

Population Studies

The discussion of fertility has already led us from family studies to population investigations. It is obviously important from the medical and social points of view to assess the frequency with which different mental illnesses occur in the population as a whole, in different regions or social groups, and in the same region at different times. From the genetical point of view this information is important too. Without knowing the incidence of schizophrenia in the general population it is difficult to assess the significance of morbidity figures obtained for the relatives of schizophrenics. What is required here is not the crude incidence at a given time, but the number of persons born who might be expected to have had the condition after having lived long enough for it to manifest itself.

Hospital admission statistics are not entirely suitable for calculating the general risk only a proportion of psychotics and defectives reach hospital. However, Norris has been able to extract from hospital data a good deal of useful information regarding the incidence of mental disorders in London. By going further afield, estimates can be obtained along three rather different lines. These we may call: (1) the genealogical method, (2) the census method, and (3) the biographical method.

Genealogical Method

The first of these to be developed was the genealogical method. This is really no more than the family method applied to a selected group of persons who are supposed to be representative of the normal population. Hospital patients and their wives are comparatively accessible and have often been used in this kind of investigation. For example, Luxenburger studied the wives of patients with general paralysis (G.P.I.) in Munich and their families. As the disease is not genetical but due to syphilis, he assumed that these women were no more likely to be psychiatrically abnormal than others of the general population; in fact their families had rather more than their share of G.P.I On the Danish island of

Bornholm, Stromgren studied the sibs of general hospital patients and persons referred to a T.B. clinic.

Census Method

The samples chosen in the genealogical studies have in some ways not been very widely representative; and this method has been partly superseded by the cross-sectional census survey. The aim of this second method of population study is to ascertain all cases of psychiatric abnormality in a defined area at a given time. The families of the cases notified by official and unofficial sources can then be investigated too. This will bring to light further secondary cases and give information of genetical value. Thus Sjogren made an intensive cross-sectional study of a typical Swedish peasant population and supplemented it by genealogical research. He utilized for this purpose the very full information that can be obtained from old Swedish parish registers which go back to the seventeenth century.

Among other census-type investigations, we may mention that of Roth and Luton in Williamson County, Tennessee, and E. O. Lewis's well known study of mental deficiency in two urban, two rural and two mixed areas in England. A more recent British example is Mayer-Gross's investigation of the incidence of mental disorders in Dumfriesshire. In this work a psychiatric Social Worker, Marjorie Brown, inquired about all patients discharged from the Crichton Royal Hospital during the previous ten years and about their families, and those of present patients. The co-operation of Public Assistance officers, teachers and social workers and ministers of the Kirk was then sought in an effort to ascertain other cases of mental abnormality; and children who had obtained an I.Q. of less than eighty in the eleven-plus examinations were investigated. It is perhaps the use of this last group that is the most distinctive feature of Mayer-Gross's study. It was interesting that the proportion of dullards and defectives among the schoolchildren was twice that found in the total material. The main explanation given for this was that subnormals can easily lead a useful life in that particular community, so that their handicap is hardly noticed after leaving school. In the whole population of 56,000 some 9 per cent were reckoned to be psychiatrically abnormal.

Mental health surveys are most frequently made in rural areas. Here populations are more static than in large towns; people are better known to one another and to those in authority; economic conditions are relatively more uniform. This is all to the good so far as genetic investigations are concerned. But it may be that results obtained in rural areas do not hold good for large towns. A town may perhaps contain less mental defect but more cases of neurosis.

One theoretical difficulty with the census method is that of calculating expectancy rates from the crude figures. Most persons in the population have not reached an age when one can say they will not develop a manic-depressive psychosis let alone a senile one. Further, psychotics, and especially schizophrenics, have an excessive mortality rate and so will be underrepresented in a living sample.

Biographical Method

These difficulties can be met by the third method of population survey the longitudinal biographical method. Here all persons born in a given year are taken as the starting point of the investigation and then followed up. With this there are even greater practical difficulties than in the census method. Klemperer was the first to try it out on persons born in Munich between 1880 and 1890, but he could trace only 70 per cent of them.

However, Fremming applied the biographical method to the Island of Bornholm. He succeeded in tracing 92 per cent of all those born there fifty-five or fifty-six years earlier, including most of those who had emigrated to the mainland. He paid some 2,000 visits to obtain information about over 4,000 persons. Fremming discovered some 12 per cent of them to have suffered from one or more kinds of mental abnormality, a rate strikingly similar to that calculated earlier for the same area by Strömgren using genealogical and census methods. The main difference in the two investigations was that Fremming's method brought to light a considerably higher proportion of manic-depressives, many of whom had never been in hospital and were quite well when seen. Slight drawbacks in the biographical method, apart from its practical difficulties, are: first, the fact that it will not represent present trends but those of a generation or two ago; and secondly no estimate can be given for involutional or senile psychoses unless an investigation group born some eighty years ago is taken.

Incidence of Psychosis and Neurosis

These three methods give estimates for the incidence of the psychoses and mental defect which are very close, considering the many differences between the different countries in which they have been tried out, the various standards of diagnosis and statistical methods used for calculating empirical risk figures. Thus schizophrenia is usually found to have a frequency of between 0.5 per cent and 1.0 per cent; epilepsy one of 0.3 per cent to 0.5 per cent. The rate for manic-depressive psychosis varies more considerably— between 0.2 per cent and 1.6 per cent— largely for methodological reasons. Mental defectives are generally thought to account for about 1 per cent of the population.

So far as neurosis and psychopathy are concerned, agreement is not so consistent, and most figures quoted are probably underestimates. Census studies give rates of about 2 per cent. Fremming gives 5 per cent, Ekblad who interviewed a large series of Swedish naval conscripts, claimed that 15 per cent of them were psychopathic; he uses the term to cover what in this country we would mostly call chronic neurosis or personality maladjustment. In spite of different methods of approach, high rates are found when the matter is gone into carefully. Russell Fraser examined a large sample of war-time workers in light engineering factories in the Midlands. He and his co-workers found that 10 per cent of them had lost work during the past six months on account of a temporarily disabling neurotic illness, and that a further 20 per cent had suffered from minor forms of neurosis during that period. Logan and Goldberg of the Medical Research Council Social Medicine Unit investigated seventy-four lads called up for National Service in a London suburb. Twelve were clearly disturbed with psychiatric treatment considered advisable, and a further nineteen, making 42 per cent in all, were also maladjusted at the time of the interview. One of the present writers, studied a sample of sixty-two pairs of ordinary twins from the L.C.C. Secondary Schools in which it was found that about the same proportion, or nearly half, had at some time or other been neurotic in a broad sense or had presented troublesome behaviour disorders.

While some recent trends in the assessment of mental health involve the intensive investigation of a few cases, Essen-Moller and three Swedish colleagues have recently shown what can be achieved in the assessment of health and personality traits by short single interviews supplemented by official records. Each psychiatrist averaged eleven to fourteen interviews a day over a period of two months, and together they succeeded in investigating personally 2,500 persons out of a total population of 2,550. The interview took the form of a conversation on the individual's medical and personal history. The area studied was a rural one which included a small municipality and the four investigators divided it equally between them. They assessed personality according to the concepts of Sjöbring. Each individual was rated on a nine-point scale on each of the three constitutional variants of personality in the Sjöbring system – solidity, stability and validity – and also on capacity (intelligence). Each variant was found to be distributed not quite normally but roughly so. Part at least of the deviations from normality could be accounted for by differences between sexes, age groups and investigators. Some small correlations between the three variants and between these and intelligence were found. No correlation was larger than could reasonably be attributed to systematic diagnostic errors. The consistency between the findings of the four different investigators suggests a fair degree of reliability, especially when the method of investigation is considered. The results are in reasonable accordance with the concept of three mutually independent lines of variation in personality and a fourth, intelligence, each with a normal distribution. Essen Moller and his colleagues also assessed the presence or absence of personality traits of a more pathological kind, asthenic states and various mental illnesses, past and present, and their inter-relations. We reproduce their cumulative table showing by sex.

Note. W = women M = men. Among "major personality deviants" are included those who are markedly aggressive, restless, indolent or eccentric. "Asthenic" states are largely characterized by fatigue and nervousness. "Chalarophrenics," in Essen-Möller's terminology, are characterized by a persisting, objective mental and motor slackness or lack of energy. In the diagram "psychosomatic" complaints are grouped with neuroses. Alcoholism is included under asocial behaviour.

Further work is needed to put population studies of personality and neurosis on a firm basis, and to allow the results of one study to be compared with those of another. Easily administered standardized personality tests, to supplement the history and personal observation and to introduce some quantitative measurement, would of course be very helpful, if they could be made reliable. Most tests, at present available, vary too much with the way the subject is feeling at the moment. It is important, also, that we should get to know the frequency, not only of neurosis, but also of those environmental factors, such as a "broken home," which are under suspicion. In researches of this kind there are good reasons for approaching the problem simultaneously from more than one point of view, genetical, social, psychiatric and psychometric.

Study of Isolates: Consanguinity Rate

Apart from surveys of the general urban or rural population, attention has also been given to isolates, or groups characterized by a high degree of in-breeding. One of the advantages of this work is that any genetically determined anomalies are likely to be homogeneous. Book recently undertook the arduous task of studying three parishes in an isolated area in the north of Sweden, some thirty miles beyond the Arctic Circle. With the help of his wife, who had been born in the region, he gained the confidence of the population and was able to estimate the frequency and the genetics of the forms of mental disorder and mental defect found there. Many of the cases of mental abnormality could be consolidated into one pedigree, traceable to thirty-one ancestral pairs.

Another investigation, with a primarily cultural orientation, was made by Eaton and Weil of the Hutterites, a religious sect living in communities of their own in the North of the United States and in Canada. Although these people appeared to be relatively free from neurotic troubles, perhaps because of their simple way of life, there was a high incidence of manic-depressive psychosis, for which the only simple explanation seems to be the genetical one.

In isolates there tends to be a high consanguinity rate in marriage, and this tends to favour the appearance of homozygotes; the result may be seen in a relative abundance of some rare recessive defect. The frequency of cousin marriage, both in the parents of trait-bearers and in the general population, is important to theoretical genetics in several ways. In the general population there are large differences between town and country. In Stockholm only about 0·4 per cent of marriages are between cousins, while in some isolated Swedish parishes the rate may be as high as 6 per cent. It is also likely to be high in minority religious groups. With the breakdown of isolates by the modern growth of communication cousin marriage is becoming less frequent.

Heredity and Environment

The extent to which a given condition tends to run in families is no measure of the degree to which genetical factors are involved. On the one hand conditions with a genetic basis which are lethal at an early age, or are commonly caused by fresh mutation, or are so common as to be nearly universal (such as senile dementia), frequently show no conspicuous familial loading. On the other hand conditions which are independent of gene differences, such as for instance the presence of nits in the hair, may show a marked tendency to a familial distribution. The plausibility of a genetical or an environmental explanation will depend on one's existing knowledge and understanding; and the appearance in siblings of, say, an inborn error of metabolism or juvenile delinquency will be judged accordingly.

The genetical hypothesis can be rejected, if it can be shown that unrelated persons, subjected to similar environments, resemble one another as much as blood relatives. Environmental factors may also be brought out in individual case studies, and by giving special attention to social environment. Were the affected members of a given family subjected to a specific stress (such as separation from their mother at an early age) while the unaffected members were not? Spouses share a family environment, but differ genetically, and resemblances between them are likely to be environmentally caused, especially where the possibility of contagion, physical or psychological, arises. On this basis, Kallmann and Reisner included the examination of spouses in their family studies of tuberculosis. However, there are two kinds of material, foster-children and twins, which are particularly suited to the investigation of environmental causes of variation.

Foster-children

The study of fostered, adopted and orphanage children, who unlike other children are not brought up with their own biological parents, enables us, in theory at least, to disentangle the effects of heredity and environment in two complementary ways. On the one hand we can observe the effect of different environments on persons (or groups of persons) who are similar in heredity, as for instance when pairs of siblings are brought up in different homes. Alternatively we can observe the effects of similar environments on persons who are genetically unlike, for example, by comparing "own" and foster-children, or by observing the range of differences among children brought up in the relatively uniform atmosphere of an orphanage.

So far research on these lines has been done mostly in the United States and in the field of intelligence. Woodworth in his monograph entitled *Heredity and Environment* has summarized and discussed in a clear and fair-minded way the findings of research on foster-children carried out by Freeman and others in Chicago, Burks in California, Leahy in Minnesota, Skodak and Skeels in Iowa and others.

Attempts have also been made, in particular by the Iowa school to measure the improvement in I.Q. following adoption from an inferior into a superior home. However, the reliability of I.Q.s tested in the early years of life is notoriously low and an improvement in test score after some years might in part be due to the greater security of the child in its new home. Even if it is reliably estimated that adopted children have a higher I.Q. than their (often below-average) mothers, this might well be an instance of the expected "regression to the mean."

Other difficulties in planning and carrying out investigations into foster-children include the practical ones of following up an adequate sample of children placed away from home early in life; moreover, information about their own families is liable to be inadequate, especially in the case of the fathers of illegitimate children. The usefulness of this kind of research is limited too, because the range of foster- home environments tends to be limited.

Among theoretical snags is selective elimination: when one investigates the adopted children of defectives, for example, one finds that their less promising children have not been adopted but retained in institutions, so that the adopted ones are not a fair sample. Selective placement is equally important: if the best children go to the best foster-homes, as is indeed intended when an attempt is made to match the child to the home, this would invalidate the findings. One investigator reports a correlation of 0·3 between "own" parent education and adoptive parent education.

Some investigators emphasize the fact that a good environment can raise by a few very worth-while points the I.Q. of children who come from an unfavourable background. The effect of different kinds of environment on the mean I.Q. of children, believed to be free from the effect of selective placement, is shown in the following findings of Freeman:

- 45 foster-children in *good* foster-homes scored an average of 112 points.
- 39 foster-children in *average* foster-homes scored an average of 105 points.
- 27 foster-children in relatively *poor* foster-homes scored an average of 96 points.

The following table from Leahy shows an apparent influence of the occupational level of the adoptive father on the intelligence scores of adopted children; but it will be seen that there was much less variation between the five adopted groups than between the five groups of "own" children, and that the children adopted into semi-skilled and relatively unskilled families actually did a good deal better on intelligence tests than children born into such families.

Table 4.5. Mean I.Q. of Foster-children and of "Own" Children in Homes of Different Occupational Categories

Occupation of Father	Adopted children		Control ("own") children	
	Number	Mean	Number	Mean
Professional	43	113	40	119
Business management	38	111	42	118
Skilled trades and clerical	44	111	43	107
Semi-skilled	45	109	46	101
Relatively unskilled	24	108	23	102

The greater resemblance between parents and their own children than between parents and children adopted even early, is also borne out by the work of Burks, who gives her findings in the form of correlation coefficients:

	Foster group Parents and adopted children		Control group Parents and own children	
	r	N	*r*	N
Father's mental age	0.07	178	0.45	100
Mother's mental age	0.19	204	0.46	105

Burks concluded that heredity accounted for about 75 to 80 per cent of the variance in intelligence, under the environmental range from which her sample was taken. Woodworth is of the opinion that, despite their apparent differences, the various studies of the intelligence of adopted children have yielded comparable results; that the method is adequate to bring out any large differences due to the environment; but that scientific precision is not to be obtained.

We may end this section by referring to one of the rare studies of traits other than intelligence which have been studied by this method. It bears out the remarks of Woodworth. Burks and Mittelmann reported on the emotional and social adjustment as adults of persons placed for adoption when under ten years of age by a large New York adoption society on account of their parents being alcoholic or psychotic. However, the majority of them either could not be traced or did not co-operate in the study. Over one third of those seen showed evidence of various sorts of maladjustment, but with few exceptions they were living useful lives. Only very few were professional workers, though many of the foster-homes were of professional standing. This is probably not a bad result, all considered, and it is perhaps better than would have been expected if the children had remained in their unstable home environments. But as the persons with whom no contact was made may well have included an undue proportion of social failures, even so tentative a conclusion as that is hardly justified.

Twins, The Two Kinds

Twins can give us information both about specific environmental factors and about the relative importance of heredity.

This is because there are two kinds of twins. There are the uniovular or monozygotic (MZ) pairs, which are derived from a single fertilized ovum, which has split into two (or sometimes more) individuals at a very early stage; and there are the binovular or dizygotic (DZ) pairs, formed by the fertilization of two different ova by two sperms. The latter are no more alike genetically than an ordinary pair of brothers or sisters, and are often known as fraternal twins; they can expect to have no more than half their genes in common. Monozygotic twins, however, should be duplicates of one another in respect of each and all of their genes, and can be regarded as genetically "identical." MZ twins are sometimes rather different in appearance, and DZ twins can be extremely alike, so that it is occasionally difficult to allot a pair of twins to their correct biological class. The usual and best method of determining ovularity is to test the pair for similarities in respect of a number of traits, of a kind in which genetical causation predominates, such as eye colour, blood groups and fingerprints. By such means the probability of an error in classification can be reduced to a level at which it can have no material effect in the comparison of two series.

Differences between Monozygotic Twins

When we compare MZ twins, we know that differences between them must be due to non-genetical causes. Some differences might be due to factors operating before birth, rather than to the post-natal environment. Influences of this kind are perhaps rather liable to occur in twins. Asymmetrical features, for example, such as the hair whorl going in opposite directions or one twin being left-handed and the other right-handed occur more frequently in twins than in the singly born. With monochorionic pairs one twin may secure for himself more than an equal share of the placental circulation and this can lead to a significant difference between identical twins in birth weight. Both these factors should be borne in mind in interpreting the findings of twin studies. However, their influence in psychiatry is probably not very great; they might be more important in connexion with congenital abnormalities. Twins of both kinds, particularly MZ twins, have a lower birth weight and are less viable than non-twins; the mean I.Q. of twin children is 5 points below the average for all sizes of family. But if they survive the initial risks they probably grow up to form a fairly representative cross section of the population; except possibly for certain forms of mental defect and epilepsy, the incidence of mental illness is not raised in twins. For instance, twins are no more often referred to the Maudsley Hospital than are singly-born persons. When we investigate a complete series of twins with a single condition we are probably making a fair sample of that condition. Information about the post-natal environment can be obtained from identical twins in a number of ways.

Co-twin Control

According to Gesell's "co-twin control" method, one infant twin is trained in an activity such as stair-climbing, while the other twin is not given the training, and the effect of this is observed. The possibility of much direct experimentation in this way is of course limited, but the method could perhaps on occasions be applied, and not only to children. In cases where a pair of adult MZ twins have the same illness equally severely at the same time the effect of different treatments can be studied.

A less experimental application of the co-twin control method consists in making careful observations of twins in infancy and predicting the possible consequences of the similarities and differences and personal relationships noted at the time. In follow-up studies these predictions can then be tested.

In psychiatric twin studies, as in ordinary clinical work, the retrospective case history method generally has to be used. Here the life histories of a pair of twins are compared and any differences between them in psychiatric status are related to their past experience or way of life. From the study of many pairs on these lines one can perhaps reach conclusions of general relevance to the causes and prevention of mental ill-health.

Twins Brought up Apart

One limitation of twin research as a means of assessing the influence of the environment is that we are normally confined to pairs who have been brought up in the same home and so have had similar experiences; and differences between MZ twins brought up together must often be attributed to the relations between them rather than to wholly external factors. However, twins brought up apart are very hard to come by. Over a period of years Newman, Freeman and Holzinger in America succeeded in investigating only nineteen such pairs of MZ twins, and to obtain this number many had to be bribed by a free visit to the World Fair in Chicago. Newman and his colleagues found that these twins, who were mostly adult, resembled one another in intelligence less closely than MZ twin schoolchildren who had been brought up together in Chicago, but they resembled one another more closely than DZ twin schoolchildren. There was a high correlation between the amount of formal education received and Binet I.Q. The difference between the MZ pairs brought up apart and those brought up together can be accounted for very largely by a few pairs where there was a rather extreme difference in their backgrounds. Thus in one of these pairs, one twin had only two years' schooling while her partner had a college education and was herself a schoolteacher. They differed by 24 points in I.Q. Small inter-family differences had little effect on intelligence. In personality, correlations between twins were lower than in intelligence; this may have been largely because of the tests used, but here again the separated identical twins were on the whole no less alike than those brought up in the same home, and a number of clinical similarities were noted.

Craike and Slater have described a pair of MZ twins who were separated at nine months and who both developed paranoid schizophrenic illnesses later on. Kallmann has also described a pair of this kind, and yet another case has recently come to the notice of our Unit.

Through a television programme the B.B.C. recently brought to light a considerable number of normal MZ twins brought up apart, and some forty of these have so far been investigated at the Maudsley Hospital. They include all degrees of separation during childhood. Thus, there is a pair in which one twin was adopted by a well-to-do family in Chile and married a Frenchman. The other was brought up mostly in Denmark in poor circumstances with a psychopathic father, and she married an Englishman. In another pair, twin boys were brought up in separate homes from birth, but by different aunts living only next door to one another. It is interesting to compare the effects of different degrees of separation. The cases where the separations were not very extreme, such as those where one twin was brought up by mother the other by grandmother, are important for the opportunity which they give for assessing the significance of such factors as the age and personality of the mother, the presence of other children in the family, a town or country environment and the mutual influence of the twins.

From the results so far, age at separation does not appear to be of very great importance – the few pairs separated after the age of four differed as much in personality as the majority who were separated soon after birth. Nor does childhood contact with the twin appear to have made for greater similarity. One of the most strikingly similar pairs had no knowledge of one another until they were reunited by the research at the age of 36. On the whole the kind of home made a bigger difference than the degree of separation. In the pairs that differed most psychiatrically there was generally some definitely unsatisfactory feature in the early environment of the twin who had the poorer mental health. Differences in social class, though not marked in the series, could be seen to have an effect in causing differences of behaviour. However, the respective foster-parents of the two twins could differ quite a lot in age, personality and ideas of bringing up children, without this necessarily resulting in any obvious differences between the twins. Many striking similarities in speech, gesture, interests and temperament were noted. The results of a simple personality questionnaire, devised for us by Professor Eysenck, lend support to the observation that twins brought up in different homes can resemble one another closely in personality. For extraversion there was a positive correlation between twins of 0.60, for neuroticism one of 0.52. For intelligence the correlation was 0.77 on a non-verbal test.

Comparison of Resemblances within MZ and DZ Pairs

If MZ twins are alike in a particular respect, one cannot conclude that this is because of their possessing the same genes; it might be due to their similar environment. To help us decide this point we have the DZ or hereditarily non-identical pairs. If sex is a significant factor then the DZ pairs of the same sex can be compared with the MZ. One could hardly find individuals brought up in more similar environments than twins. Both kinds are born into the same home at the same time with all that this implies; they are more alike in this respect than ordinary siblings. If, in a representative series of pairs, the average resemblance between the MZ twins is markedly greater than that between the fraternals, then there is a strong case for the view that the genetical constitution has an important bearing on the condition in question, at least under present circumstances.

Psychological factors. An objection sometimes raised against a comparison of MZ with DZ twins is the fact that the former tend to go about together in childhood and are sometimes unusually closely attached to one another, while fraternal twins often develop more independently and so do not have quite so similar psychological environments. The influence of this might be quite important in some conditions, particularly in childhood; but in others it would be negligible. However, any difference of this sort between the two kinds of twins is largely a reflection of the innate needs of the twins themselves. Everyone tends to make his environment for himself, as well as to be influenced by it. One can, of course, test by observation whether those MZ twins who are most closely attached to one another are in fact more similar psychologically than the others. From our own experience with normal London schoolchildren this did not seem generally to be the case. There is, however, another psychological factor one making for difference between MZ twins; this is the tendency with many of them for one to be the dominant partner, the other to be more submissive. Certainly it would be most implausible to explain any differences in resemblance between MZ and DZ twins entirely by external environmental factors, such as the ways mothers treat their twins. For this to be the true explanation, nearly all mothers would have to treat their MZ twins in exactly the same way, but handle DZ twins of the same sex very differently indeed. This does not appear to be the case at all. Some tendency of this kind may be forced on the parents by the twins themselves, but it is probably to a considerable extent offset by a reaction in the opposite direction. Mothers of MZ twins often like to think of their twins as different so that they may regard them as separate individuals. The mothers of DZ twins generally make the most conscientious efforts to give their twins the same of everything. Points such as these can often be clarified by actual case studies of twins. Further, as we have seen, the findings on twins brought up apart vindicate some of the presuppositions of the traditional twin method.

Unselected series. It is just as important in collecting a twin series as in other types of family investigation to guard against bias in selection. The field from which the collection is made must be defined, and within it the collection should be unselective and as comprehensive as possible. It has been shown that reliance on published case reports leads to a gross bias, as pairs of twins in which both members show the trait greatly preponderate. In any investigation in which there is any casualness or informality in ascertainment the same sort of bias is likely to arise; for some reason nearly everybody, including doctors, find twins who resemble one another much more interesting than twins who differ.

If an unselected series can be obtained, then estimates of *concordance rates* become interesting. A pair of twins is said to be concordant in respect of some trait if both members are alike in showing or not showing it, discordant if one shows it while the other does not. If the trait in question is wholly genetically determined, we shall expect all MZ twins to be concordant, but the concordance rate in DZ twins will depend on the mode of inheritance and frequency of the gene in the population. Thus, if we collect twins who (1) belong to blood group O, (2) have Huntington's chorea, (3) have phenylketonuria, the concordance rates which we shall expect to find in their DZ partners will be respectively (1) 70 per cent, (2) 50 per cent, (3) 25 per cent. From this it follows that no sound measure of degree of genetical determination can be obtained by simply setting the concordance rates in MZ and in DZ pairs in relation to one another. In the case of continuously distributed variables, the correlation coefficients within MZ and DZ pairs may be contrasted; and Holzinger has suggested his h^2 formula to combine both in an estimate of degree of genetical determination. This too cannot be regarded as fully reliable; and the best plan is to consider the meaning of the concordance rates found, in the total setting of the experiment.

From studies of twins alone one can obtain no information about the mode of inheritance. For this the twin and family methods can usefully be combined; a series of twins is obtained, and then not only their twin partners but other members of their families are investigated. Such a study will also provide information, through a comparison of probands with their singly born sibs as well as with their DZ partners, about early environmental influences; if these are important, DZ partners should be more alike than proband and sib.

Twin series of any useful size can only be obtained if the trait investigated is a common one; but within this field the method is a most useful one, particularly if the aetiology is obscure. A comparison of concordance rates in MZ and DZ twins provides a similar, fell one side of the line of legality in one twin, on the other side in the other; or one might find the socially acceptable equivalent of what in the other became a transgression. By and large, it could be shown that whereas personalities resembled each other closely, the range of behaviour available to anyone of a given personality was surprisingly wide.

These were considerably more alike at all levels in MZ than in DZ pairs but the figures suggest that it can fairly often happen that one of the MZ twins is merely an above-average consumer, while the other ranks as an addict or chronic alcoholic.

Rosanoff's findings on *juvenile delinquency* show the very high concordance rate of 86 per cent for MZ twins but an almost equally high one of 75 per cent for the same-sexed DZ twins. These findings resemble those of measles and mumps, rather than schizophrenia and epilepsy. Environmental factors have to be ranked high in importance, and among them, especially in juvenile delinquency, we have to take into account the influence of one twin on the other. On the borderlines of neurosis, we note that *behaviour disorders* in children are not so concordant in DZ pairs as is juvenile delinquency; such phenomena are likely to be a closer reflection of the personality than is delinquent behaviour in the young.

Neurosis. Twin studies in this field have been surprisingly deficient in number and scope. In published material from our Unit, in only two out of eight MZ pairs was the second twin likewise neurotic or psychopathic. In a subsequent study of schoolchildren, it was found that most MZ twins, while far from being replicas of one another psychologically, tended to be similar in temperament, and that when both had neurotic traits these were generally of the same kind. Even more striking were the differences within DZ pairs; if both of such a pair were neurotic, the symptoms were usually different. On the other hand, the appearance of behaviour disorders in a family was related to the poorness of the psychological environment. To over-simplify somewhat: type of reaction seemed to depend a good deal on constitutional factors, whilst severity was more closely related to the environment.

In continued work at our Unit, we have found concordance rates of about 53 per cent in MZ twins and 25 per cent in DZ twins. This is using the objective but possibly somewhat trivial criterion of having been referred to a psychiatrist or, in the case of children, to a juvenile court. Such an arbitrary definition of "neurosis" does not have much meaning; and the crude concordance rates do not do justice to the personality resemblances.

These figures show that hereditary constitution is a factor of some significance in neurosis; and detailed case study can add information on the variability of expression of some constitutional characteristics. But such material is also interesting in providing the means by which one may analyse the environmental causes of neurosis, by investigating the histories of twins who have differed. Even the concordant pairs are of use in this connexion, as there are frequently marked differences in the degree of a neurotic reaction. It would seem inapposite to classify all these reactions as pathological, or abnormal in more than a statistical or social sense. They are modes of behaviour which lie within the potentialities of the average normal person; and their causation is invariably multiple and complex. The twin method proves a very useful method of separating out some of the threads which enter into the tangle.

Psychology and Genetics

In the sections illustrating the various modes of inheritance and methods of research, we have made reference to many of the salient investigations in the field of psychiatric genetics. In this final section we propose to cover in a brief and synoptic way the present state of our knowledge of hereditary factors as they enter into particular types of psychological abnormality.

Abnormalities of Perception

Defects of *vision* may be caused by abnormalities of any part of the visual apparatus, from the cornea back to the higher association centres in the brain. Errors of refraction, long-sightedness, short-sightedness, astigmatism, are of course common, and frequently involve the participation of genetical factors. A man with a good "eye" may not necessarily be one who can see the moons of Jupiter, but rather one whose speed and accuracy in oculo-motor co-ordination enables him to excel at, say, tennis or cricket. The investigations of Galton have shown that proficiency in sports of many kinds runs in families, and this cannot be solely through a favouring family tradition. We have discussed colour-blindness under sex-linked inheritance; the defect is probably of a biochemical kind, involving the deficiency of a pigment in the retina. *Retinitis pigmentosa* is a disease affecting the retina, genetically determined, and leading to progressive loss of vision proceeding from night blindness to total blindness. Alstrom found that about 10 per cent of the persons admitted to the Swedish government's school for the blind suffered from some form of blindness due to the same recessive gene. As an example of a defect in the highest nervous centres we have congenital *dyslexia* or word-blindness, which Hallgren has shown to be almost certainly due to a dominant gene.

Defects of *hearing* are most commonly caused by infections of the middle ear, and so are essentially non-genetical. However a chronic disease of the middle ear, otosclerosis, tends to run in families, and is responsible for a large group of persons who become deaf in later life. Hereditary factors are more extensively involved in diseases of the inner ear and of the auditory nerves and their connexions, but little is known of their genetics. Among higher nervous abnormalities deaf-mutism when genetically caused is generally due to one of a number of different recessive genes. Tune deafness may be due to a dominant.

Of *other sense deficiencies* still less is known. Taste blindness to phenylthiocarbamide is due to a recessive gene, and the inability to smell potassium cyanide is possibly due to a sex-linked recessive gene. According to Malan, differences in the capacity for spatial orientation are largely inherited.

Abnormalities of Intelligence

The observed normal variation in intelligence can be satisfactorily accounted for by polygenic inheritance, with environmental factors playing a smaller but still substantial role. Variation of a pathological kind, in the I.Q. range below 50 per cent and including idiots and imbeciles, may also arise from genetical causes as well as from environmental ones such as birth trauma. Genetical factors are likely to be of the single-factor kind, such as the recessive gene of PKU. Twin studies have shown that genetical

Table 4.6. Twin Research: Mz and Dz Concordance Rates in a Variety of Conditions, Mostly Psychiatric

Condition investigated (author, year)	Number of pairs			Percentage positively concordant (to nearest 1 per cent) * = corrected for age	
	Total	Monozygotic	Dizygotic	Monozygotic	Dizygotic
Infectious diseases					
Measies	1,163	600	563	97	94
Mumps	190	92	98	78	73
Paralytic poliomyelitis	47	14	33	36	6
Tuberculosis (New York)	308	78	230	62	18
Tuberculosis (England)	202	54	148	30	13
Mental deficiency (institutionalized cases)					
Rosanoff	366	126	240	91	53
Juda "Endogenous" cases only All cases	189	60	129	100	58
	220	71	149	97	56
Schizophrenia					
Luxenburger	81	21	60	67	3
Rosanoff	142	41	101	67	10
Essen-Moller	31 (35)	7 (11)	24	22-71	17
Slater	156	41	115	68	11
				76*	14*
Kallmann	691	174	517	69	10
Kallmann	953	268	685	86*	15*
Kallmann and Roth: Pre-adolescent schizophrenia	52	17	35	71-88	17-23
Manic-depressive psychosis					
Luxenburger	139	56	83	84	15
Rosanoff	90	23	67	70	16
Kallmann	75	23	52	96	26*
Kallmann	85	27	58	100*	26*
Slater: Endogenous affective disorder	38	8	30	50	29*
				c57*	
Da Fonseca: Endogenous affective disorder	60	21	39	75	38

Involutional depression Kallmann		96	29	67	61*	6*
Senile psychosis Kallmann		108	33	75	43*	7*
Epilepsy Rosanoff		107	23	84	70	24
Conrad:	Idiopathic	161	22	97	86	4
	Symptomatic		8	34	13	0
Lennox and Jolly:	Without brain damage	173	51	47	88	13
	With brain damage		26	49	35	12
Homosexuality, Crime, Behaviour Disorder, Neurosis, etc.				Same-sexed pairs		Same-sexed pairs
Male homosexuality (Kinsey Scale, 3 or more): Kallmann		63	37	26	100	12
Adult crime: Lange, Rosanoff, Kranz, Stumpfl, Borgstroem —combined results		216	103	113	68	35
Juvenile delinquency: Rosanoff		67	42	25	85	75
Childhood behaviour disorder, etc.: Rosanoff: Behaviour disorder		107	47	60	87	43
Kranz: Juveniles with personality disorder requiring institutionalization		14	11	3	71	0
After Kent: Emotional disorders		13	7	6	100	67
Shields : Behaviour disorder or marked neurotic traits (based on 62 unselected pairs of twin-school-children)		41	23	18	74	50
Hysteria: Stumpfl		18	9	9	33	0
Neurosis, Psychopathic personality: Slater		37	8	29	25	14
Neurosis, Psychopathic personality: Slater and Shields: New series, provisional		70	38	32	53	25
Alcohol addiction: from series of 201 twin-pairs whose drinking habits were studied		82	26	56	65	30

sensitive test of significant genetical causation. For this reason, such studies have proved particularly valuable in psychiatry, for psychiatric abnormalities tend to be very common, and also to be obscure. The table above shows some of the concordance rates which have been found in a great variety of conditions, from which a lesson may also be learned on how to interpret these figures. If, for instance, we contrast the rates in measles with those in mumps and in polio, a shift in the degree of genetical participation will be seen, even though in all three the specific cause of illness is a foreign agent. In the case of measles, it would seem that nearly everyone who meets the germ gets the illness, and that there is very little variation in individual susceptibility. In the case of mumps, there is much more variation in susceptibility, but, since there is little difference between MZ and DZ concordances, this variation must be largely non-genetical. Only in the case of polio, of these three, is there a strong suggestion that hereditary constitution may be a matter of moment.

Psychiatric Abnormality in Twins

Mental deficiency. The best investigation in the field of mental deficiency is that of Juda. She studied the children attending Special Schools in Munich, and made a complete ascertainment of the twins among them. Excluding cases where the defect was caused by birth injury or other possible exogenous causes, the MZ pairs showed 100 per cent concordance; that is to say, in every case the twin partner of the *propositus* or index case was also mentally defective to some extent. In fact, in fifty-five out of sixty twin pairs both had the same grade of deficiency. In the DZ pairs 58 per cent of the partners were concordant, but in only half of them were both twins affected to the same degree. The findings are consistent with the view that most cases of undifferentiated mental defect are of primarily genetical origin, and that environmental factors, at least those that can vary within the family, are of little significance. Juda's findings are in good agreement with those of Rosanoff in the U.S.A., who, without distinguishing cases of defect of known aetiology, found concordance rates of 91 per cent for MZ pairs, 53 per cent for DZ pairs, in a series of three hundred and sixty-six twin pairs.

Schizophrenia. The work of Luxenburger in this field is the pioneer work on psychosis in twins. He drew attention to the necessity of working systematically, and recommended the ascertainment of the twins in a mental hospital population by checking in the birth registers. Doing this in a defined population of 16,000 schizophrenics, he discovered twenty-one who had MZ twin partners who had survived into an age of risk; in fourteen of these pairs both members were schizophrenic or probably so, in the other seven only one member was affected. Very similar figures have subsequently been found by Rosanoff, Kallmann and Slater; but in cases where a twin partner has not yet fallen ill allowance should be made for age at observation, and where this has been done age-corrected figures are given in the table.

A very large initial clinical material must be investigated before a large enough number of MZ twins with a given diagnosis and with a surviving partner can be assembled. Fraternal twins are of more frequent occurrence, but if the condition is one in which they are not often concordant, the sampling error of the concordance rate may be high. Thus in Luxenburger's series there were forty-eight DZ pairs, and in not one was the partner certainly schizophrenic. Kallmann and Slater, on larger material, have each found a concordance rate of 14 per cent, which is also given by Kallmann for the incidence in the sibs of schizophrenics. Kallmann's latest report is based on no fewer than nine hundred and fifty-three schizophrenic twins and their families. In accounting for the discordant MZ twins — only about 14 per cent — Kallmann lays great stress on body build and weight. He found that when one twin fell ill and the other did not, or when one twin was much more severely ill than the other, it was the more asthenic twin who fared worse.

In the mental hospital material we have investigated from the Maudsley Hospital, we found a somewhat lower MZ concordance rate than Kallmann, one of 76 per cent; twenty-eight of the MZ partners of forty-one schizophrenics were also affected. Besides many close clinical similarities there were also some striking differences. For example, in one case one twin spent eighteen years in hospital, the other four months only. In about half the pairs the twins fell ill within two years of one another; but in one case one girl became schizophrenic at 16, her twin not until 47. This material was given a detailed analysis and description, so that some conclusions could be drawn about the features of the environment and of the personality associated with differences in mental health, and about the features of the illness which showed or did not show indications of genetical determination. The modern trend in twin research recognizes the value of detailed individual analysis, in addition to mass statistics.

Another detailed study is by Essen-Möller. He investigated a small but representative series of twins from a psychiatric clinic in Sweden, and brought to light many differences in severity. However, when both twins had some psychiatric disorder in which there were schizophrenic features in one, these tended to be present in the other too. He found it necessary to formulate the diagnosis in a more fluid way than the other workers mentioned, as many of the psychotic states were atypical. It is not easy to say just what the concordance rates were.

Affective psychoses. Studies on manic-depressive twins have not been carried out on such a large scale, but those that have been made give similar results. Kallmann found in twenty-three MZ pairs that twenty-two of the partners were similarly affected, against figures of 26 per cent for DZ twin partners and 23 per cent for sibs. Once again he found that the physical constitution was important, the less severely affected individuals being less obese. His work on involutional psychoses indicates that they should be distinguished from manic-depressive syndromes. MZ twin partners of involutional depressives were similarly affected in 61 per cent of cases; but he found also a raised incidence of schizophrenia among their relatives. In previously reported work from our Unit, we have had too small a number of manic depressives to draw any conclusions. But in a recent series of sixty pairs, investigated here by da Fonseca and recently published in Portugal, results on the whole are in conformity with those of other studies. Da Fonseca's concordance rates as given in the table include partially concordant cases, *i.e.* those where the co-twin had an abnormal personality of a depressive or hypomanic kind. If overt illness is taken as the criterion the percentages concordant are reduced to 60 per cent and 31 per cent for MZ and DZ pairs respectively. Concordance for cyclothymic personality was higher than that for affective illness.

Senile psychoses and senility. It is once again to Kallmann that we are indebted for twin work in this field. He found a concordance rate in MZ twins of 43 per cent as against 6·5 per cent for DZ twins; and the incidence of such conditions in their other relatives was higher than in the general population. Studying a series of twins, selected only for having outlived the age of 60, he found that MZ pairs, even those who had lived apart for many years, showed a closer resemblance in intelligence, longevity and manner of ageing, than DZ pairs.

Epilepsy. The two principal investigators in this field have been Conrad in Germany and Lennox in the U.S.A. The work of the former is a model of thoroughness, but it is restricted to institutionalized epileptics. Lennox's material includes out-patients. In both studies a remarkably high concordance is reported for MZ twins, 86 and 88 per cent when cases of epilepsy due to acquired brain damage are excluded. Where there was a known or probable cause of local brain damage, the MZ rates were very much lower. This provides an example of the use of twin studies to throw light on the validity of diagnostic classification, and shows that the now somewhat suspect term "idiopathic epilepsy" does have a real meaning. It seems unlikely that, however far our methods of neurological investigation progress, we shall find a specific local cause for every case of epilepsy; in a considerable proportion of cases a constitutional instability must be the main factor.

Male homosexuality. A number of workers have reported single cases, or small series of cases, of homosexuality occurring in twins; however, Kallmann's series is the only thoroughly systematic one. He and his team had great difficulty in carrying it out, as their contacts showed the greatest reluctance to come to the Research Institute, and wished to be interviewed, if at all, in resorts which were familiar to them.

Out of Kallmann's eventual total of forty-five MZ twin pairs, only one was discordant; and in that case the homosexual twin was also, unlike his brother, schizophrenic. The other *propositi* in this series were confirmed homosexuals with a high rating on the Kinsey scale. A full classification of the DZ twin partners has only been given for the first twenty-six pairs; of them one reached a grade of 5 or 6; two a grade of 3 or 4; eight a grade of 1 or 2; and fifteen were in the 0 grade. This is no higher an incidence of homosexual traits than Kinsey found for the white male American population on which he worked. It is possible that Kallmann's material is influenced by a selection in favour of severity and constitutional predisposition, and that his figures would have been different if he had started with younger homosexuals. Nevertheless, the evidence is, of course, very strongly in favour of a genetical factor in the type of homosexuality which Kallmann studied.

Suicide. As a contrast with the above figures, we may mention Kallmann's work on suicide. A prolonged search of the literature disclosed no case of both of a pair of twins committing suicide— unless it were together in a suicidal pact; eventually one such case did come to his notice, and another has recently been reported by Dencker. Though heredity may perhaps play some part in causing a melancholy disposition, suicide itself must require precipitation by accidental factors, such as sudden environmental pressures. This illustrates the relationship and the contrast between personality and behaviour, which have been more intensively investigated in the field of crime.

Crime. The first study of significance was carried out by Lange, who was so impressed by his findings that he entitled his report *Crime as Destiny*. Only three out of his thirteen MZ pairs were discordant, and in very few of the DZ pairs were both twins criminal. These results have not been subsequently confirmed, and later workers, such as Kranz and Stumpfl, have found concordance rates of about 60 and 40 per cent in MZ and DZ twins respectively.

The difference is not so great as to make one think that heredity plays any strongly preponderant role. The high concordance in DZ twins underlines the significance of early family background; and the 40 per cent discordance in the MZ twins supports the idea that special opportunities and temptations have to be regarded as important.

However, detailed clinical studies show that accident plays a smaller part, and personality a larger one, in the case of severe and persistent offenders. Some of the subjects were of a kind to drift naturally into a criminal career, and if so, the MZ twins generally resembled each other in this too. Crimes of violence in one twin would be matched by violence in the other; or both of the twins might be confidence tricksters or swindlers of a similar type, or petty larcenists, or sexually deviant. In some cases, behaviour, though factors are important in cases of deficiency that find their way into institutions and special schools.

To this evidence we may add the results of twin researches in the physiological range, in which intelligence tests have been used. In the earlier work on these lines ovularity diagnosis was generally inadequate. However several workers have found that MZ twins show a closer resemblance in I.Q. than DZ twins. For instance, Newman *et al.* tested fifty MZ and fifty-two DZ pairs of schoolchildren with the Binet test, and obtained correlation coefficients of 0.88 for MZ and 0.63 for DZ twins.

Holzinger introduced the statistic h^2 as an index of heritability, the environment being held constant. This is calculated from the formula $(r_{MZ} - r_{DZ})/(1 - r_{DZ})$, a procedure which is not free from logical objection, although it has been much used. On Newman's material, h^2 was 0.68

Eysenck has stated that correlations between the factor score derived from a battery of intelligence tests would give a truer picture than a single test. Blewett carried out a study on these lines, using five scores from Thurstone's Primary Mental Abilities test (verbal, space, reasoning, number and fluency) and Furneaux's tests of speed and power. His factor scores gave rather lower correlations than those obtained by Newman, 0.76 $_{MZ}$ and 0.44 $_{DZ}$. The hypothesis that the factor score would prove to be more highly determined by heredity than any of the scores from single tests was not borne out. A higher h^2 was obtained for verbal (0.68), fluency (0.64), and reasoning (04) than for the factor score itself (0.58). However, Eysenck, analysing the results of tests applied by both Blewett and McLeod to the same twins, found that tests of finger dexterity and rigidity had high loadings on intelligence. Including these tests, the factor score gave higher correlations, 02 $_{MZ}$ and 08 $_{DZ}$; h^2 = 01.

The use of a test such as Thurstone's P.M.A. should enable one to discover whether one aspect of intelligence is more highly inherited than another. Thurstone and his colleagues ranked the separate abilities in the order of the significance of the difference between the scores of forty-eight MZ and fifty-five DZ pairs; the order was space, verbal, fluency, number and reasoning. Vandenberg makes a rough comparison of the within-pair variance of forty-five MZ and thirty-seven DZ twins for a variety of psychological and other traits, diagrammatically and without giving numerical results. Of the traits probably related to intelligence the largest MZ-DZ difference was in P.M.A. sentence completion, followed successively by the Stanford spelling test, the W.I.S.C. vocabulary test, P.M.A. arithmetic, Raven's Progressive Matrices, and finally, with very little difference between the two kinds of twins, mechanical insight. The results of these investigations are not easily compared with one another, owing to the different ways in which the findings are presented. In all of them, however, verbal ability shows up as one of the most highly inheritable aspects of intelligence within the family.

Taking intelligence as a whole, a number of attempts have been made to estimate the proportion of the total observed variance which can be attributed to heredity on the one side and environment on the other. We have already mentioned Burks's estimate of 75 to 80 per cent attributable to heredity. Burt, in a paper published in 1943, summarizes extensive work done on this subject under his supervision; and more recently he has given his opinion that very nearly 90 per cent of the variance in intelligence exhibited by a complete age group is attributable to the genetic constitution of the various individuals, while approximately half of this could be predicted from the characteristics of near relatives. Godfrey Thompson, Hogben and others have estimated the contribution by heredity as rather lower, nearer to 60 per cent. In connexion with all such estimates, it must be remembered that only that degree of genetical and environmental variance which obtained in the circumstance of the experiment will be measured, and that this will be, on both sides, very much less than what obtains in the population at large. A group of L.C.C. schoolchildren, for instance, must come from a much more homogeneous environment than the population of Great Britain as a whole, not to speak of the population of the world. Generalizations on this subject must, therefore, be made only with great caution. Other authorities consider that the interaction of heredity and environment is so complex that it is probably futile to try to inquire into the extent of hereditary determination. Nevertheless much can be learned from attempts to do so.

Abnormalities of Child Development

There is a wide range of normal variation in the rate and pattern of maturation. This is to a large extent genetically determined. Twin studies show that MZ twins resemble one another more closely than DZ twins in the age at which they begin to talk and in the tests of development of Hetzer and Buhler. Russian studies on a small number of pairs showed that the height of jump attained by four-year-old twins was much more alike in MZ than DZ pairs. The Vineland Social Maturity Scale has been administered to twins by von Bracken, Wilson and by Troup and Lester. All report negligible differences between MZ twins and larger ones between DZ twins. There is probably an important genetical element controlling the rate of sexual maturation as shown for instance by the greater mean difference in age of first menstruation reported by Petri for DZ twins (12.0 months) than for MZ twins (2.8 months). However, mothers and daughters showed no closer resemblance in this respect than pairs of unrelated women, thus suggesting, as Stern points out, that differences in family environments and differences between one generation and the next are important too.

It is not suggested that any of the above developmental stages are entirely genetically determined or that they are simple, well-understood processes. But the combined influence of heredity on many aspects of development must be considerable and will play its part in determining many abnormalities of development, for example in psychosexual maturity. Luchsinger reports that speech development, especially retardation in speech, is largely hereditarily determined. We have already had occasion to refer to Hallgren's detailed study of backward readers. In her series of twins at Special Schools in Munich, Juda found three cases of MZ pairs where both were genuine late developers. In Kallmann's large twin material he discovered fifty-two cases of schizophrenia commencing before the age of 15. Twelve out of seventeen MZ co twins also developed schizophrenia under the age of 15, and six out of thirty-five DZ co-twins. Pre adolescent schizophrenia appeared to be a special case of adult schizophrenia, and three MZ and two DZ co-twins became schizophrenic after the age of 15.

Turning to minor disturbances of development, as seen for example in some of the commoner neurotic and behaviour disorders of children, the influence of the genes can perhaps be seen in the observation of Shields that when a pair of twins both have some trouble of this nature the symptoms are generally of the same kind in MZ twins but different in DZ twins. For instance, he reports six pairs where enuresis occurred in a MZ pair and in four of these both twins were similarly affected. There were ten DZ pairs where this symptom occurred and in none of them were both twins enuretic, though in some cases the twin partner had some other trouble. In a recent monograph Hallgren has attempted to clarify the part played by the constitution in this disorder, finding quite strong grounds for believing there to be a considerable genetical element in primary enuresis. However, childhood behaviour disorders are very common, often transient and often demonstrably reactive to unsatisfactory external circumstances. Faulty learning habits are also no doubt often to blame. The role of the genes will be relatively indirect.

Psychophysiological Traits

Jost and Sontag showed that similarities in autonomic response increased with the degree of genetic relationship. Earlier work on pulse-rate and blood-pressure in twins received confirmation and elaboration when Eysenck extracted an "autonomic" factor from the data of Blewett and McLeod. The scores of MZ twins on this factor had a correlation of 0·93, those of DZ twins of like sex one of 0·72; the factor was highly influenced by sex. Carmena tested the psychogalvanic reflex of thirty-six MZ and twenty-four DZ twins and concluded that nervousness and kindred temperamental traits were the result of hereditary influences. According to Kanaev MZ twins show striking similarities in the ease with which they can be conditioned. Similar abnormal electro-encephalographic records in relatives have been reported, though the work of Harvald shows the mode of inheritance of EEG pattern to be a complex matter. Nevertheless, Lennox considers that in certain circumstances EEG patterns can be used as a criterion to distinguish MZ from DZ twins.

Personality

The relationship between autonomic factors, P.G.R., conditionability and EEG on the one hand, and personality characteristics, such as nervousness, extraversion and aggressiveness on the other. Body build too, possibly through its relation with autonomic functioning, has well-known associations with personality and is genetically determined to a substantial degree. But the connexion between physiological make-up and personality is one of some fluidity. Thus Whelan reports a pair of MZ twins, both of whom had similarly abnormal EEGs of an epileptic kind; yet one behaved in an extremely psychopathic way, aggressive, antisocial and subject to fugues, while the other was psychologically and socially within normal limits.

When attempts are made, generally by means of the twin method, to investigate personality characteristics at the level of motor activity, positive findings as regards heredity are usually found. Thus Luchsinger found heredity to be an important determinant of posture, throwing movements and mimicry. Lehtovaara made cinematographic records of twins watching a film. The course, character and intensity of the mimical process was much more alike in the MZ pairs. Also using film studies of twins, Spindler found an important hereditary basis for emotional and expressive mobility in adults, but not for voluntary movements. MZ twins are frequently reported as having indistinguishable voices. Gedda and his colleagues have found that when recordings of their own voices and those of their twins were played back to a group of uniovular twins, they were as a rule unable to tell one from the other. Family resemblance in physique predisposes towards similar interests and abilities in sport and athletics such as are often found in father and son, in siblings, and particularly in MZ twins. Galton's observations on the subject have already been noted and Grebe has made some interesting observations on sporting abilities in twins and other relatives. MZ twins are more alike than DZ twins in tests of motor skill and mechanical ability. Thus expressive movements, speech characteristics and preferred activities all of which are closely related to personality appear to be largely genetically determined.

Questionnaire tests of neurotic tendencies, interests, etc. generally show lower levels of correlation, but such tests often lack reliability, and validity. On the basis of such studies alone one cannot justifiably conclude, as has sometimes been done, that personality characteristics are much less highly determined genetically than intelligence.

Table 4.7. Twin Research: Results, Expressed in the Form of Correlation Coefficients, of Selected Psychological Tests Applied to Monozygotic and Dizygotic Twins Reared Together

Test	r_{MZ}	r_{DZ}
Intelligence tests		
Wingfield (National Intelligence Test and McCall's Multimental Scale)	0.90	0.57
Herrman and Hogben (Otis)	0.84	0.48
Newman, Freeman and Holzinger (Binet)	0.88	0.63
Blewett (factor score)	0.76	0.44
Eysenck (data of Blewett and McLeod) (factor score)	0.82	0.38
Other psychological tests		
Mechanical aptitude (Brody)	0.69	0.28
Motor skills (McNemar)	0.79	0.43
Bernreuter's neurotic inventory (Carter)	0.63	0.32
Woodworth-Matthews' neurotic tendencies (Holzinger)	0.56	0.37
Strong's vocational interests (Carter)	0.50	0.28
Autonomic factor (Eysenck, data of Blewett and McLeod)	0.93	0.72
Neuroticism factor (Eysenck and Prell)	0.85	0.22
Extraversion factor (McLeod)	0.77	0.03
Extraversion factor (Eysenck, data of Blewett and McLeod)	0.50	-0.33

Besides self-ratings, the opinions of others have been used to investigate similarities and differences between twins. According to Lassen teachers' ratings on a large number of social and moral characteristics have much higher correlations between MZ than DZ pairs. This may have been influenced by a halo effect. Similarly H. E. Jones reports that parents more often perceive personality differences in the case of DZ than MZ twins. However, Jones considers that these opinions of the parents of the twins may have the effect of producing an environment in which greater similarities come to be expected of MZ than of DZ twins. This stereotyping process might, he thinks, be of importance in maintaining or increasing the similarity of twins in certain traits.

Instead of using a single test, Eysenck and Prell used a variety of tests of different kinds, all purporting to discriminate between neurotic and normal subjects, and extracted the factor which they had in common. The tests were given to twenty-five pairs each of MZ and DZ twin schoolchildren and to a "criterion" group of children from a child guidance clinic. The score for the factor of neuroticism had a higher correlation between twins than the scores of any of the separate tests. r_{MZ} for factor score was 0.85, and r_{DZ} 0.22; h^2 was 0.82—even higher than h^2 for intelligence. The authors concluded that their factor of neuroticism was a biological reality and not just a statistical artefact, and that it was highly inheritable as a whole.

Two years later, Blewett repeated the experiment of Eysenck and Prell on a fresh sample of twins, using a largely different set of tests, but these did not intercorrelate in the expected way and no factor of neuroticism could be extracted. However, McLeod tested the same twins with tests designed to measure extraversion-introversion and found a very large difference between the two kinds of twin in their resemblance in factor score ($r_{MZ} = 0.77$, $r_{DZ} = 0.03$; $h^2 = 0.77$). Eysenck reanalysed the combined data of Blewett and McLeod and, in addition to factors for intelligence and autonomic function, extracted an extraversion factor which gave a r_{MZ} of + 0.50 and a r_{DZ} of - 0.33; the difference was significant at the 2 per cent level. The very low correlations between DZ twins in the study of McLeod and the negative one in that of Eysenck may possibly be attributable to the small size of the sample.

Cattell devised an ingenious experimental design to analyse the contributions of heredity and environment, and of any correlation between them, to the variance of scores on personality tests. This makes use of (*a*) MZ twins in their own families, (*b*) siblings in their own families, (*c*) siblings, each member of a pair in a different family, (*d*) pairs of unrelated persons brought up in the same family, and (*e*) unrelated persons in different families. From their scores a series of equations can be solved for heredity and environment, both within and between families. Unlike other statistical methods hitherto proposed, such as Holzinger's h^2, this multivariate design takes into account any correlation between the single variances. Two years later Cattell and his colleagues reported on the first attempt to apply this design to the scores of schoolchildren on twelve personality factors from his "Junior Personality Quiz." He was, however, unable to obtain a sufficient number of pairs under group (*c*) above. The results are rather difficult to interpret. However, Tender-mindedness, General Neuroticism and Somatic Anxiety were among those factors found to be determined predominantly by the environment. Cyclothymic factors and General Intelligence were predominantly determined by heredity. Although considerable advances have been made in methodology, it cannot yet be claimed that objective tests of personality have given consistent results when applied to problems of heredity.

Deviations of Personality

The relevance that findings based on measured personality factors would have to the genetics of neurosis and psychopathic personality lies, of course, in the widely held view that these conditions consist for the most part of deviations along one or a number of different dimensions of personality. The problem can, however, be approached more directly, though not in such a quantitative way, by investigating along more traditional lines.

There have been a number of family studies, in which workers have investigated the incidence of all kinds of psychiatric abnormality among the relatives of persons showing some particular deviation of personality: von Baeyer on the relatives of pathological liars and swindlers, Brown on the families of anxiety neurotics, hysterics and obsessionals Cohen on "neurocirculatory asthenia," Edith Rüdin on obsessional neurotics, and Ljungberg on conversion hysteria. All of these workers have found an excess of psychiatric abnormality, compared with the general population, among the relatives of these people, but not always of specifically the same kind. Thus von Baeyer found among the relatives of his pathological liars no large absolute number of swindlers of a similar kind, but rather an excess of persons showing similar personality traits, *i.e.*, an excess of extreme extraverts, of cyclothymics, and people with marked hysterical traits. Brown found, among the relatives of the anxiety neurotics, an excess of anxiety neurotics, but also an excess of hysterics and of emotionally unstable people. Such findings as these led Slater and Slater to postulate not only a multifactorial but also a multi dimensional genetical basis for the so-called neurotic and psychopathic deviations of personality. The hypothesis enables one to understand, on the basis of a simple working model, such facts as the shading off of the neurotic or psychopathic into the normal, and the clinical finding that most patients show weaknesses or handicaps of personality of more than one kind. The point has been effectively made by Williams that, if we take the 95 per cent level as the line of demarcation between "normal" and "abnormal," only 60 per cent (0.95^{10}) of people would be normal for all of ten characters, and less than I per cent for all of a hundred.

There is also a probability that specific genetic factors may cause a deviation of personality not amounting to illness. Thus among the relatives of schizophrenics there is an excess of persons of schizoid personality, which might be explained if they were heterozygous for the hypothetical schizophrenic gene. A similar phenomenon may hold also in the families of manic-depressives. Personality deviations may also arise from purely environmental causes of many kinds, from birth trauma and organic illness in childhood, to defects in upbringing and conditioning in the widest sense.

Interesting studies of superior personalities and their families have recently been made by Juda and by Roe. Roe studied sixty-four prominent American-born scientists and compared them with a control group of university faculty members of lesser distinction. As might have been expected, a combination of hereditary and environmental factors appeared to be responsible for the superiority of the *élite* group. Juda's material consisted of two hundred and ninety-four German-speaking men and women of the most outstanding achievement in the arts and sciences during the past three hundred years. Nearly all came from families with other signs of talent, and many were related to one another. The rate of mental abnormality in the relatives was raised by only a small amount; and though the incidence of abnormalities of personality among the subjects themselves was well above average expectations (about 20 per cent), yet one could still say that the great majority of them were healthy and normal. The view that practically all creative workers are psychopathic or insane is shown to be a travesty of the facts. Both Juda and Roe found an excess of first-born among their superior subjects.

Psychosis

We have already mentioned the hypothesis that a dominant gene with reduced manifestation plays an important part in the causation of *manic-depressive psychosis*. This theory, rather than one of multifactorial inheritance, is favoured by the fact that the tendency to endogenous mood swings seems to have a bimodal distribution. In the families of manic-depressives one rather frequently comes across persons who, though not necessarily psychotic, show marked depressive moods at times, or hypomanic phases, which occur spontaneously and without any clear environmental cause. Other members of the same families show no such tendency, and one can draw usually a fairly clear line between them. The presumption is that in those subject to endogenous mood swings, the temperamental deviation is attributable to the same gene as the psychosis, and that classification as a psychotic depends on the mood swing being long and severe enough to need psychiatric treatment.

Quite distinct, clinically, from the tendency to endogenous mood swings, is the tendency to overreact emotionally to strains and stresses of both a physical and psychological nature. The depression which may result is usually diagnosed as "reactive"; but some psychiatrists do not recognize the distinction between "reactive" and "endogenous."

It is probable that manic-depressive, or cyclothymic, disorders are not the only forms of affective psychosis which may have a hereditary basis. So-called involutional depression is probably a heterogeneous group of illnesses, including some manic-depressives, some schizophrenics, and perhaps also a nuclear group of a specific kind; this latter group would consist of people who fall insidiously ill on the basis of a rigid and obsessional, rather than a cyclothymic, personality. However, the most recent study of the genetics of involutional depression, that of Stenstedt, failed to confirm this association between involutional depression and schizophrenia. While agreeing that involutional depression was aetiologically heterogeneous, environmental factors playing an important role in many cases, the results of his work were to support the older view that in so far as it was genetical it could not be distinguished from manic-depressive disorders. However, the milder cases did not differ aetiologically from severe (psychotic) depressions.

While there is a great deal of evidence from twin and family studies that hereditary factors are of considerable importance in *schizophrenia*, there is still no general agreement on the mode of inheritance. Kallmann, who has done more on the subject than anyone else, postulates a recessive gene whose effects are influenced by modifying genes, but a dominant gene with reduced manifestation has its supporters. There may not be as much difference between these views as might at first appear. Kallmann supposes that there is some degree of manifestation in the heterozygote, *e.g.*, as a schizoid personality; and this would bring the mode of inheritance near to an intermediate type.

In his study of a North Swedish population, Book calculated that his data could be explained by a gene manifesting itself in all homozygotes and in about one in every five heterozygotes. This hypothesis has been further examined by Slater; and it was shown that the principal data supplied by Kallmann and Elsässer were in conformity with a gene of this intermediate type. At a gene frequency of 0.015, with manifestation in 26 per cent of heterozygotes, the theoretical expectancies of schizophrenia in the sibs of schizophrenics, the children of one schizophrenic, the children of two schizophrenics, and in the children of cousins were, respectively, 0.144, 0.143, 0.396, and 0.008. The corresponding observational findings are 0·.142 (Kallmann), 0.164 (Kallmann), 0.392 (Elsässer), and 0.011 (Nixon and Slater). On this basis, some 70 per cent of all persons carrying an adequate genetical predisposition to schizophrenia would not fall ill, leaving therefore a considerable margin for the operation of environmental factors. The fact that schizophrenia is a relatively common disease as well as a biologically malignant one could be accounted for on this theory if there was some degree of heterozygotic advantage.

This is probably not the only genetical model which could be constructed to account for the available data, but it supplies an adequate working hypothesis. Attempts to demonstrate genetical heterogeneity for schizophrenia have not been entirely convincing so far. It seems unlikely that there will be any decisive answer to the problem without advances in other fields, e.g. the biochemical basis of schizophrenia.

Organic States and Epilepsy

Some forms of brain damage, including senile dementia and Huntington's chorea, are due very largely to the genetic constitution, and their psychological consequences depend closely on the extent of the brain damage. Genetical factors also play a part, but a more remote one, in the causation of arteriosclerotic dementia; they enter into the causes of arteriosclerosis, but other factors may determine how far the brain itself is damaged and hence how much psychological change there is. Most brain tumours are non-genetical. The psychological consequences of head injuries are of course primarily accounted for by the site and the amount of damage done; but brain injuries may also precipitate psychoses or bring out latent personality traits in predisposed persons.

One of the consequences of brain injury may be epilepsy, but in most epileptics no plausible external cause can be found. The genetical constitution is quite important in determining how easily a person develops epilepsy. This is probably a graded characteristic. The capacity to respond with a major convulsion to certain stimuli is universal in man, and this fact is made use of in the treatment of depression with E.C.T. But the threshold at which a fit occurs ranges from those who are most resistant down to those who suffer from "idiopathic" epilepsy. All investigations of the relatives of idiopathic epileptics have shown an increased incidence of epilepsy, and the genetical factor has also been demonstrated by twin studies. However, Ounsted has shown that the incidence of epilepsy in other members of the family is related to the nature of the fits; and the most trivial cases, such as infantile convulsions, often have the heaviest family loading. Ounsted found that 25 per cent of the sibs of the children who had had infantile convulsions had some form of convulsive disorder. When adult epileptics are investigated, lower rates for the incidence of epilepsy in sibs have been found, usually around 4 per cent.

Studies with the EEG by Lennox and others indicate that electrical patterns of brain activity have a genetical constitutional basis. Lennox found that there was a high incidence of *cerebral dysrhythmia* in the parents of epileptics, and he postulated that this was connected with the possession of a dominant gene. Epileptics would then be constitutional dysrhythmics, who had suffered in addition some environmentally caused trauma sufficient to bring on epilepsy. However, there is too much individual variation in brain-wave patterns, even when taken under standardized conditions, for dysrhythmia to be a satisfactory unitary concept; and abnormalities of the pattern may also take a great number of different forms. The best measure of instability of brain physiology is obtained by submitting the subject to a graduated increasing dosage of a convulsant drug, given by intravenous injection; the level of dosage at which, first abnormalities in the EEG, and finally a convulsion, occur then becomes the required measure. Individual variation in this respect shows every sign of being a graded character, its genetical basis being then of a probably multifactorial kind.

Conclusion

We have presented the genetical contribution to the study of abnormal psychology in very largely psychiatric terms. There are of course abundant reasons for this, into which we need not enter. One of them has been the fact that most of the genetical work on psychological abnormalities has been concerned with psychiatric syndromes, rather than with psychological concepts, such as perception, memory, emotion and learning. It is probable that those who are concerned with human genetics in the first place will continue to work along the same lines, for, as must have been seen, there are many pressing unsolved problems. Genetics, however, has another contribution to make, that of providing the framework for primarily psychological investigation, such as is seen in the work of Eysenck and his associates.

We began the chapter by asking in what sense and to what extent can physical heredity be offered as an explanation of psychological abnormality, or rather of various specific kinds of abnormality, for there can be no general answer. From the discussion which followed it can perhaps be seen that genetical studies try to answer three different but related kinds of question: the mode of inheritance (formal genetics), how the genes manifest themselves (developmental genetics), the relative share of heredity and environment (analysis of variance). The importance we attribute to heredity depends on which question we are most interested in, and this in turn depends on the nature of the condition under investigation and the point of view of the inquirer. The first of these questions will be asked most often of specific non-normally distributed conditions. Ideally, the answer should be given in Mendelian terms, and with some estimate of the frequency and the distribution of the gene in the population. The influence of factors other than the specific gene, both those of a genetical and environmental kind, will appear in reduction of the manifestation rate or variabilities in expression. The greater the variability of expression, the more difficult the analysis becomes; and the lower the manifestation rate, the less important and less useful. Answers will be interesting to to the geneticist, and of relevance to the eugenist. The second question relates to the mode of interaction between heredity and environment. The work involved stretches from biochemical investigations on the action of single abnormal genes, over such work as Grüneberg's on embryo rats, to social and psychological studies of twins. The results are of the greatest interest to the practical clinician; they may affect his work, from the theoretical side of the classification of diseases to the purely practical aspect of treatment. Abnormalities due to single-gene differences will occupy pride of place; but deviations form the norm caused multifactorially will become increasingly accessible. The third question is one which has dominated psychologists, particularly educational psychologists, in the past, as it has considerable social significance. Its importance, however, will diminish as our capacity to answer the first two questions improves. It has been, and still is, a battleground for debate, not always either dispassionate or sensible. The question is still worth asking about conditions which are graded in degree, can be measured with reasonable reliability and accuracy, and are universally distributed; and the answers obtained may be very important, though only in a limited field. They also suffer from being entirely provisional. As we have already mentioned, they can apply only to a limited population, extrapolation being more than usually dangerous, and they are rendered obsolete at once by any large and general change on either the genetical or environmental side. It is probable that, as our knowledge increases, we shall turn more and more in other directions.

5

Models of Abnormal Behaviour and Psychology

Introduction

The biological model of abnormal behaviour is also referred to as the organic model, the traditional medical model, or the disease model. In this model it is assumed that the various abnormal behaviours that people with a particular syndrome display are symptoms of a specific disease with a discrete cause, a unique course and prognosis, and for which a specific physical treatment will ultimately be identified. This model evolved within a medical tradition where there were numerous examples of physical conditions involving a syndrome of signs and symptoms that could be explained by a discrete cause, such as an infection or metabolic dysfunction. Syphilis is a good example of a condition where a discrete physical cause (syphilitic infection) causes a psychological syndrome (general paresis of the insane) and can be treated by specific physical methods (inoculation). In 1897 Richard von Krafft-Ebing (1840-1902), a German neurologist, following the work of Louis Pasteur (1822-1895), inoculated patients with general paresis, with pus from syphilitic sores, and this halted the development of the degenerative condition which typically culminated in insanity. The success of this work gave impetus to the biological model of psychiatry. Not surprisingly, the biological model has been championed by psychiatry more than other mental health professions.

The diathesis-stress model is a subtler variant of the biological model. In this type of model it is assumed that psychiatric illnesses or psychological problems occur when people who are biologically vulnerable to such difficulties are exposed to particular stresses.

Achievements

The biological or medical model has led to a number of important achievements. The first of these has been the development of mental health legislation. This legislation makes provision for the involuntary detention and/or treatment of people with psychological disorders whose judgement is severely impaired, especially if they are a danger to themselves or other people. Suicidal behaviour and extremely violent behaviour are recognized within mental health legislation in most countries as possible reflections of impaired judgement and possible grounds for involuntary detention or treatment in a psychiatric treatment centre.

A second important achievement of the biological or medical model has been the development of widely used classification systems. This began with the painstaking work of Kraepelin (1896) who, through careful observation, catalogued symptoms characteristic of different groups of patients. Psychological problems are currently classified in the World Health Organization's *The International Classification of Diseases — Tenth Edition: Classification of Mental and Behavioural Disorders* (ICD10) and in the American Psychiatric Association's *Diagnostic and Statistical Manual of Mental Disorders* (now in its fourth edition). These two systems ICD 10 and DSM IV are now used widely throughout the world and provide a way for clinicians and researchers to communicate with each other in a relatively unambiguous manner. This was not always the case and in the past there has been wide variation in diagnostic criteria used in different countries. For example, in the US a very broad definition of schizophrenia was typically used up until the development of DSM III in 1980. The extraordinary differences in rates of diagnosis are highlighted by the results of the US-UK project presented in Table 5.2.

The use of scientific methods and quantitative techniques to study abnormal behaviour is a third achievement of the biological

Table 5.1. Model of Abnormal Behaviour

	Biological model	Psychoanalytic model	Cognitive behavioural model	Family systems model
Cause of abnormal behaviour	Central nervous system abnormality	Unconscious psychopathology	Learned habits	Dysfunctional family system
Therapy goal	• Rectify CNS abnormality	• Resolve unconscious conflicts	• Learn more adaptive habits	• Alter problem maintaining family interaction patterns and beliefs
Therapy process	• Pharmacological • ECT • Psychosurgery	• Long-term one-toone psychoanalysis	• Short-term cognitive behaviour therapy	• Short-term marital or family therapy
Achievements	• Liberation of insane • Mental health legislation • Classification • Scientific method • Medical technology • Pharmacological and physical treatments	• Discovery of unconscious • Makes madness meaningful • Discovery of transference • Legitimized talking cure • Inspired other models of personality and therapy	• Brief and effective • Permits evidencebased practice • Has specific interventions for specific problems • Scientifically rigorous	• Highlighted social context of abnormal behaviour • Brief and cost-effective • Permits evidence-based practice • Permits integration of biological, psychological and social factors

model. Case-control studies, longitudinal studies, and randomized controlled trials are three common research designs used in studies conducted within the medical tradition.

Case-control studies may be used to determine the unique characteristics associated with a particular psychological disorder. In case-control studies a group of diagnostically homogeneous cases, about which the researcher is trying to find out more information, is compared to another group of patients with a known condition or to a normal control group. This was the method Kolvin used to differentiate between childhood schizophrenia and autism. He found that, compared with childhood schizophrenia, autism was associated with an earlier onset, delayed language development, catastrophic reactions to environmental changes, gross stereotypic behaviours, and the absence of delusions and hallucinations.

Table 5.2. Rates of diagnosis of schizophrenia in US and UK

	Hospital diagnosis	Project diagnosis
US	61%	29%
UK	34%	35%

Longitudinal studies may be used to determine the course of a psychological disorder. In longitudinal studies the researcher assesses a group of diagnostically homogeneous cases at repeated time points. This was the research design used by Robins to establish the course of conduct disorder. He found that about a third of cases developed antisocial personality disorder and a third adjusted well in adulthood. The remaining third had a more variable course.

Randomized controlled trials are used to evaluate the effectiveness of specific treatments. Diagnostically homogeneous cases are randomly assigned to treatment or control conditions. All cases are assessed immediately before and after treatment and then a number of months after treatment has been completed. Standard assessment procedures are used for all cases at all three time points. If the group that receives treatment shows greater improvement than the control group, then the treatment may be said to be effective. This design is typical of studies reviewed in books such as *A Guide to Treatments that Work* and *What Works with Children and Adolescents*.

The development of sophisticated methods for monitoring activity within the central nervous system is a fourth achievement of the biological model. These include brain imaging systems such as the CAT (computerized axial tomography) scan, the PET (positron emission tomography) scan, the SPECT (single photon emission tomography) scan, and fMRI (functional magnetic resonance imaging). Imaging techniques have thrown light on those areas of the brain associated with particular disorders. For example, studies using SPECT have found increased metabolic rates in the basal ganglia in people with obsessive-compulsive disorder.

A fifth achievement of the biological model is the development of physical treatments for psychological problems. These include psychopharmacological advances such as neuroleptic medication for psychoses; antidepressant medication for unipolar mood disorders; and lithium carbonate for bipolar disorder. Electroconvulsive therapy is also an effective physical treatment for major depression which does not respond to medication and psychotherapy. Psychosurgery has been found to be effective in extreme cases of OCD. The development of physical treatments, particularly psychopharmacological treatments, has depended upon hypotheses in which dysregulation of neurotransmitter systems has played a central part for example, the dopamine theory of schizophrenia.

Limitations

Despite these major achievements, the biological model is not without its limitations. First, much abnormal behaviour is not caused exclusively by organic factors. Rather, for conditions such as anxiety, depression and schizophrenia, people with a genetic vulnerability to a particular condition develop abnormal behaviour if they are exposed to particular stresses within their environment. This observation has led people working within this tradition to move away from a purely biological model to a diathesis-stress model of psychological problems. Such models acknowledge the importance of psychosocial factors such as family environment, gender, social class and culture in the development of abnormal behaviour. For example, confusing and unsupportive family environments, the societal inequalities that favour men over women, membership of a disadvantaged ethnic minority, or membership of a low socio-economic group may all contribute to the stress experienced by individuals who are biologically vulnerable to particular psychological conditions and who as a result develop psychological problems.

Second, much abnormal behaviour and experience is not neatly organized as a set of discrete syndromes with an under-lying biological cause. Boyle has shown, for example, that schizophrenia does not meet the specified criteria for a medical syndrome. Furthermore, much abnormal behaviour is normally distributed within the population. Thus dimensional rather than categorical conceptualizations of specific conditions are probably more valid for many conditions. For example, conduct disorder can probably be most validly conceptualized as instances where youngsters show extreme levels of externalizing behaviour problems, which fall on a continuum, with most children showing a moderate number of these types of difficulties. Also, trait conceptualizations of personality disorders are probably more valid than categorical conceptualizations.

Third, many psychopharmacological and physical treatments have harmful or unknown side-effects. For example, many widely used neuroleptic antipsychotic agents lead to an irreversible neurological movement disorder known as tardive dyskinesia. Electroconvulsive therapy (ECT), which is commonly used to treat major depression which is unresponsive to antidepressant medication, invariably leads to memory loss and confusion. The long-term effects of stimulant therapy such as Ritalin (methylphenidate), which is widely used to treat ADHD, are currently unknown.

Fourth, in some instances abnormal behaviour is a reaction to stresses inherent in family structures, such as oppressive, neglectful or abusive patterns of family organization. In others, abnormal behaviour is a reaction to stresses inherent in the structure of society at large, such as poverty, injustice, prejudice, racism, sexism, ageism and intolerance for non-conformity. The biological model, with its exclusive emphasis on organic factors in the etiology of psychological problems and its privileging of physical treatment, draws attention away from important psychosocial and political changes that may be required to alleviate psychological distress and to preserve civil liberties. By insisting, from the privileged position of a high-status profession, that abnormal behaviour is a reflection of mental illness requiring physical treatment, proponents of the biological model prevent society from addressing injustices, stresses and intolerance for non-conformity at a political level.

Fifth, the development of asylums has led to the exclusion of people with psychological problems from society. This in turn has promoted stigmatization and marginalization of large groups of people who engage in abnormal behaviour. The stigmatization and marginalization may further reinforce the difficulties of people with psychological problems and coping difficulties.

Sixth, mental health legislation, which emerged within the biological and medical tradition for understanding abnormal behaviour, has been abused so as to limit the freedom of people with psychological problems. Szasz has argued that imprisoned criminals have more liberty and fewer violations of personal rights than people with psychological problems who are involuntarily detained.

Seventh, because the biological model of abnormal behaviour and practices based upon it are championed by biologically oriented psychiatry, non-medical professions, including clinical psychology and psychotherapy, have often been marginalized in the development of mental health services.

Psychoanalytic Model

Assumptions

The psychoanalytic or psychodynamic model assumes that abnormal behaviour patterns are symptoms of underlying unconscious conflict or psychopathology. As a child develops, according to classical psychoanalytic theory, primitive sexual and aggressive urges of the unconscious 'id' become gradually controlled by the rational 'ego'. The ego is guided by an internalization of society's standards: the 'superego'. However, intrapsychic conflict is inevitable. Conflict occurs between the sexual and aggressive impulses of the id and societal standards as reflected in the superego.

Such conflict is managed unconsciously by using various defence mechanisms, the function of which is to keep the forbidden sexual and aggressive impulses from consciousness. For example, a man who is angry at his boss at work may sing his superior's praises, thereby using the defence of reaction formation.

However, defences are compromises between the forces of the id and superego and often carry costly side-effects. For example, the man who is angry at his boss may eventually develop chest pains and anxiety, as a result of repressing rather than acknowledging the anger felt towards the superior.

Furthermore, the psychoanalytic model argues that relationship styles learned early in life are transferred in later life to other relationships, notably relationships with authority figures, sexual partners and psychotherapists. These relationship styles or 'transference phenomena' as they are called in psychoanalysis are coloured in part by feelings aroused and partially resolved during the Oedipus complex phase (for boys) or Electra complex phase (for girls). These developmental phases refer to the psychoanalytic hypothesis that children in early life desire their opposite-sex parent and harbour aggression towards the parent of their own gender. However, these sexual and aggressive impulses are repressed and the child eventually identifies with the parent of the same gender for fear of the consequences of acting them out. In later life, patients, such as the man with chest pains referred to earlier, experience feelings towards significant others and deal with them in a manner similar to that which occurred during the oedipal phase of development. So the man with chest pains experienced aggression towards his boss, and later towards his psychotherapist in a similar fashion, and dealt with this using reaction formation in a manner similar to that with which he handled the oedipal triangle as a child.

Psychoanalysis and psychoanalytic psychotherapy provide a context within which patients can experience transference towards a psychotherapist and then through interpretation gain insight into the transference and related defences which underlie their psychopathology. The analyst or therapist and client meet frequently according to a strict schedule. The patient reports in an uncensored way his or her contents of consciousness. Eventually the client develops transference and the analyst interprets this repeatedly over time until the patient has gained insight into the transference and related defences and worked through related unresolved feelings. Concurrently, the patient's symptoms abate.

In order to be able to practise psychoanalysis, therapists must undergo their own analysis so that they have a first-hand understanding of the process, and so that they will recognize transference feelings that they have towards patients (counter-transference). Traditionally strict selection criteria are used for psychoanalysis and typically YAVIS (young, adult, verbal, intelligent and single) patients only have been deemed suitable. However, this has changed in recent years with developments like object relations approaches to conditions such as borderline personality disorder.

Achievements

The most outstanding achievement of the psychoanalytic model is the discovery of the unconscious. Freud drew together a set of ideas from a wide range of sources and crystallized them in the notion of the unconscious, not as a passive repository of irretrievable memories but as an active set of psychological processes. According to the psychoanalytic model of the unconscious, people can make themselves forget things or keep them outside awareness.

Second, psychoanalysis gave meaning to apparently meaningless behaviour. For example, Freud showed how, in phobias, fears of one stimulus (*e.g.* one's father) could be displaced onto other stimuli (*e.g.* horses). He also showed how unconscious processes which explained psychological disorders could also explain peculiar everyday behaviour.

Third, psychoanalysis introduced the ideas of transference and countertransference into the practice of psychotherapy. This idea that people have a limited number of relationship-maps, which they learn early in life and transfer onto significant others in adulthood, has been supported by recent empirical work on continuity in patterns of attachment from childhood to adulthood.

Fourth, psychoanalysis established the place of the 'talking cure' in mainstream mental health practice. It also provided a model of the development of private long-term outpatient treatment of patients with moderately debilitating psychological difficulties.

Finally, Freud provided a model for developing a theory of personality and therapy which spawned a wide range of neo-

Freudian derivatives including those of Jung. Adler, Horney, Stack-Sullivan, Reich, Fairburn, Klein, Erikson and many others.

Limitations

Classical psychoanalysis has many limitations. First, many of its hypotheses were untestable due to the imprecision of the constructs or the imprecision of predictions entailed by the psychoanalytic theory. Also, for some considerable time there was little evidence for the effectiveness of psychoanalytic psychotherapy. In recent times, attempts have been made to address this by developing rating scales to evaluate defence mechanisms and formulations of core conflictual relationship themes, and by conducting controlled research trials to evaluate the effectiveness of psychodynamic psychotherapy.

Second, Freud's speculations about infantile sexuality were not borne out by subsequent developmental research and in particular by research on child sexual abuse. It is quite likely that many of Freud's patients who reported sexual contact with a parent had in fact been sexually abused and were not simply fantasizing about seducing their parents in oedipal dramas.

Third, as a model for practice, classical psychoanalysis is too time-consuming and expensive. Classical psychoanalysis involves multiple sessions each week for a number of years. It is therefore not sufficiently cost-effective for routine use in a public mental health service where resources are limited. However, in recent times attempts have been made to use psychoanalytic ideas and practices as a basis for brief psychodynamic therapy.

Cognitive-behavioural Model

Assumptions

The cognitive behavioural tradition incorporates a range of psycho-therapeutic theories and practices, including behaviour therapy, behaviour modification, cognitive therapy and cognitive-behaviour therapy, all of which have their roots in learning theories. Within the cognitive behavioural tradition, it is assumed that abnormal behaviour is a set of habits. Psychological disorders are clusters of learned behaviours, cognitions and affective states. Within the broad cognitive behavioural tradition it is assumed that abnormal behaviour is learned through the same processes as normal behaviour. These processes include operant and classical conditioning, imitation and insight.

Therapy involves coaching clients in such a way that they learn to replace abnormal with normal behaviour patterns. This coaching process is based on the principles of learning theory. So the small constituent habits that make up large clusters of behaviour, cognition and affect are identified through careful interviewing and observation. The antecedents, co-occurring beliefs, and consequences associated with individual habits are identified.

Treatment programmes include interventions that alter antecedents which signal the onset of abnormal behaviours; interventions that challenge non-adaptive beliefs and styles of information processing that accompany abnormal behaviour; and interventions that change the consequences of behaviour so that normal alternatives to abnormal behaviour patterns are reinforced. In the behavioural treatment of depression, antecedents of low mood may be altered through inviting clients to schedule pleasant events regularly throughout their day. In the cognitive therapy of depression, anxiety and personality disorders, clients are coached in how to identify and challenge negative automatic thoughts and to identify the use of cognitive distortions. With conduct-disordered children, reward programmes are used so that prosocial behavioural targets are routinely reinforced. Imitation and operant procedures may be used to help individuals with skills deficits learn social, communication and problem-solving skills. Skills training is routinely used when working with people who have schizophrenia and their families.

Treatment programmes also include procedures based on classical conditioning. For example, with systematic desensitization for people who have phobias, increasingly threatening stimuli are paired with the experience of relaxation. Another example of a classical conditioning-based intervention is the use of urine alarm programmes for nocturnal enuresis in which bedwetting is paired with the sound of an alarm. Through this procedure, the child learns eventually to awaken when the bladder is full.

Within the cognitive behavioural tradition, specific treatment programmes are developed for specific symptoms and detailed assessment of the impact of treatment on abnormal behaviours targeted in treatment is routinely made. This tradition is championed by clinical psychologists.

Achievements

The cognitive behavioural tradition has made a number of important contributions to the understanding and treatment of psychological difficulties.

First, this tradition has led to the development of a brief, effective approach to therapy which is applicable to a wide range of patients. Typically cognitive behaviour therapy is brief, ranging from 1 to 30 sessions, depending upon the nature and severity of the problems.

Second, the cognitive behavioural tradition has shown empirically that its treatment strategies are effective. It therefore facilitates evidence-based practice. More than any other approach to treating psychological difficulties, the cognitive behavioural tradition has generated an enormous volume of empirical research to test the effectiveness of a wide variety of treatment programmes for a broad range of problems in adults and children.

Third, the cognitive behavioural model has led to the development of specific psychological treatment packages for specific types of problems. For example, exposure-based treatments have been developed for anxiety disorders, and cognitive therapy has been developed for mood disorders.

Fourth, methodological and scientific rigour has characterized cognitive behavioural research on psychological problems and their treatment.

Limitations

The main limitation of the cognitive behavioural model is the risk it entails of trivializing psychological problems. When people are suffering and in profound psychological distress, it may seem to them and others that to construe their difficulties as bad habits does not do justice to the gravity of their situation.

Two other possible limitations deserve mention. First, there is the danger of disregarding the possible role of organic factors in the etiology of psychological difficulties, and second, there is the danger of not taking the role of the patient's wider social context into account. Having noted these two dangers, it should be mentioned that these have been addressed by various members of the cognitive-behavioural tradition at different times. For example, Eysenck in his conditioning model of neurosis argued that people with high levels of neuroticism and introversion were more conditionable and so more likely to develop phobias and that these two traits were 50 per cent heritable. Eysenck's position, therefore, while essentially behavioural, acknowledges the role of biological factors. With respect to social context, the work of Falloon and others on reducing family stress in schizophrenia is a good example of social-context-sensitive cognitive behaviour therapy.

Family Systems Model

Assumptions

The family systems model assumes that psychological problems are maintained by patterns of interaction and belief systems within the family and the wider social system of the patient. Historical, contextual and constitutional factors may predispose family members to engage in these interaction patterns and adopt these belief systems. The many family therapy schools within this tradition may be classified in terms of their central focus of therapeutic concern and in particular with respect to their emphasis on (1) problem-maintaining behaviour patterns; (2) problematic and constraining belief systems; and (3) historical, contextual and constitutional predisposing factors.

With respect to the first theme, some family therapy schools highlight the role of repetitive patterns of family interaction in the maintenance of problem behaviour, and advocate practices which aim to disrupt these patterns of interaction. Schools that fall into this category include the MRI brief therapy approach; strategic therapy; structural therapy and functional family therapy.

With respect to the second theme, some schools of family therapy point to the centrality of belief systems and narratives which subserve repetitive interaction patterns that maintain presenting problems. Practices that facilitate the emergence of new belief-systems and narratives which liberate family members from problem-maintaining interaction patterns are espoused by these schools. Schools that fall into this category include the Milan school; solution-focused family therapy and narrative therapy.

With respect to the third theme, a number of family therapy traditions highlight the role of historical, contextual and constitutional factors in predisposing family members to adopt particular belief systems and engage in particular problematic interaction patterns. Such schools advocate using practices that specifically address these historical, contextual and constitutional predisposing factors, including working with members of the extended family and wider social network as well as coaching individuals to manage historical, contextual and constitutional constraints. This category contains transgenerational family therapy; psychoanalytic family therapy traditions; attachment-theory-based approaches; experiential family therapy; multisystemic consultation, which includes reference to the wider system and psychoeducational approaches.

Elsewhere I have argued that an integrative approach to family therapy may be taken so that, for any problem, a formulation may be constructed using ideas from many schools of family therapy, in which the pattern of family interaction which maintains the problem is specified; the constraining beliefs and narratives that underpin each family member's role in this pattern are outlined; and the historical and contextual factors that underpin these belief systems and narratives are specified. In parallel with this, a similar formulation may be constructed to explain why the problem does not occur in exceptional circumstances, which, while similar to problematic situations, differ in important key respects. In light of these formulations of the problem and exceptions to it, a range of interventions may be considered. Some interventions aim primarily to disrupt problem-maintaining behaviour patterns or amplify exceptional non-problematic patterns. Others aim to help family members change the personal narratives that make them repeat the same problematic behaviour patterns, and develop more liberating and flexible belief-systems which underpin exceptions to the problem. Still others aim to modify the negative impact of historical, contextual and constitutional factors or to draw on family strengths in these domains.

In family systems therapy, assessment and treatment involve the patient and the family participating in multiperson meetings. Multiple perspectives on the problem and related interaction patterns, belief systems and predisposing factors are therefore available to the therapist. Furthermore, there is the possibility of multiple people being involved in therapeutic change. Because of this, it is a fundamental assumption of family systems therapy that a small intervention may lead to a big change. It is therefore not surprising that family therapy is usually brief, with treatment rarely extending beyond twenty sessions. Furthermore, family therapy is dominated neither by clinical psychology nor psychiatry. Many disciplines are involved including social work and nursing.

Achievements

Family therapy has made an important contribution to the understanding and treatment of abnormal behaviour. First, in a field dominated by essentially individualistic models of practice, it has highlighted the role of the patient's social context in the etiology and treatment of psychological difficulties. Second, family systems therapy is a brief, affordable form of treatment well suited to public health services. It is highly cost-effective. Where different family members have problems they may all be treated by the same therapist or team. Third, empirical research shows that family systems therapies are effective with a wide range of problems in children and adults. Thus, there is a sound foundation for evidence-based practice. Fourth, systems theory can offer an integrative framework for comprehending not just the role of social factors but also those of biological and intrapsychic factors in the understanding and treatment of psychological difficulties. Fifth, in clinical practice, an integrative approach to family systems therapy is particularly useful in managing complex cases in which multiple family members have multiple problems, since often these are interconnected, a point missed by individualistic conceptualizations of abnormal behaviour.

Limitations

The main limitations of the family systems model are a danger of vagueness, a danger of losing sight of the individual, and a danger of failing to take account of organic factors.

Summary

The biological, psychoanalytic, cognitive-behavioural and social systems models are each based on a unique set of assumptions, and have each resulted in a unique set of achievements; but each is limited in its usefulness by a specific set of shortcomings. With the biological model it is assumed that each set of abnormal behaviours constitutes the symptoms of an underlying brain disease, which follows a unique course, and has a particular prognosis, and for which a discrete cause and physical cure may ultimately be identified. The biological model's greatest achievement was the liberation of people with psychological problems and the creation of asylums where those in psychological distress received humane treatment. Mental health legislation, widely used classification systems such as the DSM and the ICD, a commitment to scientific study of abnormal behaviour, and the development of psychopharmacological treatments are among the major achievements of the biological model. The limitations of the biological model include the facts that much abnormal behaviour is not caused by organic factors; many psychopharmacological treatments have harmful side-effects; asylums have led to social exclusion; and mental health legislation has been abused.

The psychoanalytic model assumes that abnormal behaviour patterns are symptoms of underlying psychopathology. Psychotherapy gives insight into the conflicts, defences and transference phenomena which constitute this psychopathology. Achievements of the psychoanalytic model include the discovery of the unconscious; the demonstration of continuity between the normal and abnormal behaviour; and the establishment of talking therapy as a valid method for treating psychological problems. Classical psychoanalysis, however, is too expensive to be a viable approach for routinely treating people in the public health services. This and the fact that it is diagnostically vague, many of its propositions are untestable, and it pathologizes everyone are its major limitations.

The cognitive behavioural model assumes that symptoms are learned through conditioning, imitation and insight and that therapy involves changing patterns of learned behaviour using specific treatments that have been developed for specific symptoms. The development of a brief, effective approach to therapy, which is applicable to a wide range of patients, and for which there is empirical evidence for effectiveness, is the main achievement of the cognitive behavioural model. However, the risk of trivializing psychological problems and the risk of paying insufficient attention to organic or social factors are its principal limitations.

The systems model assumes that psychological problems are maintained by patterns of interaction and belief systems within the family and the wider social system of the patient. Historical, contextual and constitutional factors may predispose family members to engage in these interaction patterns and adopt these belief systems. In family systems therapy, assessment and treatment involve the patient and the family. In terms of achievements, empirical research shows that family systems therapies are effective with a wide range of problems and that systems theory offers a framework for integrating biological, psychological and social factors. However, the main limitations with this approach are a danger of vagueness, a danger of losing sight of the individual, and a danger of failing to take account of organic factors.

6

Cultural and Sub-cultural Issues in Abnormality

Introduction

The term '**culture**' refers to 'a learned system of values, beliefs, meanings, rules and practices that are passed from one generation to the next in patterned ways. Culture provides a way of looking at the world and of experiencing it'. As such, it will affect beliefs, values, attitudes, ideologies, rules, practices (such as child-rearing, for example), language, family systems, social structures, art, technology and artefacts - in short, ways of thinking and ways of living.

Two other terms are often confused with culture (although they are not equivalent), and will therefore be clarified here. '*Race*' implies membership of a group that is distinct biologically or genetically from other groups. This term is rarely considered appropriate nowadays, since many groups in society are biologically diverse, and genetic differences within apparent racial groups are often greater than those between them. The preferred term is '*ethnicity*', a subjective term referring to the sense of belonging to a particular group, which may be based on race, religion or culture. *Subculture* is a subdivision within a cultural group, which shares distinctive behaviours, beliefs and attitudes. In this chapter we will be exploring the implications of cultural and subcultural differences by looking at mental disorder in different ethnic and national groups, and at differences associated with gender, age and social class.

Relevance

Anthropologists refer to the organised bodies of knowledge passed on to individuals by their culture as *cultural meaning systems*. According to Castillo 'a cultural meaning system generally structures cognitive reality for an entire society'. These meaning systems serve four functions, as follows:

- **Representational function** They provide systems for symbolically representing the world and for communication between individuals. Language (written and spoken) and art are examples.
- **Constructive function** Through communication, cultural entities are created. These are socially agreed rituals, explanations or ways of doing things; examples are marriage, property and the family. The diagnostic categories used in DSM can be seen as cultural entities, in the sense that they are arrived at through the consensus of a committee of experts, and then by general social agreement they are applied universally and become reality for all those involved.
- **Directive function** The cultural entities created through group consensus then have an effect on the way that people in that culture (and sometimes outside, as we shall see) live their lives. A particular diagnosis will affect the individual concerned (*e.g.* an elderly person diagnosed with the beginnings of Alzheimer's disease will undoubtedly be distraught), will evoke a response from others (which may be positive and helpful or negative and stigmatising), and may lead the clinician to apply a particular form of treatment.
- **Evocative function** The cultural meaning system also provides rules about how to feel. Thus in Western culture generally, losing your job or failing an exam would be regarded as cause for feeling unhappy, but only for a prescribed period of time.

Cultural Differences in Behaviour

Differences in cultural and subcultural backgrounds can therefore be seen as having a profound influence on all aspects of life, including our views about what is normal, expected behaviour and what is not. For example, in some cultures (such as the Mediterranean) the expression of emotions is valued and encouraged, whereas in others (such as the English and Chinese) it is frowned on and considered inappropriate behaviour. There is also considerable variation in the emphasis on an *individualist* versus *collectivist* outlook. In Western individualist cultures the emphasis is on the self, achievement of personal happiness and status. In collectivist cultures, the family and community come first, and everything the individual does is for their benefit rather than for himself. He must avoid bringing shame on them at all costs.

Cultures have a range of *social norms* that specify appropriate behaviours for different groups of persons in that culture. Behaviour outside those norms may be acceptable if it forms part of a '*rite of reversal*' (such as a carnival), *i.e.* it takes place in a specified setting. Communing with the ancestors and hearing their voices would be acceptable in North American Indian culture; entering trance states or other altered states of consciousness is acceptable, or even desirable, in many cultures, given the right context. White, Western cultures, however, have a strong emphasis on the existence of objective reality, and regard hearing voices as abnormal behaviour. In some cultures, treatment involves religious and spiritual practices; in others, it would be visiting a clinician (although some would still see this as a disgrace).

Culture and Mental Disorder

Given these differences, the aim of *transcultural psychiatry* (a discipline that has sprung up to link the fields of psychiatry and anthropology) has been to look at the nature of mental disorder in other cultures. If abnormal behaviour is culture-free, and biologically determined, then it should take exactly the same form in all cultures, known as *absolutism*. This extreme view is unlikely to be tenable, for the reasons mentioned earlier, hence the debate mainly revolves around the other two possibilities. *Universality* is the view that mental disorders, as outlined in DSM, are found in all cultures, and in essentially the same form, although there may be some variation in expression in different cultures. *Cultural relativism* argues for a much more significant role for culture than does universality, to the extent that syndromes found in some cultures do not appear elsewhere - these are known as *culture-bound syndromes*. There are several different areas of research that can be brought to bear on this issue. Helman notes that culture may affect mental disorder in four ways:

- it defines what is normal and abnormal in a particular society;
- it may influence the prevalence and expression of particular disorders;
- it may be a cause of the development of particular disorders;
- it may determine the way the disorder is explained and treated in a given culture.

How Culture Defines What is Normal and Abnormal

In this section we are considering the ways in which culture affects our decisions about what is normal and abnormal. At one point in history, for example, certain groups of people in certain societies considered it desirable to flagellate (whip) themselves regularly. Nowadays that would be regarded as undesirable behaviour.

So are there differences between cultures in ideas about mental health? According to Fernando, in many Eastern cultures mental health is associated with integration and harmony with the family, environment, society and religious values. In the West, the aim is self-sufficiency, autonomy, efficiency and the enhancement of self-esteem. When it comes to mental disorder, ideas also differ about what is unusual or unacceptable.

Response to Unusual Behaviours

In many societies, being possessed by spirits, hallucinating, and speaking in unknown tongues (glossolalia), are acceptable, provided that those behaviours occur in ways that are prescribed by cultural norms. It is when they do not that they may be regarded as problematic. The research described next attempts to demonstrate when this is likely to occur.

Several studies have explored the response of people from other cultures to psychiatric terms such as 'insane', or to descriptions of people who suffer from symptoms such as hallucinations. Africa would appear to have been the location for most research. In

Zimbabwe, Gelfand reported that hallucinations were considered to be 'real' events sent by spirits. Those who experienced them were not rejected by society, showed reduced levels of distress, and good recovery rates. Collomb in Senegal found 90% recovery rates, for example. Other less developed countries such as Columbia have shown similarly low levels of stigmatisation and good outcomes. In Nigeria, the Yoruba were presented with vignettes describing case studies of mentally ill persons, one of whom was a paranoid schizophrenic. Almost all Americans would identify such a person as being mentally ill, but only 40% of the Yoruba group did so; 30% said they would be willing to marry such a person. Educated Nigerians, however, presented a different picture, in that 31% said such a person should be expelled, and 16% said they should be shot. Thus education (and Westernisation) had led to a decrease in tolerance.

Research in Laos showed that the term 'insane' ('baa') was applied only after several years to disruptive, violent individuals who displayed bizarre behaviours. Hallucinations were not considered a problem. Even those who were considered insane would still be given food, clothing, shelter and care. Edgerton in East Africa also found that hallucinations were not considered a problem. The term 'psychosis' ('kichaa') was applied to those who commit murder, arson, theft or show themselves naked. Depending on the area, they may be treated with rituals and tranquillising herbs, starved, expelled or battered to death. In Malaya, only violent people will be termed 'mad' ('gila') and banished from the village.

Differences in Interpretation of Symptoms

There are also societies in which particular symptoms may be seen in different ways. For example, in Hindu and Buddhist societies depression is not seen as an illness, but as a spiritual insight about the world. Thus it is an accomplishment. In Micronesia, depressive feelings are always traced back to some personal loss to do with relationships, and they are seen as normal even if the depression goes on for a long time. In Britain, Furnham and Malik found that middle-aged Asian immigrants did not see depressive symptoms as an illness, whereas a British sample and a sample of younger immigrants from Asia did. In societies that place a high value on ritual purity, *e.g.* Israel and India, fear of contamination and hand washing may be more acceptable than in the West. In the Swat Pukhtun of Pakistan, which is a violent and competitive culture, paranoia would not be an appropriate diagnosis, since people *do* plot against one another. Nor would antisocial personality disorder be considered unusual, since extreme egocentrism is the norm. The 'macho' behaviour associated with histrionic personality disorder in DSM is considered to be appropriate in Latin cultures.

Conclusion

Such research clearly shows that there is only very limited consensus about what is abnormal behaviour. Extreme behaviours, which would in many cases be dealt with by the legal system in Western society, are generally agreed to be unacceptable in most other cultures, but many of the behaviours that we would regard as indicative of severe mental disorder are accepted. Indeed, in some societies they are even accorded high status. Rogler and Hollingshead report that Puerto Rican schizophrenics may rise in status if they visit a spiritualist, as they are seen to have psychic faculties themselves. They may then become more acceptable as husbands. The differences in prognosis in other cultures also indicate that for such persons in Western society, the disorder itself is only part of their problems.

Differences in Prevalence and Expression of Mental Disorders

Cultures and subcultures can be compared in terms of differences in prevalence (rate of occurrence) of mental disorders in the population and in the ways that mental disorders are expressed.

Differences in Prevalence in Different Cultures

Reading about the history of mental disorder reveals that disorders come and go at different historical periods. In the Middle Ages, there were mass outbreaks of lycanthropy feeling that one is turning into a wolf and growing fur - but this disorder is virtually unheard of nowadays. In late 18th- and early 19th-century Europe somnambulism (sleepwalking) was quite common. Could there be a similar variation between different cultures at the same point in time? Remember that if there is significant variability in frequency of occurrence, this will go against the notion of cultural universality of mental disorder.

The anthropologist Kleinman noted that many adult disorders such as depression and manic depression, schizophrenia, dementia and anxiety disorders do seem to occur universally. Some studies have been carried out to ascertain whether the prevalence of specific disorders is different in different countries. One problem that faces researchers in this area is whether to accept the diagnoses of practitioners from other cultures (who may use different diagnostic systems, as they do in China, for example), or whether to insist that all diagnoses are carried out by Western-trained clinicians according to our standards. It is very unlikely that the same results will be obtained in the two cases.

Schizophrenia

A study for the World Health Organization by Sartorius found that there was in general a 1% risk of developing schizophrenia between the ages of 15-54. However, this varied in different cultures, from as low as 0.53% in Honolulu to as much as 1.74% in rural India. This research has been criticised on the grounds that the coverage of cultures was limited, and it may therefore have underestimated the full range of possible variation. There is also the problem of applying Western criteria that do not carry the same negative connotations elsewhere - hallucinations and delusions often represent a belief in the supernatural, for example, which is considered perfectly acceptable in other cultures. Another study found similar rates of occurrence in 10 countries, including India, Britain, Denmark, Russia, Nigeria, Japan, America, and the Czech republic.

Dissociation

This is regarded as being virtually ubiquitous, although in most cultures it is seen as being an important part of cultural rituals, rather than a problematic disorder.

Alcoholism

Helzer compared the rates of alcoholism in five cities in different countries, and found a range in lifetime prevalence for males of between 23% for Koreans to 7% for Taiwanese. This compared with a rate of 19% in Edmonton, Alberta. Given the different cultural usage of alcohol, it is not surprising that there are different risk factors. Although some countries have a higher rate of consumption than others (*e.g.* France), alcohol is typically taken in small amounts with meals over the course of the day. In other countries (*e.g.* America) it is used at the end of the day for the purposes of intoxication. In others (*e.g.* Muslim countries) it is expressly forbidden on religious grounds. In Indian, American Indian and Saudi cultures, abstinence is defined as ideal behaviour, and drinking is not a normal part of social life. In Ireland, Japan and Puerto Rico, heavy alcohol use is expected in males, and they would be considered socially impaired if they did not participate.

Anorexia Nervosa and Bulimia Nervosa

These are far more common in modern, industrialised societies such as America, Canada, Europe, Australia, Japan and New Zealand. This difference has been attributed to the culturally promoted images of ideal female beauty in Western countries. A study by Nasser showed that Egyptian students studying in London were more likely to develop an eating disorder than a group of controls studying in Cairo, which lends some support to this explanation.

Major Depressive Disorder

Depression does not seem to be much in evidence in Asian cultures. This may well be, according to Rack, because Asians only consult for the physical symptoms associated with depression. The emotional experience, as noted in a previous section, is not seen to be a problem. The prevalence of depression is lower in Taiwan and Hong Kong than in the West, which has been attributed to the extra social support available in those countries.

The Cross-national Collaborative Group reported that depression is increasing in prevalence generally, and occurring at younger and younger ages, although there is cultural variability. The cumulative rate of occurrence in America, for example, is much higher than that in the Lebanon and Taiwan. Breakdown of social support systems, lack of opportunity for young people and the negative socio-cultural construction of the elderly, are among the explanations offered for the increase in modernised societies.

Anxiety

This presents more evidence of cultural variability, particularly when generalised anxiety is assessed. However, there is more agreement with object phobias. Davey reported agreement on the stimuli that are phobia-related in Japan, Britain, America, Italy, Scandinavia, India, Korea and Hong Kong.

Obsessive-compulsive Disorder

The most common forms of this disorder have been found in England, Egypt, India, Israel, Taiwan and Puerto Rico, indicating cultural similarity. However, clinicians need to bear in mind the prevailing cultural norms when making a diagnosis, as in many cultures, such as Egypt, India and Israel, ritual purification and washing are important parts of religious observances, and therefore are not considered abnormal.

Conclusion

Research into cultural differences in prevalence was begun in 1904 by the father of modern psychiatry, Emil Kraepelin, who travelled to Java to see if dementia praecox (now known as schizophrenia) and manic depression were found there. His conclusions, like those of many modern researchers, were that there was some universality, and some aspects of disorders that were culturally distinctive. Given the internal diversity of most countries, it should not be too surprising that this is the case, if culture is accepted to have an influence.

Weisz attempted to explain cultural differences such as those noted earlier with their *suppression-facilitation model*. Based on learning theory principles, they argue that behaviours that are rewarded within a culture will be observed frequently (facilitated), whereas those that are discouraged will be suppressed. Studies of children in America and Thailand who had been referred for the treatment of behaviour problems found that the behaviour they showed most predominantly was an exaggeration of that preferred by the parents. In America this was assertive behaviour, which manifested itself as problem behaviours such as aggression and distractability. In Thailand this was quiet, controlled behaviour, which manifested as overcontrolled behaviour such as anxiety and fearfulness. Thus the cultural values and expectations of the parents had led to different patterns of problem behaviour in the two countries, or more accurately, to different patterns being perceived as problems in the two countries.

Differences in Expression in Different Cultures

Again, it can be seen that there is historical variability in the expression of disorders. A good example of this is multiple personality disorder, which was initially seen in the form of 'double consciousness'. Based perhaps on the Christian concept of good versus evil, early cases in the mid-19th century manifested as two alters. In the modern world, where life is generally more fragmented, cases have been observed with hundreds of alters. Could such variability be observed across cultures at the same time?

Schizophrenia

Schizophrenia has again received the most attention. In developed countries, the disorder seems to occur in a more severe form; 40% of cases are severe compared with 24% in developing countries. This, however, could be due to differences in diagnosis, as some of those seen in the developing countries recovered so quickly that it was unlikely that they were suffering from true schizophrenia in the first place. In 1979, the WHO compared the symptoms of schizophrenia in nine different countries. Some symptoms were common: lack of insight was found in 97% of cases seen; hallucinations were found in 70%. However, when the subtypes paranoid, hebephrenic and catatonic were explored, differences emerged. Catatonic and hebephrenic types were found to be more common in developing countries such as India, and paranoid types in more urban, Western, developed countries such as Japan.

Other cultures may also show completely different symptoms from those found in Western cases. The Inuit, for example, have a syndrome that appears similar to schizophrenia (*e.g.* it includes talking to non-existent people) but also includes other symptoms such as killing dogs. The content of schizophrenic delusions will also vary, by definition. DSM IV defines bizarre delusions as those that 'are not understandable and do not derive from ordinary life experiences'. The supernatural powers accepted by many other cultures may seem bizarre to Western eyes.

Experiences may also be described in different ways. Littlewood and Lipsedge noted that 40% of psychotic Afro-Caribbean patients describe their experiences in religious terms, compared with only

20% of white British patients. Scheper-Hughes found that in rural Kerry, Ireland, religious descriptions were more common than in white American schizophrenics. Western psychotics were more likely than psychotics from other cultures to describe their experiences in terms of extra-terrestrials.

Anorexia

Anorexia, when it is found in non-Western countries, does not tend to include the symptoms of distorted body image or fear of being too fat. Since these constitute part of the criteria for diagnosis of the disorder in DSM, it is arguable whether these forms can be regarded as true anorexia. Lee found that the main fear was of stomach bloating rather than fatness in Chinese anorexics. In India, Khandelwal did not find disturbances of body image or excessive exercising, nor was there fear of fatness. Food intake was restricted on the basis of powerful religious or nutritional beliefs.

Depression

This also shows variability. In 1983, the WHO found that depressive patients from Canada, Iran, India, Japan and Switzerland showed different symptoms: 68% of the Swiss sample showed guilt feelings, and only 22% of the Iranians did, for example; 57% of the Iranians showed somatisation (physical symptoms such as headaches, weight loss, pains etc), whereas only 27% of the Canadians did. In general, somatisation is more common in the Far East and in patients of lower socio-economic status. The Taiwanese, for example, are very reluctant to express personal feelings and thoughts. Lau in Hong Kong reported that the chief complaints leading depressive patients to seek help were gastric discomfort (18.7%), dizziness (12.2%), headaches (9.8%) and insomnia (8.4%). Of their sample, 96% initially complained of somatic symptoms, and hardly any mentioned emotional problems. In Britain, depressed Asian immigrants are most likely to complain of generalised weakness, bowel problems, fear of heart attack and concern about their genitals. In Turkey, too, it has been found that somatic complaints such as insomnia and hypochondria are more common. In Britain, guilt and pessimism are common. Thoughts about suicide and suicide rates are also variable. Barraclough showed Scandinavia, Eastern Europe and some Asian countries to be highest in this respect, and the Arab countries to be the lowest.

Conclusion

When Western categories of mental disorder are recognised in other cultures, they frequently show quite marked differences in symptomatology. This makes the universal application of DSM diagnostic categories difficult.

Subcultural Differences

We will look at differences in four subcultural categories: ethnic groups; gender; class; and age. An important general point in this context is that there may be many possible explanations for any differences observed. At the very least, they may be explained by differences in help-seeking behaviour, or by bias in the assessment process and/or classification system, as well as by genuine differences in prevalence. Even genuine differences in prevalence may be the result of poor social conditions or the stress associated with prejudice, rather than being biologically based. It is also very difficult for research to separate out the effects of the ethnicity, class, age and gender of participants.

Ethnic Groups

Differences in Help-seeking

It can be stated at the outset that there are differences here in the extent to which ethnic groups use health services. Some encourage individuals to seek professional help, others insist upon the denial of problems; some tolerate problem behaviours, others develop physical symptoms and seek medical help for those rather than for their emotional problems. In America, it has been found that African ethnic groups use services more and Hispanic and Asian groups use services less, compared with Caucasians. Orientals are more likely to seek medical help than psychological help.

Kendall and Hammen attribute these differences to variation in cultural attitudes about such problems and where to seek help. Another possible explanation has been proposed by Kirmayer in Montreal, who found that when levels of psychological distress were controlled, immigrants were ¼ to 2 less likely to seek mental health care. When questioned about this, the most important factor was found to be 'ethnic mismatch'. By this the immigrants meant their expectations that they would be unable to see professionals from their own ethnic group, that they would not be understood by those they did see, and that they would encounter prejudice. In Britain, Frederick reported that Black persons participating in the study were less likely to have sought help of their own accord. Afro-Caribbean women have also been found to be more critical of GPs, and Afro-Caribbeans are also less likely than other groups to be referred for help by GPs.

Rates within Immigrant Groups

Looking at general levels of mental health, Guarnaccia compared Puerto Ricans living in Puerto Rico with those living in cities in America. The rates of disorder and reported symptoms appear to be higher in the immigrant groups, and higher in Puerto Ricans than in other disadvantaged groups. The researchers argued that this is due to the culturally accepted way of responding to stress in Puerto Rico. Called 'ataque de nervios', this involves fainting, seizures and heart palpitations. Clinicians may well interpret such symptoms as being indicative of mental health problems if they use the current classification system without making any allowance for the effects of culture.

In Britain, Cochrane found that the psychiatric admission rates for Polish, Irish and Scottish immigrants to England and Wales were higher than for those born in those countries. Early research into other ethnic groups, such as Asians and Afro-Caribbeans, produced conflicting findings, but more recent, better-controlled studies are more consistent, although the picture is still variable for Asian groups. For example, Carpenter and Brockington found higher admission rates for Asian groups, while Hitch found that Pakistani-born groups had higher rates and Indian-born groups had lower rates. This may be due to comparing them with different control groups, however; the first study used White Britons, and the second Asians born in Britain.

Stress or Selection?

Immigrants may also represent a special case, since immigration itself may be a stressful process (stress hypothesis) and those who choose to do it may have more problems than most (selection hypothesis).

There is some support for both of these explanations. As regards the latter, Schaechter in Australia found that 45.5% of a sample of immigrants admitted to psychiatric hospitals had a record of mental illness prior to migrating. This figure was increased to 68.2% when possible cases were included as well. As regards the former, the difficulties faced by immigrants can perhaps be most clearly seen in the Irish statistics. Irish immigrants to mainland Britain have been shown by Cochrane and Bal to have the highest incidence of diagnosis for most categories of disorder - psychoses, neuroses, depression, personality disorder and alcohol abuse. Psychiatric admissions, for example, are 1080 per 100,000 compared to 504 per 100,000 for English people. Pilgrim and Rogers attribute this to two groups of factors: first, material factors such as poverty, forced migration and unstable social and political conditions; and second, cultural factors such as oppression by the church and a history of English colonialism, both of which have led to crises of identity for the Irish people. Littlewood and Lipsedge argue that different immigrant groups have different risk factors due to their specific circumstances. Some appear to be more at risk than others, such as Afro-Caribbeans. Refugees, who are often forced to leave their country, suffer trauma before leaving and cannot return, may be particularly at risk.

Rates in Different Ethnic Groups

Another approach is to look at the rates of disorder in ethnic groups compared with those of the population as a whole. Looking at Afro-Caribbeans, they appear to be consistently overrepresented in psychiatric hospital admissions given their numbers in the population in general. According to Banyard Black people only account for 5% of the population, but they constitute 25% of those in psychiatric hospitals. Although hospital admissions are not generally good indicators of the rates of occurrence of disorder, these findings are borne out by a study by Harrison, which included all patients in contact with psychiatric services.

Explanations offered for these findings have tended to attribute the difficulties faced by Afro-Caribbeans to poverty and racism. The relatively lower rates of admission in Asian communities (compared to those of Afro-Caribbeans) may be attributable to greater affluence, a more fatalistic attitude to life, or the greater stigma associated with help-seeking in Asian communities. However, such explanations cannot account for the observed differences in Irish and other groups, nor for the differences in the type of disorder noted, which is the topic we move on to next.

Differences in Type of Disorder

Many studies have now confirmed that the rate of occurrence of schizophrenia in Afro-Caribbeans in Britain is considerably higher than it is in the general population, that such differences are also found in second-generation immigrants and that they do not occur in Afro-Caribbeans who have emigrated to other countries. For example, Cochrane and Sashidharan report a seven-fold increase in incidence. Harrison estimated it to be 12-13 times that of the general population. In America the rates of admission for schizophrenia have been reported to be approximately double for Black males compared with the general population. This may also apply to Hispanic Americans, Inuit and American Indians.

Nor are these the only differences observed. Substance abuse, for example, is more common in African Americans than Whites and alcoholism is more common in American Indians. Attempted suicide is a particular problem in British Asian women. These latter conditions, however, are more objectively verifiable than schizophrenia, and more readily attributable to social conditions and lifestyles.

Why are there Different Rates for Schizophrenia?

So how can the differential rates of schizophrenia be explained? Pilgrim and Rogers suggest two processes: misdiagnosis and ethnocentric psychiatric constructs. Misdiagnosis is the misapplication of psychiatric labels, which could result from the ethnocentric views of the (usually White) psychiatrists dealing with such cases. Blake found that a case study that included a description of the patient as African American was more likely to be given a label of schizophrenia by clinicians than the same case study described as a white person. Thus Black and White people are seen differently even when they show the same behaviour. Loring and Powell found the same applied even when the clinicians were themselves Black. Fernando points out that White (or even Black) middle-class psychiatrists are unlikely to have any experience of the culture or general social conditions in which their clients are immersed. For example, Bell, reviewing studies of the exposure of Black children in American inner cities to violence, quoted research by Fitzpatrick and Boldizar showing that 70% of their sample had witnessed a shooting and 44% had seen a murder.

Ethnocentric psychiatric constructs derive from taking a Western viewpoint when devising the classification systems themselves. These systems can be viewed as social constructs, or as Fernando puts it '*psychiatric imperialism*'. Thus the norms for behaviour are based on Western expectations, and so deviations from those, such as hearing voices or going into trances, must be abnormal irrespective of the culture of the person concerned.

Conclusion

Clearly, then, even within this small area of research, there are some very complex forces at work, and the observed differences cannot readily be attributed to one single factor. Cultural norms regarding acceptance of behaviours and help-seeking, stress and clinical bias may all be responsible. What can be concluded, however, is that in one way or another, many of the factors involved do relate to culture.

Gender

Differences

Statistics relating to psychiatric hospital admissions for men and women in both England and America show similar patterns. Overall, women are more at risk than men of suffering from a mental disorder. There are, however, significant differences between disorders. Women are particularly at risk of suffering from affective psychoses (*e.g.* depression), neurotic disorders (especially phobias and panic disorders), borderline personality disorder and dementia, and 90-95% of anorexics and bulimics are female. Men are more at risk from alcohol abuse, antisocial personality disorder, pyromania, gambling problems, obsessive-compulsive disorder and (marginally) schizophrenia. These differences appear to be reducing compared with their levels in 1976. They are also far from being universal; in China, for example, women show higher rates of schizophrenia than men, and lower rates of depression and neurosis than Western women. Cross culturally, men show a slightly greater incidence of depression than women. However, the differences are still significant enough to warrant investigation.

Table 6.1. Rates of admission to hospitals in England per 100,000 population by sex and diagnostic group. From a Sociology of Mental Health and Illness

Diagnosis	Males	Females	Excess of female over male rate (%)
All diagnoses	364	468	+29
Schizophrenia	66	58	?12
Affective psychoses	35	68	+98
Other psychoses	32	44	+37
Senile and presenile dementia	33	55	+67
Alcohol psychoses and alcoholism	45	20	?55
Drug dependence	9	8	?11
Neurotic disorders	22	42	+91
Personality and behaviour disorders	28	32	+14
Other conditions[1]	89	142	+60
Rates for all diagnoses (1986)	364	468	+29
Rates for all diagnoses (1976)	320	447	+40

Explanations

Several explanations can be considered. First, there is the possibility that the differences observed are biologically based. It has been argued, for example, that women are less prone to schizophrenia than men because they are protected by the hormone oestrogen. The equal rates for schizophrenia in persons who are beyond menopausal age would suggest that this could be the case, but there is little other evidence to support this explanation. Hormonal fluctuations in women during the menstrual cycle, in pregnancy and as a result of the use of contraceptives have also been blamed for depression, but again the evidence is far from conclusive. For example, Cooper found a slight increase in depression in women who had just given birth, but it was still lower than that in non-pregnant women. Given the range of differences observed, several biological mechanisms would need to be postulated, and it seems unlikely that this would be the case.

A second possibility is that women express distress in different ways from men. The Western gender roles allow women to be emotional, whereas men are expected to be dominant, independent, rational and controlled. Women are expected to be concerned about weight and appearance, whereas men are expected to pursue their goals aggressively. These differences would seem to fit in with the observed patterns as regards different disorders.

Another view would be that they reflect differences in help-seeking behaviour. Women generally seek help, both medical and psychological, more often than men do for the same disorders. Men have often been referred to as suffering from the 'John Wayne syndrome', meaning that the gender stereotype to which they are expected to conform precludes them from seeking help, especially for psychiatric problems. Since the research generally relies on hospital admissions or community surveys of use of mental health services at best, this is a significant problem and cannot be dismissed. However, it cannot account for the different types of disorder noted. Recent studies also indicate that women do not always recognise mental health problems such as post-natal depression as significant enough to lead to help-seeking.

A fourth explanation relates to social causation of the differences. Here a variety of mechanisms have been postulated. Cochrane notes that the rate of child abuse for girls is much higher than that for boys, and that up to 70% of depressed patients admitted to hospitals have suffered abuse as children. That, combined with the general incidence of abuse (up to 46% of children may be affected, according to some estimates) Cochrane considers sufficient to account for the gender differences in levels of depression. Brown found that 2% of the sample of depressed women they studied had suffered neglect or physical or sexual abuse during childhood. Brown suggests that such experiences also increase the chance of suffering from anxiety in adulthood, and could account for the finding that depression and anxiety are often found together. Williams found that at least 50% of women using the mental health services they reviewed had been sexually and/or physically abused as children and/or as adults.

Other life experiences that relate to gender roles have been implicated. Women's roles are frequently linked with powerlessness, submissiveness and lack of opportunity to achieve except vicariously through their husbands. These are conditions associated with the concept of learned helplessness, which produces behaviour akin to depression in animals. The circumstances in which this may be most marked are those noted by Brown and Harris in their findings on risk factors for depression in women lack of employment outside the home, presence of three or more children under the age of 15 years, absence of a confiding relationship with a partner and loss of mother before the age of 11 years (which is also one factor associated with an increased likelihood of child abuse). Low self-esteem, chronic social difficulties such as shortage of money, and feeling humiliated and trapped by the situation also contribute to the problem. Cochrane adds that whereas men cope with such problems by active achievement (*e.g.* at work), by obtaining social support (usually from women) or by substance abuse, depression may be the more likely form of coping in women. It could be, for example, that it is more acceptable in view of their gender roles.

It should not be forgotten in this connection that the male figures also require an explanation. Schizophrenia is slightly more likely in men than in women overall, but between the ages of 15 and 24 it is twice as likely. It has been suggested that this may be because this is the time when work and career-related stress are at their peak. Men are particularly vulnerable to suffering psychiatric problems as a consequence of unemployment.

The fifth explanation of the gender differences would be that clinicians are biased in the way that they diagnose mental disorders. Broverman found that if clinicians were asked to identify the characteristics of the healthy man, the healthy woman and the healthy adult, they placed women in a separate group, describing them as ideally dependent, submissive and emotional. Men and adults were independent, assertive and decisive. Looking specifically at diagnoses, Ford and Widiger gave clinicians case studies describing histrionic personality disorder and antisocial personality disorder. Each case study was labelled as either male or female when presented to different clinicians, and they were asked to diagnose the conditions. When labelled as male, antisocial personality disorder was correctly identified 40% of the time, compared with under 20% of the time when labelled as female.

Histrionic personality disorder was correctly diagnosed 80% of the time when labelled as female, and around 30% of the time when labelled as male. Thus the behaviours were interpreted in accordance with the expectations for that gender - women should be emotional (histrionic) and men should be aggressive (antisocial).

Finally, it is also possible that the classification system itself is biased. For some syndromes, the diagnostic descriptions appear to link closely with typical behaviours of one gender or the other. It should not therefore be too surprising that those syndromes are more commonly diagnosed in those genders. Chesler goes further than this, and argues that the female role demands behaviours that are clinically neurotic; rejection of the role, on the other hand, is seen as deviance. As Busfield puts it, 'Women are likely to be viewed as disturbed if they "act out" either masculine or feminine roles; men only if they act out feminine roles.' There is a double standard for mental health, with the result that women will inevitably show a higher level of disorder – exactly what the statistics show.

Social Class

Differences

There is variation in the incidence of most disorders according to social class. The Midtown Manhattan Study by Srole was one of the first to show that the lowest levels of psychiatric disorder could be found in the upper classes, and the highest in the lower classes. In Britain, Cochrane and Stopes-Roe obtained the same findings. Bruce found that over a 6-month period a sample of people living below the poverty line were more than twice as likely as others to have developed a substance abuse disorder, or an affective disorder, and 80 times as likely to have developed schizophrenia. Many other studies have confirmed that the major disorders such as schizophrenia are more likely to occur in the lower social classes. For example, Faris and Dunham found schizophrenia to be seven times more likely in poor inner-city dwellers than in those from middle-class suburbia. The same results have been found in Denmark, Norway and England.

Suicide, and substance abuse are more common in the unskilled and unemployed. Depression and Alzheimer's disease are also more common in the lower classes. Manic depression may be more common in the middle classes. Also more common in the middle classes are the neurotic disorders, and anorexia nervosa.

Explanations

Again, several explanations have been considered. First, there is the *social drift hypothesis*, which suggests that persons suffering from severe mental disorders will move down the social scale because of the debilitating effects the disorder has on their ability to function. Thus being low-class is a consequence of the disorder, not a cause. Schizophrenia, for example, may begin later in life than some other disorders, and the individual may have had a successful career prior to its onset. The evidence here is inconclusive, however. Hollingshead and Redlich did not find any evidence for drift. Goldberg and Morrison found that the fathers of schizophrenics were of a higher social class, indicating downward mobility; Turner and Wagonfeld, on the other hand, found that even the fathers were low, which would limit the scope for downward mobility.

Second, there is the *sociogenic hypothesis*, which argues that social conditions are responsible for the differences observed. According to this, poverty, unemployment, poorer physical health and environmental conditions all add up to increased levels of stress in the lower classes, who may in addition have fewer coping resources at their disposal and may feel less in control of their lives. The middle classes can afford pleasurable experiences such as holidays to alleviate their stress, for example, and may more readily be able to obtain social support or seek professional help. Halpern notes that there is an increase in mental disorder in those living in high-rise blocks; this may be due to social class, or simply to the fact that in such blocks there is less social contact. Wilkinson points to the perception of inequalities as a source of considerable stress, especially when it is combined with lack of control or ability to take effective action to change one's circumstances. Brown and Harris found that a high level of stress tended to be associated with a high level of mental disorder in general. Fryer found that unemployment increases the chance of mental disorder not only in the individual concerned, but also in other family members.

In order to test the two latter explanations, Dohrenwend compared established groups of European immigrants to Israel with recent groups of African and Middle Eastern immigrants who would have suffered more prejudice. For schizophrenia, they found that the social drift hypothesis was supported, in that the former group showed higher rates, especially those in the lower social classes. Social causation was linked with higher rates of depression in women, and substance abuse and antisocial personality disorder in men in the latter, disadvantaged groups. Thus it may be that different explanations apply to different disorders.

The final explanation relates to clinical bias. It is also possible that clinicians give less favourable diagnoses to those people from the lower social classes. Umbenhauer and DeWitte confirmed this, and also showed that upper-class patients were more likely to be offered psychotherapy rather than pharmacotherapy. In a review of the research, Johnstone found that people from the lower social classes were regarded as being less able to benefit from verbal therapies, because they were less articulate, and were often given a poorer prognosis.

Age

Differences

Certain disorders are so strongly associated with particular age groups that they are described as such in the classification system; disorders of childhood (such as autism) and old age (such as dementia) constitute distinct categories. However, the expectations that people have of children will differ according to culture, as shown by Whiting and Edwards in a study of six different cultures. For many other disorders, there is the implication that the behaviour displayed is inappropriate for a person of a particular age. Children may talk to imaginary friends, for example, but adults may not. Most disorders, such as depression and anxiety, could occur at any stage of the life cycle. Depression is in fact uncommon in children below the age of about 9 years. Carlson and Cantwell argue that this is because they cannot express their feelings in ways that clinicians would understand, and that would relate to the diagnostic criteria. Major depression has been found to increase in incidence between 15 and 19 (in females particularly), and in those over 90. The median age of onset for bipolar disorder, panic disorder, obsessive-compulsive disorder, phobias, substance abuse, schizophrenia and antisocial personality disorder has also been found to be around late adolescence/early adulthood. In Britain the prevalence of depression has been found to be around 11-15% in the over 65s. In old people's homes this may rise to 38%.

Explanations

As with the other differences we have discussed, there are a variety of possible explanations. The first group relate to social and physical conditions. For example, it has been argued that in young adulthood there are more pressures—educational, occupational and social—and young people do not always have the experience to cope with them all. Old people, on the other hand, are often suffering from physical illnesses as well, which will inevitably reduce their satisfaction with life. Dover and McWilliam found that in their sample of elderly depressed patients only 3% of men and 20% of women were physically well. Many had serious complaints such as cancer or cardiovascular illness. The drugs given for these conditions may in turn lead to depression.

Older people also suffer from other social conditions that may be associated with depression. Those in residential homes may suffer from lack of stimulation, as well as loss of personal autonomy and control over the environment in which they live. Material adversity, and loss of social relationships, may also occur. Blaxter found, for example, that the psychosocial well-being of older people is associated with social class. Lowenthal found that having a stable confiding relationship protected elderly people against depression. As many as 30% of those reporting the lack of such a relationship have been found to be depressed.

Another view would be that the diagnostic system is itself biased, as Carlson and Cantwell argue with respect to young children. Research into the clinical experiences of the elderly is lacking, since they have been excluded from most of the research carried out to date (which could in itself be viewed as a bias).

Conclusion

This section has demonstrated that across cultures there are marked differences in the recorded prevalence of different mental disorders, and in the way that disorders are expressed. These differences can also be seen at the subcultural level in different ethnic, gender, social class and age groups within a culture. Some explanations have been considered for these observed differences, but they are likely to be complex and multi-causal. In the next section we will examine the evidence for culture-bound syndromes.

Culture-bound Syndromes

One innovative feature of DSM IV compared with its predecessor DSM IIIR is that it has made explicit attempts to address cultural issues. A National Institute of Mental Health working group was set up to look into the issues of culture and diagnosis when DSM IV was being drawn up. As a result, version IV includes an outline for cultural formulation and a glossary of culture-bound syndromes. The first of these is an attempt to help clinicians to apply the DSM criteria in a multicultural environment. It suggests that the clinician should take into account the individual's cultural background by making notes on the person's cultural identity, cultural explanations of the presenting illness (*e.g.* spiritual possession), culturally relevant social factors (*e.g.* stressors, social support), cultural elements of the relationship between the individual and the clinician, and cultural considerations related to diagnosis and care. The DSM glossary attempts to provide an account of syndromes that are not found in all cultures, and it is this we are concerned with here. We will also consider Western (DSM) syndromes that do not occur elsewhere, and criticisms of the cultural formulation of DSM.

Definition

Culture-bound syndromes are defined by DSM as 'recurrent, locality-specific patterns of aberrant behaviour and troubling experience that may or may not be linked to a particular DSM-IV diagnostic category.' This definition has been criticised for its vagueness, which can be seen in the use of terms such as 'aberrant' and 'troubling', and in particular the phrase 'locality-specific'. The last, for example, does not clarify how to deal with syndromes that are not universal but are nevertheless found in a range of different areas. The syndromes identified by DSM include the following:

Amok is a south-east Asian trance or dissociative syndrome that occurs only in males and is characterised by a period of depressive brooding, often precipitated by an insult and accompanied by persecutory ideas. This is followed by a violent, often homicidal outburst that may last for several hours and ends in a state of exhaustion. Amnesia for the episode follows. In Laos, some

Polynesian islands and the Philippines it is known as 'cafard'. Locally, it is attributed to interpersonal conflict and loss of honour.

Ataque de nervios is associated with Latin cultures in America and the Mediterranean. It occurs most frequently in women, but can also be found in men. It involves extreme anxiety, shortness of breath, crying, trembling, numbness in the hands, aggression and possibly fainting, convulsions or suicidal gestures. It may occur as a result of a stressful experience such as a bereavement, and there may be amnesia for the episode later. The attack is often attributed indigenously to an attack by evil spirits, as well as to grief or conflict.

Bilis/colera involve nervous tension, headaches, trembling, screaming, loss of consciousness and stomach disturbances, followed by chronic fatigue. This occurs in Latin cultures and is associated with strong feelings of rage.

The patient was a Dominican female who was being treated in America. She seemed very frightened, alternately screaming, remaining silent or mumbling to herself. She also heard voices telling her to kill herself. At times, she would try to snatch valuables from other patients. It emerged that she had recently been told that her ex-husband had remarried, and she was afraid of being left unsupported. When she found out that he would still pay her child support, her symptoms disappeared.

Boufee delirante is found in West Africa and Haiti. It is characterised by an outburst of agitation and aggression, associated with confusion, hallucinations and paranoia.

Brain fag is found in West African students, who complain of difficulties in concentrating, thinking and remembering, associated with somatic symptoms such as blurring of vision, and feelings of pressure or heat in the head.

Dhat is an Indian syndrome associated with anxiety, depression, fatigue, headaches, loss of appetite and suicidal feelings. It is attributed locally to the loss of semen, which is described in Sanskrit literature as being one of the essential elements that make up the physical body. Thus excessive masturbation or sexual intercourse could lead to these symptoms. Western-trained psychiatrists often diagnose this as major depression.

Falling out occurs in Black persons in southern America and the Caribbean, and involves a sudden collapse. The person affected lies with eyes open but is unable to move. They report that they can hear what is going on around them, but cannot see. In Haiti this is known as 'indisposition'.

Ghost sickness is found in American Indians, and is characterised by a preoccupation with death and deceased persons. Symptoms include bad dreams, feelings of danger, fainting, anxiety, hallucinations, loss of appetite and a feeling of suffocation.

The client was a 45-year-old cloth merchant, married with four children. He began to masturbate every day when he was a student, and started to worry that he was losing too much semen. In later life, if he had intercourse with his wife too often he developed the symptoms of depression and the physical symptoms associated with Dhat syndrome. He himself felt that his early overindulgence and constant daydreaming of sexual activity had led to him developing bad habits involving too much sexuality. This made him physically weak, and mentally weak to an even greater extent.

Hwa-byung is a Korean syndrome that shows itself as fatigue, depression, insomnia, panic, anorexia, indigestion and aches and pains. It is attributed to conflict in relationships, and other sources of unexpressed anger, and hence is often referred to as 'anger syndrome'. It is most common in middle-aged women who have little education and domineering husbands or mothers-in-law. Such women are expected to fulfil their role as wife without complaint, and are not allowed to express anger towards either husband or in-laws.

Koro is seen in south-east Asia and southern China and is a recognised syndrome in the Chinese Classification of Mental Disorders. The sufferer fears that the penis, vulva or breasts are shrinking back into the body, and will cause death. Men may resort to tying a string around the penis to try and prevent this happening. Koro leads to extreme anxiety, fainting, palpitations, sweating and numbness in limbs. It often occurs as a localised epidemic. Indigenously, it is attributed to excessive or inappropriate sexual intercourse, or exposure of the penis to cold. Although it appears to resemble panic or another anxiety disorder, Tseng found that the personality profile of koro patients differed from that of a group of patients with anxiety disorders in significant ways.

Latah is found in many places in south-east Asia, including Malaya, the Philippines, Japan and Siberia. It is a trance syndrome shown as a response to fright, and includes automatic obedience, echolalia (repetition of the speech of others), imitation of the movements of others, violent body movements and striking out.

Locura is a severe chronic psychotic disorder that includes symptoms such as incontinence, agitation, hallucinations and unpredictable violent outbursts. It is a term applied in Latin America, and the condition is attributed to life events and inherited vulnerability.

Mal de Ojo is an illness in Mediterranean, Muslim and Latin cultures that is attributed to the 'evil eye', a glance from an envious person. Found mostly in children and females, it involves diarrhoea, vomiting, crying for no reason, fever and disrupted sleep patterns.

Piblokto q (Arctic hysteria) occurs in Inuit communities, and is more frequent in women . It starts with a period of withdrawal or irritability that may last for hours or days. There is then a dissociative episode lasting from 5 minutes to 1 hour involving extreme excitement, during which the individual may tear off their clothes, scream incoherently, break furniture, eat faeces or run out onto the ice naked. This may be followed by convulsions and coma for up to 12 hours, after which there is amnesia for the event. Indigenously it is attributed to intense fear or personal abuse, real or imagined. According to Dick there are only around 25 published accounts of this syndrome, and it may well be that those were the result of sexual exploitation of Inuit women by explorers.

Qi-gong psychotic reaction is also included in the Chinese Classification of Mental Disorders. It is a brief episode of psychotic, dissociative or non-psychotic symptoms that follows excessive participation in the Chinese practice of qi-gong (movement and breathing exercises, relaxation and sensory awareness techniques that aim to tone muscles, boost circulation and brain activity and shape the spirit).

Rootwork/voodoo death/mal puesto are symptoms such as anxiety, chest pains or gastrointestinal disorders that result from fear of witchcraft or voodoo in which a curse has been placed on the sufferer by a sorcerer. It occurs in the southern states of America, and in Latin and Caribbean cultures.

Sangue dormido is found in Portuguese Cape Verde Islanders and involves numbness, paralysis, convulsions, heart attacks, infections and miscarriages.

Shenjing shuairuo (neurasthenia) is another disorder recognised in China, and consists of fatigue, dizziness, headaches, memory and concentration loss, and sleep, gastrointestinal and sexual disturbances. It accounts for over half of all psychiatric outpatients in China.

Shenkui is also Chinese, and refers to a syndrome where there are anxiety or panic symptoms together with somatic symptoms such as dizziness, backache, fatigue, insomnia and sexual dysfunction. It is attributed to excessive semen loss through intercourse, masturbation or the loss in white urine. This is felt by sufferers to be a loss of vital life essence and therefore dangerous.

Shin-byung is Korean, and starts with anxiety and somatic complaints such as gastrointestinal disorders, which then lead to dissociation. It is attributed to possession by ancestral spirits.

Spell is a trance state found in southern America, during which the individual communicates with the spirits of the dead. Brief personality change may also occur.

Susto (or 'magical fright') is a Hispanic and Latin American syndrome that combines anxiety, depression, dissociative and somatic symptoms, including vomiting, anorexia, sweating, phobia and irritability. It is attributed to soul loss after a frightening experience (although it may not occur until some years after the event), which has caused the soul to wander and become detached from the body and dcath is thought to result if treatment is not given to return the soul.

Taijin kyofusho is Japanese, and is a phobia that the body is offensive to others in terms of appearance, smell or movement. It leads to social withdrawal, and is included in the official Japanese Classification of Disorders. Anthropophobia appears to be the Chinese equivalent; it is a fear of being looked at.

Zar is found in Ethiopia, Sudan, Iran, Egypt and other countries in the North African region. It refers to possession by spirits, which may lead to apathy and withdrawal, including refusal to eat or to work, shouting, weeping and singing, or dissociative experiences. However, zar is not seen as a problem locally.

The above disorders are all listed in the appendix on culture-bound syndromes in DSM IV, but there are others. For example, grisi siknis is found in the Indian culture of Nicaragua, and is a trance syndrome that involves assaulting others and self-mutilating with machetes. This is attributed to spirit possession. Nangiarpok is an Inuit syndrome that involves intense fear of capsizing and drowning in a kayak, which can lead to social withdrawal and suicide.

Evaluation

The debate here is between whether all cultures basically display the same disorders (universalism) or whether there are real differences in the disorders found in different cultures (relativism).

Universalism

Some writers dispute the existence of the above syndromes as distinct disorders. They take the view that mental disorders are universal and do not show cultural differences. For example, Kiev considers that they can be adequately categorised within the other DSM axes. Koro and susto can be seen as types of anxiety disorder, voodoo death as a phobia and amok as a dissociative state. Ataque de nervios may be considered to be a brief psychotic episode. If this is accepted, then the Western categories are universal. Another view is that they should be seen as distinct symptom patterns rather than as diagnostic categories; in this view the diagnostic categories themselves are universal.

The case for cultural differences is weakened because the extent to which many culture-bound syndromes are recognised within the cultural group concerned still needs to be established in many cases. For example, Windigo psychosis (a depressive disorder in which sufferers believe that they have mutated into cannibalistic monsters) had been identified in North American Indians; Marano subsequently argued that it had never existed.

Allied to this is the issue of establishing reliably what the syndrome entails and which symptoms are typical. Guarnaccia, for example, were able to show that although seizures and suicidal gestures have been associated with ataque de nervios. There may also be identifiable subtypes, and social conditions that are associated with onset may be determined. Ataque de nervios, for example, is associated with unemployed, divorced women over 45 with little educational background, who have recently lost a family member.

Another view on this would be that many culture-bound syndromes are in fact very similar. McCajor

Hall has classified them into 10 groups according to symptoms - *e.g.* possession, mass assault and exhaustion syndromes.It has also been found that some of the culture-bound syndromes may in fact occur elsewhere; that is to say, they are not culture-bound at all. Tobin, for example, has reported on a case of koro in an Irish male.

Relativism

Other critics, arguing the case for cultural relativism, consider that incorporation of these syndromes into DSM requires too much distortion of the existing categories. They have also pointed out that DSM IV has not met its goals of being a multicultural document. There are several reasons why this is the case:

- Many of the proposals of the working group were not incorporated in the new DSM IV document, particularly those emphasising the importance of social context when determining diagnosis and treatment.
- Some syndromes do seem to be widely accepted in other cultures. For example, Canino established in a large-scale study in Puerto Rico that 16% of the population had suffered an ataque de nervios.
- There is an assumption that the Western syndromes represent the standard and those of other cultures are presented as 'exotic' or anomalous; as such, they are only presented as a brief glossary of 25 syndromes drawn from a much larger list. McCajor Hall lists 36, although it may be the case that, as described earlier, many of these can be grouped together.
- The possibility that any of the Western syndromes may also be 'culture-bound' has been largely overlooked. For example, anorexia nervosa and premenstrual syndrome are relatively infrequent elsewhere in the world.
- There is still little acceptance of cultural variation within societies rather than between them. Class, for example, and age, still receive little attention. This suggests an even greater role for relativism, but raises the issue of how far it is possible or necessary to take such differentiation.

A Synthesis

Fernando argues that rather than seeing culture-bound syndromes as those where culture has distorted the way the disorder manifests itself, the term should be used as 'a shorthand for identifying a condition where a cultural understanding is a sine qua non for bringing any practical help to the individual that is identified as "suffering" from the syndrome.'

It may also be possible to see mental disorders, including both Western and culture-bound syndromes, as falling along a continuum. This could range from those that are locally recognised and do not appear to correspond to syndromes that are more generally observed (*e.g.* amok), through to those that may so correspond (*e.g.* ataque de nervios). Outside this group would be other disorders that may subsequently prove not to exist at all, *e.g.* windigo.

Conclusion

Cultural variability can be observed in the types of mental disorder that occur. However, it is disputed whether these syndromes represent distinct disorders, which DSM has failed to acknowledge adequately, or whether they should be subsumed within the existing system.

Progress Exercise

For each of the countries/regions/ethnic groups given below, give the names of the culture-bound syndromes that may be associated with them: Japan; China; Korea; south-east Asia; Africa; India; Caribbean; Latin countries; American Indian; Inuit.

Differential Treatment according to Culture

Although detailed coverage of treatment issues is beyond the scope of this book (see *Therapeutic Approaches in Psychology* by Susan Cave), it is useful to conclude this chapter with a brief consideration of the implications for treatment of the cultural variations we have been discussing. First, treatment differentials will be discussed for the different subcultural groups considered earlier. We will conclude by looking at non-Western treatments for mental disorder.

Treatment Differentials

Persons from ethnic minorities and from the lower social classes are less likely to utilise mental health services. If they do seek help, they are more likely to see junior doctors, receive somatic therapy rather than psychotherapy and be placed in locked wards. Responsiveness to different treatments also varies; Asians, for example, are slower to metabolise some antidepressants and faster to metabolise others. An entire field of research, known as *pharmacogenetics*, is devoted to the study of ethnic differences in response to drug treatments. Hence for each group, it is useful to consider not only what is typically offered by way of treatment, but also what appears to suit each group. Fernando has provided a summary of the research findings. Dropout rates are also influenced by *cultural responsiveness factors* - whether the therapist and client share culture and language. Sue found in a large-scale study that *matching by ethnicity* was associated with lower dropout rates and more treatment sessions for Asians and Mexicans (though not for African Americans). Language match was also beneficial. These points indicate that it should be possible to develop services for the treatment of mental disorder that take more account of cultural variability than those that exist at the present time.*Client-centred treatment* has been advocated in order to address some of the concerns raised in this chapter. The aim is to provide treatment appropriate to the cultural identity of the client. Such treatment will also require the increased training of minority-group therapists, or therapists who are specialised in working with minority groups. This can be regarded as part of a general need to develop services that display *cultural sensitivity*. According to Sue the key requirements for such a system are:

- parallel services for different ethnic groups;
- fit of characteristics (training more ethnic providers);
- cognitive fit (matching therapists to clients carefully);
- provision of guidelines for culturally competent care at the level of the provider (therapist), agency (organization) and systems (political level).
- Self-assessment by clinician of ethnocentric biases.
- Assessment of client's culture and experience.
- Assessment of own knowledge of the client's background (especially deficiencies in that knowledge).
- Pre-therapy intervention (explanation of process to client).

- Hypothesise and test hypotheses.
- Attend to credibility and giving.
- nderstand the nature of discomfort and resistances from the client's perspective.
- Develop a strategy for intervention.
- Address (un)willingness of clients to consult.
- Educate the community at large about issues involved.

Non-Western treatments

In other cultures, a variety of treatments exist for mental disorder that differ from those available in Western cultures. In some countries, such as China, they operate alongside the institutional treatments based on the Western model of psychiatry.

Forms of treatment

In non-Western cultures, folk healers (*e.g.* shamans, curanderos) generally deal with mental disorder by becoming possessed by spirits during a trance. In this state they can master the spirits, and exorcise or neutralise the spirits that possess others. Also important in folk healing is *symbolic healing,* which is the use of accepted symbols such as herbs, rituals and chants, to transform experience and provide understanding of the problem.

South Asian shamanism considers mental disorder to be the result of possession by ghosts and demons. The shaman, employing rituals, aims to become possessed by powerful gods with enough status to banish them. The patient also has a trance state induced, so that the shaman can converse with the demon directly and encourage or force it to depart. Symbols used include recitation of mantras (sacred verses), costume props for the shaman to assist with taking on the form of a particular god, offerings to the spirits or ritual burnings (*e.g.* of hair clippings) to symbolise the removal of the demon. The patient is highly suggestible while in the trance state, and this encourages an *existential shift* (change in the way in which the mental disorder is conceptualised and experienced).

A curandero may treat susto in South America by having an initial diagnostic session with the client to identify the cause of the initial episode, which will be agreed with the client. Then there will be a healing session, in which the soul is coaxed back into the patient's body by massage and sweating treatments.

Other cultures may also employ different forms of medicine from those used in the West, such as Ayurvedic medicine (Asia), Chinese medicine, Yoruban (Africa) and Tibetan medicine. Generally, they do not view the mind and body as separate, and treatment is given for both. This may involve herbs, rituals or acupuncture.

Are the Treatments Effective?

That these may be effective is acknowledged by Prince, who reported a case of severe neurosis that had not responded to 4 years of both Western and non-Western treatment. The patient was eventually cured by a Yoruba healer using sacrifice and ritual. Prince concluded that 'Western psychiatric techniques are not in my opinion demonstrably superior to many indigenous Yoruba practices'. Similarly, Finkler found that spiritualism in rural Mexico was helpful in the treatment of neuroses.

Further support comes from the finding that schizophrenics do better in less developed countries than in Britain, America and Denmark. They found that 25% of schizophrenic patients fell into the best two outcome categories in developed countries, compared to 39% in less developed countries. In developed countries 65% fell into the worst two categories, compared to 38% in the less developed countries.

How do the Treatments Work?

Treatment of mental disorder in the West is based on a view of disorder that is focused on the individual. In other cultures, the disorder is viewed as a social problem that involves the community at large - what Kleinman refers to as *cultural healing*. This aims to resolve conflicts, reintegrate the individual and restore the cohesion of the group. Sorcery, such as the casting of spells or curses for example, may be blamed for the disorder, but may in itself be the result of social conflict that needs to be addressed. Thus group ties are strengthened by treatment, unlike the situation in the West. Murphy notes that the shaman is psychotherapeutic because he reinforces the shared beliefs of the group, involves both the individual and the community in treatment, shows a personal ability to master spirits, identifies the source of the illness (*e.g.* breaching a taboo) and prescribes acts that will remedy the problem.The positive outcomes have also been attributed to the level of *expressed emotion* shown by the families of patients in the different countries. This is the amount of criticism and hostility shown and has been shown to lead to re-admission in Western patients who have been discharged from hospital. In other cultures, such as India (23%), it is found to be lower than in Britain (48%). Another explanation is in terms of modern versus premodern *meaning systems* In premodern meaning systems, symptom causes are located externally to the individual (*e.g.* possession by an outside force). Modern meaning systems locate the causes internally, in the form of illness, relieving the individual of responsibility. Antonovsky refers to the concept of *coherence* in healing. This is the idea that the environment (internal and external) is predictable and can be controlled, providing hope for the future. The three components of coherence are:

- Comprehensibility (the understanding of the source and mechanism of the problem; this will differ according to culture, and may refer to a disease process, as in the medical model, or a spirit attack).
- Manageability (feeling that the situation is not out of control, and can be treated whether by rituals or drugs).
- Meaningfulness (providing a sense of purpose to the experience, such as a religious meaning; the medical model is poor in this respect).

According to Dow this amounts to inducing an existential shift. This means changing the way the problem is conceptualised and experienced, which then provides opportunities for change. If the therapist and client share cultural schemas related to the problem, there will be better understanding and more change.

Conclusion

It is clear from the research considered in this chapter that 'we have failed to see others clearly but have instead treated their cultural worlds like funhouse mirrors that hold up distorted reflections of our own cultural preoccupations'.

As Fernando makes clear, all psychiatries have a common purpose in different cultures - to maintain the mental health of individuals. This, rather than the maintenance of any particular system of psychiatry, must be the focus for the future. We have taken a wide-ranging perspective on the influence of culture and subculture on mental disorder. In the first section, we have seen how cultural meaning systems affect the ways that different cultures view behaviour. The role of transcultural psychiatry in exploring the effects this has on mental disorder has been outlined in terms of absolutism, universality and cultural relativism. Cultural differences in response to unusual behaviours demonstrate that in non-Western cultures behaviours such as hallucinations are not recognised as problems. Different cultures also show differences in the prevalence of and mode of expression of disorders. Within a culture, too, there are marked differences between subcultural groups. The ultimate expression of these differences in disorders is in culture-bound syndromes, found in some cultures but not elsewhere. Different cultural groups also have different ways of treating mental disorder, and within a culture they may receive differential treatment. It is concluded that there is a need to ensure culture-appropriate treatment for all.

7

Abnormalities of Motivation and "Ego-functions"

Introduction

It seems to the present author that certain consistencies may be traced in at least three adjacent experimental areas of considerable importance to abnormal psychology, which are referable to the interaction of such higher processes with stress and the arousal of affect or motivation on the one hand, and with individual differences on the other.

Before these interrelationships can be described, however, some consideration must be given to the terms which will be involved in the description. The notion of higher process is invoked simply to take into account the fact that the adult human being is capable of behaving in relation not only to changes in external, and in simple internal, stimulation, but also is capable of behaving in relation to an immense, and an immensely complex, range of self-produced stimulations or "symbols."

Berlyne has discussed the usefulness of the notion of self-produced stimulation in, for example, relating experimental data concerned with "knowledge" within the framework of a stimulus-response psychology. He suggests that the way of talking about such self-stimulation, or "symbolizing," formulated by Osgood provides at least a good beginning.

Osgood states that, "a pattern of stimulation which is not the object is a sign of the object if it evokes in an organism a mediating reaction, this (*a*) being some fractional part of the total behaviour elicited by the object and (*b*) producing distinctive self-stimulation that mediates responses which would not occur without the previous association of non-object and object patterns of stimulation." Berlyne goes on to point out that, "Osgood's scheme thus follows this pattern – where S is the sign, r_m the mediating reaction (a part of the response pattern made to the signified object), and Rx is the overt behaviour evoked by r_m. It will be seen that r_m is the behavioural equivalent of the 'concept' or 'meaning' which a sign, in traditional accounts of symbolization, 'conjures up' in the interpreter's 'mind.'"

It is not only "knowledge," however, that can be conceived in these terms. Certain aspects of "emotional" or "orectic" behaviour can also be so conceived.

To put it at its simplest, when one "learns a word for X," one does *not* simply learn to connect noises or marks on a piece of paper with their referent in a neutral sort of way. A wide range of symbols are primarily emotive by nature. Even those which are ordinarily neutral can, of course, acquire emotional overtones by appropriate manipulation.

The need for recognizing *both* cognitive *and* orectic aspects of symbolizing has been pointed out, for example, by Morris. He has suggested that symbolic processes may exist, not necessarily exclusively, in several different "modes of signifying."

Symbols in the "prescriptive" mode, for example, are of primary importance in human *cognitive* behaviour. These include symbols which are mainly concerned in arousing fractional anticipatory skeletal responses. The *orectic* aspect of behaviour is mainly the concern of symbols in the "appraisive" mode of signifying. In Osgood's terms, if the r_m initiates mainly drive-producing or emotional responses, it is an "appraisor."

In human abnormal psychology the appraisive content of symbolic processes (both verbal, pre-verbal and non-verbal) which are concerned with anxiety mediation are of very considerable importance. Such mediators, in the case of man, may not only be conditioned, "at the first level" so to speak, on simple tissue-injury-avoidance, as they may be with lower organisms. They may, in fact, be so remote from this primary level as to appear as mediating many different "kinds of drive." Recently, however, Brown has suggested that there may, in fact, be a relation between anxiety drive and such higher-level motives as, for example, "self-esteem." He suggests that: "The important motivating component of many of the supposed acquired drives for specific goal objects is actually a learned tendency to be discontented or distressed or anxious in the absence of these goal objects. On this view stimulus cues signifying a lack of affection, a lack of prestige, insufficient money, etc., would be said to acquire, through learning, the capacity to arouse an anxiety reaction having drive properties." This way of looking at human motivation is important on at least two counts. Firstly, it permits us to regard human motivational processes in the same light as the motivational processes of lower organisms. They may be different and more numerous in *kind*, especially in view of the vastly complex mediation systems used by man. We need not, however, regard them as being different in *source*, as is sometimes suggested by such expressions as "ego-involvement," and the like.Secondly, it suggests that, in the consideration of individual differences, we may expect certain common elements to run through all aspects of, for example, "motivational intensity." In terms of personality structure some of the important individual differences may be, for example, (i) neuroticism, which will determine the strength of the primary drives upon which anxiety may be secondarily conditioned and which will, in turn, then provide the basis for further learned drives; and (ii) introversion-extraversion, which, will determine the strength of the conditioning of the secondary, and other, drives.The connexion between anxiety and socialization has been discussed by Mowrer while the importance of personality variables has been emphasized by Eysenck. They have suggested that the process of socialization, *i.e.*, the acquisition by the individual of a certain set of standards of conduct and behaviour may be considered to be mediated by a process of conditioning. Now, if the process of socialization is based on a conditioning procedure, then the extreme introvert, subjected to a standard process of cultural indoctrination, should become over-socialized compared with the average sort of person. The extreme extravert, on the other hand, subjected to the same process, should become under-socialized compared with the average person. The contribution of neuroticism to this picture would be, perhaps, a basic "over excitability of the autonomic nervous system, particularly the sympathetic branch." This would result, for the introvert, in an over-driven, over-socialized individual; in other words in the tense, conflict-full dysthymic. The extravert would become over-driven and under-socialized; he would be typified, in fact, by the explosive hysterico-psychopathic individual It would follow from this argument that the appraisor elements related to "higher-level drives" in any individual's behaviour repertoire would be partly determined by his personality structure. In the introvert we would expect these to be strong and numerous, in the extravert, few and weak. It is to be argued in this chapter that an important part of human orectic behaviour is related to the "handling" of such appraisive mediators, and that certain experimental data can be interpreted in terms of individual differences in dealing with such mediators under varying degrees of stress.The principal consideration will be given to that method of dealing with stress in which it may be said that individuals initiate avoidance reactions to their own anxiety-producing covert responses. It will become apparent that this formulation is akin to suggestions which have been put forward at various times, for example by Sears, Angyal, and by Dollard and Miller and others, in an attempt to provide a behavioural interpretation of Freud's notion of "repression." Reviews of the evidence for such a formulation have been made by Sears, Zeller and Farrell. There are, however, several important differences between previous adumbrations and the present chapter—

i. In the first place, it is not the intention of the writer to review the evidence for, or against, "psychoanalytic theory" as such. It seems more worth-while to attempt to relate experimental data which have hitherto been more or less discrete rather than to recount attempts which have been made to evaluate virtually untestable "clinical hypotheses."

ii. Secondly, previous authors have tended to discuss the elimination of anxiety-producing responses in terms of the more-or-less passive inhibition of such processes. The present writer wishes to emphasize rather the influence of active *avoidance* behaviour. It is to be suggested that the paradigm for the elimination of anxiety-producing mediating responses is to be found in experiments involving "escape-activity" rather than in experiments dealing with the simple exclusion of unrewarded responses.

Thus, in an animal like the rat, whose mediators are (comparatively speaking) few, anxiety-producing stimuli are mainly located, so to speak, externally. Hence they may be dealt with by straightforward. overt avoidance behaviour.

In man, however, both the anxiety-producing stimuli and the behaviour initiated for the reduction of anxiety may be much less overt, and may, in fact, consist in the suppression or avoidance of certain symbolic activities.

iii. Thirdly, it must be taken into consideration that such avoidance-activity may have a more or less beneficial influence on the organism's repertoire of responses. Commonly symbols may fulfil both "appraisive" (emotional) and "prescriptive" (cognitive) functions. By initiating too much avoidance, therefore, the individual may deprive himself of certain problem-solving "tools" and so may reduce the efficiency of his adjustment. On the other hand, insufficient avoidance may be equally maladaptive, since the consequent increase in the emotive properties of a situation may also be disruptive of efficient behaviour.

iv. This latter view, that certain avoidance behaviour can be practised too little or too much leads to a fourth important consideration which has, in general, been ignored by previous writers. This relates to the interaction to be expected between situations of differential stress and differential individual susceptibility to stress.

It has emerged from several studies that adequacy of performance may not be a simple linear function of drive-strength. There may, in fact, be an *optimum* level of drive for the execution of any task, and, in general, the more complex the task the lower the optimum drive level required for its efficient execution. The general form of the relationship between drive and efficiency is curvilinear, taking the form of an inverted U-curve.

The avoidance of anxiety-mediating self-stimulation may be regarded as a kind of problem-solving task. It may be argued, therefore, that stress and the personality variables related to susceptibility to stress have a similar effect upon the achievement of an adequate "solution" involving the *avoidance* of anxiety-mediators, as they may have upon the efficient positive execution of other behaviours.

This notion agrees with the conclusion reached by Iverson and Reuder in their review of studies of "ego-involvement." They say: "Generalizing from their review, the writers propose the hypothesis that varying reactions to ego-involving conditions reflect, at least in part, a continuum of motivation. The relationship between degree of ego-involvement and efficacy of response appears to be a curvilinear one, inhibitive or disruptive at the extremes and optimally facilitative near the middle. There also appears to be a common personality dimension which is responsive to ego-involving conditions."

In view of the working hypothesis adopted here it is suggested that their "continuum of motivation" may be regarded as one of differential "social stress" or "socialized-anxiety-production," and in terms of the propositions which have been put forward concerning the likely relevance of personality structure, their "common personality dimension," may be regarded as falling along a composite continuum comprising, in turn, neurotic extraverts (NE), stable extraverts (SE), stable introverts (SI), and neurotic introverts (NI).

Thus, in situations of low objective "external" stress, individuals at the NI end of the composite continuum NE-NI may have already begun to initiate the avoidance of anxiety-mediators, since the motivational content of such reactions may, even at this stage, be sufficiently high for these individuals to be functioning "maximally" in respect of this avoidance activity. Such a process, under these circumstances of low objective stress may, however, be otherwise maladaptive since, as has been pointed out, it may concomitantly reduce access to other important cognitive aspects of these same mediators. Under the same circumstances of stress the individuals at the NE end of the continuum may not yet have begun to initiate avoidance behaviour.

On the other hand, in circumstances of high objective stress, the individuals at the NE end of the continuum will now initiate powerful avoidance behaviour. Individuals at the NI end, however, are now being subjected to so much stress that successful avoidance activity may be disrupted.In such a situation both the powerful avoidance activity and the inability to avoid may be maladaptive, since the first leads to the diminished availability of possibly relevant cues and the second leads to the increase of anxiety in an already stressful situation.It is suggested that this scheme may be used to relate data from three adjacent experimental areas, namely:

1. Studies concerned with "Perceptual Defence."
2. Studies concerned with the "Zeigarnik Effect" and
3. Studies of "Level of Aspiration" phenomena, which may now be considered in that order.

Studies in "Perceptual Defence"

Description of the Phenomena

Perceptual sensitization or vigilance to relate together results which they had obtained in an experiment designed to examine the connexion between associative reaction-times and recognition thresholds. In this study the association times of nineteen undergraduates were measured to ninety-nine words, some of these words being "neutral" in connotation (*e.g., clock, book,* etc.) and some "emotional" (*e.g., penis, hymen,* etc.) For each subject there were then selected the six words giving the longest, the six giving the median, and the six words giving the shortest reaction time. A fortnight later the tachistoscopic exposure time necessary for each subject's recognition of the chosen words was examined. A correlation ratio was run for each subject and in seventeen out of the nineteen cases, a significant curvilinear relationship was shown to exist between the two measures. A generalized z-score function was plotted for the group, the *eta* being 0.124 with a standard error of 0.054.

It can be seen from this figure that the relationships between association time and recognition time generate an inverted U-shaped distribution. The authors suggest that this is because, for most of their subjects, time of recognition increases as reaction-time; since, with the increase in emotionality of the stimulus, recognition is avoided as long as possible, as an anxiety-reducing technique, this constituting perceptual defence. Other subjects, however, tended to recognize more quickly words to which they had initially returned long reaction-times; they, in fact, showed perceptual vigilance or sensitization.

A further demonstration of the defence phenomenon was then reported by McGinnies. He presented sixteen student subjects with seven emotional and eleven neutral words and established their recognition thresholds for these words tachisto- scopically. He also took readings of the subjects' galvanic skin responses. The subjects reacted with G.S.R.s of significantly greater magnitude during the pre-recognition presentation of the emotional words than they did during the pre-recognition presentation of the neutral words.

They also required longer exposures for the accurate recognition and report of the emotional words.

McGinnies concludes that: "The findings are interpreted as representing conditioned avoidance of verbal symbols having unpleasant meanings to the observer. The stimulus word serves as a cue to deeply embedded anxiety which is revealed in autonomic acitivity as measured by the G.S.R.

Criticisms and Controversies

The notions of perceptual defence and vigilance have come in for a good deal of criticism, on several grounds. The main forms of criticism may be grouped, for convenience, under several heads and separately considered as follows:

Logical Difficulties

One difficulty which has been seen to lie in the notion of perceptual defence comes from the apparent paradox that, in order to know what to avoid, the subject must first recognize the stimulus which is to be avoided. This difficulty has been recognized from the beginning and was dealt with by Bruner and Postman in the following terms:

> The paradox remains only so long as we (1) restrict the definition of *recognition* to one type of response— veridical report and (2) insist that all systematic responses to the stimulus depend on the *prior* occurrence of correct recognition. Neither of these restrictive assumptions is necessary. There can be tripped off, by the presentation of a stimulus, a multiplicity of response tendencies among which veridical reporting is only one, albeit a most important one. Other systematic reaction tendencies tripped off by the stimulus may be largely affective in nature and lead to various forms of avoidance responses. Each of these

> possible responses has its own threshold, determined by characteristics of the stimulus end and by the directive state of the organism (differential "availability" of the responses). Thus, veridical report has its threshold, and affective avoidance response has its. As our experiments suggest, the threshold for affective avoidance response is frequently lower than the threshold for veridical report. If this rather reasonable assumption of the heirarchy of thresholds be accepted, a Judas eye notion of double-perception is not required to account for the phenomena of "defensive" perception in which avoidance responses seem to precede correct recognition.

Despite this proposal, which derives plausibility from work on "subception" as well as the study by McGinnies already cited, the same type of difficulty has been raised by others including Howie and also by Allport.

The former author has, however, been answered by Postman and Allport has himself noted that:

> The term perceptual defence is misleading in that it suggests that defence is accomplished *through* perception (*i.e.* through the abortive character or self-retardation of the perceptual process) an interpretation that raises the dilemma of a subconscious, preperceiving perceiver. If we could consider that some fractional stimulus element in the situation, rather than the complete and meaningful stimulus pattern, can, in short exposures, lead the subject *to avoid perceiving anything further with respect to that stimulus pattern* until long exposures give him no escape from perceiving it, the matter could be more simply explained. It would not be a case of "perceptual defence," in the sense of raising the threshold, but simply of an inhibition of perceiving that has been conditioned to certain (actually perceived) cues.

Studies by Bricker and Chapanis and by Murdock have provided evidence that, in fact, identification of words at near-threshold values is *not* necessarily an all-or-none matter so that it is not inconceivable that some such process as Allport suggests may, in fact, take place.

Word Frequency

A much more telling kind of criticism which has been levelled against the notion of perceptual defence is involved in the suggestion that the relative frequency of usage of words, as determined for example by the Thorndike-Lorge word-count is a more important determinant of recognition threshold than is the relative "emotionality-neutrality" of the words used in the experiments cited.

The principal proponents of the word-frequency criticism have been Howes and Solomon. These authors examined the problem experimentally and were able to show that the visual recognition threshold of a word, as measured tachistoscopically, is an approximately linear function of the logarithm of the relative frequency with which the word appears in a word-count, the product-moment correlations between the two variables ranging from - 0.68 to - 0.75.

An even more convincing study has been reported by Solomon and Postman which also examined the relationship between frequency of prior usage and recognition threshold. This latter study represented an advance on the Howes and Solomon experiments since it did not rely merely on an actuarial control of word-frequency. The undergraduate subjects in this experiment were required to read and pronounce different nonsense (actually Turkish) words. The number of times they were required to read the words ranged from once to twenty-five times. The subjects' recognition thresholds for these words were then compared with other words which they had *not* read before and it was found that thresholds varied inversely with frequency of prior usage. A similar experiment with equivalent results has been reported by King-Ellison and Jenkins.

Goodstein has also reported the further analysis of a set of results obtained by Aronfreed, Messick and Diggory. These authors had, in their study, confirmed that the mean visual recognition threshold for unpleasant words was significantly higher than the mean threshold for neutral and pleasant words. Goodstein was able to show that there was a parallel difference in frequency between the categories of words used.

Bresson in his brief review, also finds reasons for emphasizing the importance of frequency. His conclusion seems too facile, however, since he gives little or no consideration to those studies which provide evidence for the importance of other factors. In fact it has been recognized from the beginning that relative frequency might be an important determinant in the recognition situation. Bruner and Postman, for example, stated that

> We do not believe, of course, that perceptual defence is the only factor responsible for the impairment in recognition associated with increased reaction time. Part of the correlation, particularly in the case of very fast reaction words, can be ascribed to familiarity. The positive correlation between popularity and speed of associative responses is a well established empirical fact (Marbe's Law). A familiar stimulus will not only elicit a quick and popular response, but it is also likely to be recognized readily, since familiarity will facilitate "closure" when only part of the stimulus word is seen under rapid exposure. *Some* of our fast reaction-fast recognition words are indeed among those which are known to give quick, popular responses. Familiarity, cannot, however, account in entirety for the correlation between speed of association and speed of recognition. Many words with relatively *fast* recognition and reaction times are not among those which normally yield quick, popular responses. And, conversely, among the slow and *medium* recognition and reaction words are many which, according to the convential norms, should have evoked quick and popular responses. These discrepancies we attribute to the differential effect of perceptual defence in the face of emotionally charged stimuli.

Replies have been made, by other supporters of the notion of perceptual defence, to the charge that word frequency can account, by itself, for the phenomena observed in their experiments. McGinnies, for example, attempted to rebut Howes and Solomon's arguments on two grounds. In the first place he suggested that their assumptions, based on actuarial methods, of the frequency of usage of the emotional words were too low, and, secondly, he suggested that the correlations which Howes and Solomon reported between frequency and threshold were spurious since these authors drew a regression line through the two distributions represented by the emotional and neutral words, whereas such lines drawn *within* each distribution show no such marked relationship. The study by Solomon and Postman, noted above, appears to answer both these counter-arguments of McGinnies since they obtained results consistent with the importance of word frequency *without* employing the word-count technique and using a *continuous* range of word frequency.

Cowen and Beier however, report an experiment with fifty-nine students who were required to decipher progressively less blurred carbon copies of words, some emotional, and some neutral. They found that significantly more trials were required to achieve the correct report of the former as compared with the latter. They also found *no* significant correlation between threshold and frequency ($r = +0.003$).

Lazarus has pointed out that, after all, the two factors of familiarity and emotionality may interact; frequency itself may be partly a function of an individual's needs as well as experience.

A study has been reported by Delucia and Stagner who tested twenty members of the National Guard in an association time, and in a recognition threshold, situation in a way analogous to the method of the original study by Bruner and Postman. Delucia and Stagner provide a graph of their results which show interesting similarities to the one given by Bruner and Postman.

Delucia and Stagner point out that: "Both show an initial negative acceleration, a peak and a decline. The final segments of the two curves differ, perhaps because we have ten steps on the x-axis whereas Bruner and Postman have only five. The overall resemblance, however, seems noteworthy." It should be noted that even with frequency held constant, these authors report that recognition time is still significantly related to association time and they conclude that: "Our data seem to support both the Bruner and Postman emphasis on emotional factors, and the Solomon-Howes stress on frequency."

An ingenious experiment by Wiener used the *same* words as both threat and neutral stimuli by placing them in different contexts for example, placing the word *fairy* in a context which emphasized its homosexual connotation and in a context which stressed its supernatural connotation. Differences in threshold were shown; in this case, however, the critical words were perceived *more quickly* when they had been in a threat context than when they had been in a neutral context.

From this review of criticisms and rebuttals it can be concluded that in any well-conducted experiment designed to elucidate further the phenomena of perceptual defence it is certain that there must be taken into account the important factor of word frequency, and also, in view of the findings of McGinnies, Comer and Lacey word — *length* should be controlled as well.

It is probably the case, however, that word frequency, by itself, cannot account for all the phenomena reported and that the notion of perceptual defence cannot be explained away in terms of this factor alone.

Response Suppression

Another kind of criticism which has been made of the apparent defensive phenomena is that they may, in fact, be due, at least in part, to the deliberate withholding of responses to emotional words by the subjects until it is abundantly clear what words are being shown, simply because of the embarrassment involved in reporting words like *penis, whore,* and the like, in an experimental situation.

This type of criticism has been put forward by Howes and Solomon who, it will be recalled, are also among the main proponents of the word frequency argument.

Whittaker, Gilchrist and Fischer have published a note on data which they claim support the idea of "response suppression." When words derogatory to negroes were projected and the situation was conducted by a negro experimenter, these authors claim that the negro subjects' protocols showed evidence of "conscious suppression." Their case is somewhat weakened, however, by the fact that although this suppression effect was only noted with this S × E combination there was *no* significant difference between the mean illuminance threshold value for such words for this group of subjects and two other (white) groups also taken by a negro experimenter.

Postman, Bronson and Gropper report a more convincing study which was designed experimentally to vary the likelihood of response suppression. The subjects were ninety-six students; word frequency was controlled by the word-count method and thresholds were established by different levels of illuminance. Four different sets of instructions were used. Thus, one group was "uninformed," in that they were not warned to expect "taboo" words. A second group was "informed," *i.e.,* they were told what to expect. A third group was "facilitated"; they were given instructions designed to discourage the withholding of taboo responses. A fourth group was "inhibited," being given instructions designed to encourage the withholding of responses. The results of this experiment showed that the thresholds for the taboo words were significantly *lower* than the thresholds for the neutral words. The relative thresholds for neutral and emotional words, however, varied significantly with the nature of the instructions, as would have been predicted from the response suppression hypothesis.

The response-suppression hypothesis has also been favoured by Bitterman and Kniffen. They used a tachistoscopic procedure with forty female students and they derive support for their hypothesis mainly on the basis of the fact that there was a significant decline in threshold for taboo words as a function of order of presentation.

These authors note that: "The fact that no order effect is evident for the neutral words suggests that the order effect for the taboo words cannot be attributed to tachistoscopic practice. It must represent, instead, the development of insight into the essential nature of the situation. In the words of one subject, 'I caught on to what you were doing and then expected anything.' This result is precisely what might be anticipated on the assumption that differences in the threshold of taboo and neutral words (beyond those attributable to frequency of experience) may be accounted for in terms of differential readiness to report rather than in terms of perceptual functioning.

Lysak also favours the response-suppression hypothesis, although it does not seem to the present writer that his investigation of the effect of shock on thresholds provides crucial evidence on this point.

In other studies in which the subjects were given instructions which led them to expect taboo words, Lacy, Lewinger and Adamson and Freeman have shown that this may, in fact, lead to *lower* recognition thresholds for the taboo than for the neutral words.

In the meantime some of the data which have been produced by the supporters of perceptual defence in reply to the suggestion that their findings are explicable in terms of response suppression may be considered.

McGinnies and Sherman examined, tachistoscopically, the recognition thresholds of twenty male undergraduates for eight five-letter words of approximately equal frequency and of neutral meaning. Half of these task words were presented to the subjects immediately after the full exposure of a taboo word, half were presented following the exposure of a neutral word. These authors were able to show that the subjects' thresholds for the former were significantly higher than for the latter. They interpreted their findings in terms of *the generalization of an avoidance reaction* from the taboo to the neutral words. They argue that there can be no reason to suppose that subjects voluntarily withheld responses to stimuli which were, in fact, themselves neutral in connotation.

Cowen and Beier and Beier and Cowen have also shown that even when subjects are alerted to the fact that threat words are about to be exposed, they may still require a greater number of trials and more time for the correct report of threat words than for neutral words. These authors in one study checked on the possibility of response suppression in several ways; by warning the subjects what words they were to expect, by cross-examining them after the experiment, by estimating differences between male and female subjects and by comparing the effect on male and female subjects of like-sex and different-sex experimenters. The results obtained were, in the authors' view, more consistent with the perceptual defence hypothesis than with the notion of response suppression.

Newton has also examined tachistoscopically visual recognition thresholds for pleasant versus unpleasant words equated for word-count frequency. He found significantly fewer errors for the pleasant words. Response suppression would not seem to be an adequate explanation here since the unpleasant words (*e.g., shame, cruel,* etc.) were not such as to make it likely that the subjects would withhold verbal report simply from embarrassment.

It may be concluded, therefore, that the effect of response suppression, like the effect of word-frequency, must certainly be taken into account in any well designed experiment concerned with perceptual defence. It seems, however, that when the possibility of withholding responses has been, as far as possible, eliminated or controlled, differences in threshold and/or in response time remain, and so remain to be explained.

Personalized Anxiety

Another general type of criticism has been made of some of the material employed in some perceptual defence experiments.

Chodorkoff has pointed out that the use, for example, of taboo words does not guarantee their personal, anxiety-arousing relevance for every subject and that any adequate experiment must ensure the employment of such personally relevant threatening and neutral stimuli.

A search of the literature suggests that at least two main methods have been employed in attempts to secure items so that they contain a certain amount of personalized anxiety. In the first place, words have been employed which have elicited "complex indicator" responses (*e.g.*, delayed reaction-times) in word-association situations. Secondly, stimuli have been employed to which some anxiety-reaction has been experimentally secured (*e.g.*, by association with electric shock). A brief review may be made of such studies under the separate heads.

1. Word Association

It will be recalled that this is the method initially used by Bruner and Postman to secure their "defended against" stimuli. The same technique has been employed by Eriksen and by Chodorkoff who both obtained results consistent with the hypothesis of perceptual defence, and by Delucia and Stagner in their study.

He estimated illuminance threshold for twelve young women on two occasions to two lists of eight neutral and eight emotional words respectively. He notes that: "From each of the two tachistoscopic tests, two mean recognition thresholds were obtained for each subject; the mean recognition threshold for the eight emotional words shown (E_1 and E_2) and the mean recognition threshold for the eight neutral words shown (N_1 and N_2). The differences $E_1 - N_1$ (in the case of the first test) and $E_2 - N_2$ (in the case of the second test), indicate the amount by which the mean recognition threshold for emotional words exceeds the mean recognition threshold value for neutral words. A positive value for this difference would indicate that the mean recognition threshold for emotional words was greater than the mean recognition threshold for neutral words. A negative value for this difference would indicate the reverse." It can be seen that six subjects showed defensive reactions to the emotional words, while two showed vigilance reactions, and that most of the subjects showed consistency of reaction over the two occasions. Overall the defence effect was significant.

Mednick, Harwood and Wertheim secured five neutral and five disturbing words, controlled for frequency, for twenty-four students on the basis of word-association test responses. When it was suggested to the subjects that an apparently moving (but actually motionless) point of light in a dark room would trace out sentences containing the selected words, *fewer* of the disturbing words were reported, and when they were they showed a greater latency than did the neutral words.

It is interesting to note that all these studies took careful consideration of word frequency factors and, by ensuring the relevance of the stimuli, obtained results consistent with the perceptual defence hypothesis.

However, as Singer has cautiously put it: "In this experiment, and in several others, the objective criterion of the emotional connotation of a word has been the duration of reaction-time. Strictly speaking, the present experiment has only shown that higher thresholds (and the reverse) are obtained for words of a long reaction-time: that the words were actually emotional has not been unequivocally demonstrated. Our present knowledge indicates that two determinants are mainly responsible for the duration of reaction time: the associative strength of the stimulus word and its emotional effect on the subject."

2. Association with Shock

An experiment into the phenomena of "subception" (or "discrimination without awareness") by Lazarus and McCleary incidentally provided information of use in the examination of the problems of perceptual defence. In this study ten paralogs were presented to the subjects, and five of these were paired with an electric shock so that a conditioned P.G.R.s was obtained. When the ten paralogs were now exposed at speeds too rapid for the subjects accurately to report which stimulus was being presented, it could be shown that the syllables which had been previously paired with shock gave greater P.G.R.s than did the neutral syllables. It should be noted, however, that there was in this case *no* difference overall for the accuracy of report between shock and non-shock syllables.

An experiment by Reece used a factorial design to examine the effects of escapability and predictability of shock on the recognition thresholds and learning of nonsense syllables by seventy undergraduate subjects. He was able to show that when he expressed his results as ratios between post- and pre-learning (*i.e.*, shock-association) thresholds then there was a significant difference between these threshold ratios for the non-escape shock group compared with the escape shock group and also compared with the shock group.

Similar results have been reported by Rosen who argued that if the perception of a stimulus is painful to the organism and it cannot do anything directly to avoid it, then one consequence may be the raising of the recognition threshold for such a stimulus. This author was able to show, in accordance with prediction, that non-avoidable shock did raise the tachistoscopic recognition threshold of shock-associated words. The role of the learning process in the use of either defence or vigilance as the preferred mode of response to shock-associated stimuli has also recently been studied by Dulany.

3. Other Methods of Securing Relevant Stimuli

Various other methods have been employed in order to secure personalized anxiety. For example, a study by Eriksen showed consistency between the handling of T.A.T. themes (as regards aggression, etc.) and the perceptual recognition of such relevant "theme" words. Those subjects who, for example, blocked or showed other emotional indicators in their stories as regards aggression also had higher tachistoscopic visual thesholds than those who did not.

Neel used groups chosen for being prone to conflict over sex or aggression and compared their recognition threshold for pictures containing mild or direct sexual or aggressive content with the corresponding thresholds of a "no-conflict" control group. Her results suggest that there may be differences in the kind of response made to different *kinds* of anxiety-provoking stimuli.

An interesting application of the notion of personalized anxiety applied to a single case has been reported by Walton. Applying the method originally used by Rosenstock he was able to show that sentences containing material judged to be stressful on the basis of a patient's case-history were more defended against in terms of illuminance threshold than were similarly selected neutral items. Walton has also followed up these results on groups of patients.

A study by Carpenter, Wiener and Carpenter has shown that when anxiety-provoking words are individually chosen (from results on a "sentence completion" type of task) for subjects on the basis of their susceptibility to conflict in a particular area (*e.g.*, sex, hostility, etc.) then the defence or vigilance behaviour in the perceptual situation is consistent with the behaviour in the sentence completion situation.

Smith however, failed to show differences in the recognition of hostile and neutral words in subjects rated as hostile or non-hostile on the basis of M.M.P.I. scores and a "hostility scale."

Spielberger reports on differences in oral and written recognition for stuttered words by stutterers and a control group of non-stutterers. There were differences in oral, but not in written, recognition thresholds. The author interprets his results as favouring the response-suppression hypothesis. This experiment is based on the assumption that stuttered words are emotionally loaded for stutterers. It should be noted, however, that recent work by Cherry and Sayers suggests that factors other than orectic may be of prime importance in stuttering behaviour.

Having discussed some of the main areas of controversy which are to be found in the work on perceptual defence, we may now turn back a little to examine some apparent contradictions which have arisen and which have appeared principally in studies concerned to elucidate the possible role of response suppression. It will be recalled that certain studies which permitted the subjects to *expect* the presentation of emotional or taboo words actually demonstrated that, under such conditions, the recognition thresholds for emotional words may be *lower* than for neutral words.

In an article by Lacy, Lewinger and Adamson an experiment is reported (and its replication) in which thirty undergraduate subjects were tachistoscopically presented with neutral and obscene taboo words under three different conditions; *i.e.*, (1) no knowledge; (2) general knowledge (in which each subject was told what *kind* of words to expect); and (3) specific knowledge (in which each subject was told exactly what words were to be shown). The found recognition thresholds for the two kinds of words are best described graphically.

The differences between conditions of knowledge were shown to be significant and the interaction Taboo × Knowledge was also significant. The small apparent differences between the experimental and replication results were not significant. The authors note in their discussion of these results:

> The present experiment grew out of work which initially has been theoretically explained by the notion of perceptual defence. Competing with this conception is the explanation offered by Howes and Solomon which supposed that the slower times for the taboo words is due to the lesser frequency with which such words appear in visual experience. The present experiment enlarges the evidence with which these competing theories must deal. It is now necessary, not only to account for the longer reactions for taboo words seen under McGinnies' conditions, but also for the shorter reaction times seen under our "warning" conditions. In addition the competing theories must deal with the fact that differences in recognition thresholds involving taboo and non-taboo words disappear with habituation in experiments of this sort. The Howes-Solomon theory can account for the slowness with which taboo words are seen without warning, but it cannot explain the fact that such words are seen more quickly than non-taboo words when expectation exists. Further, the Howes-Solomon theory offers no grounds for explaining the habituation effects described above.

Looked at in the context of McGinnies' original theory the results suggest very strongly the bipolar character of the personal conditions which affect the speed with which perceptions are reported. In a sense, the experiment is a test of Bruner and Postman's views that these personal conditions are of such a nature that at some times they operate to defend against stimuli and at others to promote alertness to the reception of stimuli, whether defensiveness or alertness occurs depending upon the need prevailing in the receiver.

These authors conclude that such differences with differing instructions are explicable in terms of changing dominance of "set."Substantially the same results for forewarned subjects are reported by Freeman. This latter author has also reported a study again using tachistoscopic recognition of taboo and neutral words by students. In one experiment, forewarning was used as one of the variables, and, in another, ego-involvement was employed. That is to say, the subjects were warned that the perceptual task they were about to do was related to academic success and aptitude. The effect of this forewarning was, as before, to reverse the speed of differential perception of taboo words. The effect of ego-involvement, on the other hand, was to speed up perception generally but to leave the neutral words as the faster perceived.In fact, these findings illustrate what had been evident from Bruner and Postman's original study, that any notions designed to describe and explain the phenomena which exemplify perceptual defence must also make room for the obverse phenomena of perceptual vigilance.

Perceptual Defence and the Mediation-Motivation Hypothesis

The role of mediation-like processes in perception has been emphasized, from the "neuropsychological" point of view, by Hebb whose main concern has been to propose a model for perceptual processes which involves elements which are to some extent the neurological analogues of "mediators." Hebb adduces evidence mainly from the work of Senden and Riesen to show that apparently "simple" perceptions are in fact complex; that they depend to a considerable extent on the self-stimulation provided, for example, by oculo-motor activity, and that their apparent simplicity and immediacy is only the end result of a long learning process.Vernon has discussed the role of *schemata* in perception. Berlyne, from the Hullian point of view, has made proposals suggesting that "perception" should, in behaviour theory, be introduced as an intervening variable, and be allotted the status of a stimulus-producing response.Now the availability, to the organism, of such stimulus-producing responses in perceptual behaviour may be a function of several factors and among these the two most important are likely to be "habit strength" (*e.g.*, as determined by word frequency) and "drive status" (*e.g.*, in terms of their role as, say, "anxiety mediators"), the latter quality depending not only on stimulus quality but upon susceptibility factors within the individual. (This is in agreement with the point made by Klein and Schlesinger by Lazarus and by Eriksen among others, that one of the antecedent conditions which must be taken into account in such experiments is the "kind of individual" used as subject.) Let us now consider what seems to happen in the situations of high and low stress such as were postulated at the beginning of this chapter.

1. **Low stress.** In a perceptual situation in which the habit strength of the mediators involved is held constant at approximately asymptotic value and the drive value of such mediators approaches a minimum, then individuals at the NE end of the suggested personality continuum may not be concerned to initiate any avoidance behaviour towards such mediators. Individuals at the NI end of the continuum, however, being much more susceptible to stress, may have already begun to initiate such avoidance (*i.e.*, anxiety-reducing) activity. In terms of performance, then, individuals NE may appear to show perceptual vigilance whereas individuals NI are at this time showing evidence of perceptual defence.
2. **High stress.** In situations of similarly constant habit strength, but where the drive value is high, then, as in simple learning, the second part of the Yerkes-Dodson law effect becomes evident. Individuals *NE* now perform more markedly their mediation- avoidance activity; whereas, by reason of the fact that their drive component has now become excessive, individuals *NI* are now avoiding less adequately so that, in terms of performance, the vigilance and defence roles are now reversed.

These processes can be illustrated by their application. The advantages of this model seem to be as follows:

1. It permits the dismissal of "agency" notions since mediation may be triggered off, and presumably, therefore, *not* triggered off, by responses below the threshold of verbal report.
2. It takes into account both the components of word frequency and emotional value.
3. It reduces the apparent gulf between response suppression and perceptual defence since the explanation may now be couched in terms of different levels of readiness to report. Thus, at one level we have the avoidance of the production of overt mediators towards other organisms and, at another, the avoidance of the production of covert mediators toward the organism itself.
4. It takes into account the apparently paradoxical phenomena of vigilance and defence and deals with such curvilinear

relationships as were first noted by Bruner and Postman.

It can also deal with the apparent vigilance effects which have been noted when the subjects have been warned to expect taboo words by suggesting that the effect of such instructions is to reduce anxiety, so producing indifference to avoidance.

5. Most important of all, this model explicitly states the parameters of individual differences which are expected to be relevant to performance in the perceptual defence situation.

Certain other studies which have been carried out in the investigation of perceptual défence phenomena may now be reviewed in order to see if they can be resolved with the model proposed.

Consideration of Some Further Evidence

It is evident that an ideal experiment, specifically designed to test the hypothesis put forward would, at least:

a. control for such factors as word frequency and the likelihood of response suppression, and
b. vary systematically such factors as personality structure and the anxiety arousing relevance of the stimuli used, and also take account of their interaction.

In default of such a single experiment the results of a number of further studies from the literature may be recounted which have commonly taken a few of these considerations into account.

It should be pointed out that, in the ordinary visual threshold experiment it is likely that situations of low stress will be principally involved. That is to say, we shall be dealing mainly with the left-hand side of the postulated inverted U-distribution, and it will follow that these will mainly show a relationship between dysthymia and defence. This will arise from the fact that not only will the stimuli employed be only mildly stressful but also that the individuals used as subjects, even when they are selected as being at an extreme on some personality index, are usually students rather than, say, psychiatric patients.

There are, however, other studies which show the expected U-distribution of results. McClelland and Liberman showed such difference in threshold for "deprivation" words in subjects showing differences in "n-Achievement,"

Other relevant studies may be examined under headings provided by the principal factors taken into account in their design, as follows.

Low Stress and Personality

An experiment by Chodorkoff used an "accuracy of self-description" test (which has been shown to be related to adjustment by Brownfain and a Rorschach estimate of general adjustment to measure the personality variables. This study demonstrated that it was the less adequately adjusted individuals who showed defensive threshold phenomena. Another study by the same author, however attempted to relate anxiety to defensive phenomena with a negative outcome. It seems likely that such results are vitiated by the fact that the personality measures in this study were derived from Rorschach indices of very doubtful validity.

A study using a better measure of the relevant personality variables has been reported by Smock. He used two groups of twenty subjects; one group chosen on the basis of high scores and one on the basis of low scores obtained on the Sarason Anxiety Scale. To estimate the effects of such anxiety on the perception of anxiety-arousing words Smock used a technique similar to that employed by McGinnies and Sherman. The results obtained in this experiment confirm the present hypothesis in two respects. Firstly, anxiety level as measured by the Sarason test was positively associated with delayed recognition of words, and, secondly, the anxiety-arousing properties of the pre-task word also contributed to the elevation of recognition thresholds under all experimental conditions. The interaction which would have been expected on the present hypothesis was, however, not statistically significant.

Kissin, Gottesfeld and Dickes have also shown that persons who are inhibited (in the sense of "restrained" or "constricted") on projective tests may show raised thresholds for sexual, as compared with neutral words.

Pustell using shock-associated geometrical figures as tachistoscopic stimuli, found significant threshold differences between male and female students. The males showed vigilance, the females defence. Pustell claims that this was because the males found the shocks moderate, while the females found them severe.

High Stress and Personality

A study which appears to the present author to be illustrative of the situation to be expected on the right hand side of the postulated inverted U-curve has been reported by Eriksen and Browne. These authors experimentally manipulated the frequency of response strength of ten words for two groups of about twenty student subjects. For one of these groups they arranged that these ten words should also become conditioned stimuli for anxiety (through association with a failure experience). The groups were also divided in terms of high and low scores on the "Psychasthenia" scale of the M.M.P.I. Eriksen and Browne were able to show that while the variables of frequency and recency did, in fact, lower the perceptual recognition thresholds for the experienced words, this reduction was less in the case of the anxiety-conditioned words. They were also able to show that the group high on psychasthenia (or in our terms, in dysthymia) had a *lower* mean threshold on this occasion for the anxiety related words than did the low psychasthenia group. Eriksen and Browne suggest that this difference in thresholds was due to the presumed fact that the failure-associated words were *less* anxiety-producing for the high psychasthenic group. The present writer would suggest, however, that the reverse may be the case and that, in the high-stress area in which they were operating, the high psychasthenic groups were unable to avoid anxiety mediation and were therefore exhibiting vigilance.

Osler and Lewisohn using the Taylor Anxiety Scale and ingeniously employing paired stimuli as alike as possible, in which the difference in one letter alone made them acceptable or unacceptable (*e.g., tit-tot, bitch-botch*), also found lower thresholds for the unacceptable words in the high anxiety group. The opposite difference, which would be predicted on the basis of the present hypothesis for the low-anxiety group, did not, however, appear.

Variation in Stress

In addition to the studies already quoted in which forewarning appears to have *reduced* anxiety, some studies have been made on the effect of the experimental increase of anxiety.

In one experiment which, however, attempted to vary the stressfulness of the task situation, Stein showed that under conditions of increased anxiety there was an accentuation of either sensitization *or* defence in twenty-four neurotic patients, rather than the progressive *change* from one to the other which would be predicted from the present hypothesis.

Zuckerman tried to see whether frustration induced aggressive need had any effect on the tachistoscopic threshold for aggressive words compared with neutral words in groups of subjects in whom had been induced varying degrees of need-strength.

Higher thresholds were found for the aggressive words but these were not associated with the differing, presumably need-arousing, conditions. However, the experimental group *did* show greater *variability* in threshold phenomena than did the control group.

Blum demonstrated (in a study whose design, however, has been criticized by Smock, that, by increasing anxiety through two stages, subjects could be induced to show first vigilance and then defence for selected items from the "Blacky Pictures". The author himself interprets these results in terms of two psychoanalytic hypotheses, in which vigilance represents the effect of "the unconscious striving for expression of underlying psychosexual impulses," and defence represents the "warding off of these threatening impulses as they begin to approach awareness." It appears to the present author, however, that Blum's results may be more economically subsumed under the hypothesis advanced in this chapter, which does not invoke the personalized agencies of psychoanalytic theory. A similar interpretation might be made of Nelson's confirmation of Blum's results. Blum has also cross-culturally validated these findings on a group of Italian subjects.

Consistency of "Response Style"

Evidence for the current hypothesis should not only be traceable in studies which have used the same kind of situation (*e.g.*, visual recognition) and which have attempted to control the relevant variables; further evidence should also be available from studies in which the process of "mediation avoidance" can be said to be at work in quite different kinds of situations.

For example, Blum has demonstrated relationships between such avoidance in *recall* and in recognition. In a situation which controlled the variables of "set," familiarity and selective verbal report, seventeen graduate student subjects were required to recognize tachistosoopically selected items from the Blacky Pictures. In the series of stimuli were included pictures to which the subject had previously shown both conflict and repression (*i.e.*, avoidance tendencies such as forgetting the picture or its name in either of two recall procedures) and neutral pictures. Similar sets of scores were obtained for pictures which were *not* actually flashed (the subjects being unaware of this) so as to control for the actual avoidance within the perceptual situation. As Eriksen has pointed out, this is a very important kind of control to exercise, since it is necessary to show that the defence type of result is not obtained when subjects are tachistoscopically shown pictures other than the ones which are supposed to portray their conflicts.

There are an unequal number of subjects within each condition since all seventeen did not have pictures falling into all four conditions, for example, only six subjects obtained "conflict plus repression" scores on one or more of the "present" pictures. Blum notes that:

> Pictures representing areas of conflict and repression are significantly undercalled when the stimuli are actually present (Condition 1) in comparison to the same pictures unaccompanied by conflict and defence (Condition 2). This difference between disturbing and neutral pictures does not obtain when the stimuli are absent (Condition 3 v. 4). Two interesting sidelights also deserve mention. Though the hypothesis deals only with the combined effect of conflict and repression, the data lend themselves to a further breakdown on the effect of conflict alone. Fourteen individuals showed conflict but no defence on present pictures. Their mean number of calls per picture is 17·68, which conforms closely to the chance expectancy. Therefore the conclusion is warranted that an avoidance response cannot be expected solely from the existence of conflict, but requires as an essential component, the predisposition to avoid, namely repression.

Perhaps the best evidence concerning the consistency of response styles, and their relation to stress and personality factors, comes from the work of Eriksen. In one study Eriksen compared the effect of individual differences in the response to ego-threat in a situation involving memory for incompleted tasks with the effect of these individual differences upon the perceptual recognition of ego threatening stimuli. In the former situation college students were required simply to recall the names of tasks, half of which they had been allowed to complete and half of which they had been forced to leave unfinished. Half the subjects did the tasks under the guise of an intelligence test (*i.e.*, they were made ego-involved, or, in our terms, they were made anxious). The other half did the tasks under much more relaxed conditions. It was found that the main effect of the ego-involvement procedure was greatly to increase the group variance on the recall of completed *v.* uncompleted tasks. That is to say, compared with the non-ego-involved group greater individual differences were apparent.

Table 7.1. Mean Performance of Subjects as Related to the Tendency to Show Superior Recall for Successful or Unsuccessful Sentences

Group	Learning by trials		Learning by number of correct syllables		Recall in terms of per cent of total		Relearning by number of trials	
	S	N	S	N	S	N	S	N
Superior recall of successes	17.1	15.5	28.6	31.1	56.1	74.0	3.12	2.55
Superior recall of failures	15.5	14.9	25.8	30.7	72.1	60.0	2.60	3.34

For the second part of this study individuals were selected from the ego-involved group in terms of their scoring either a high success-to-failure ratio or a high failure-to-success ratio in the recall of tasks. Eriksen then proceeded to determine the relation between association-time (on a word association test) and the recognition thresholds for "complex-indicating" words for these individuals. Comparison showed that individuals who had responded to threat in the first situation by forgetting their failures showed a similar avoidance reaction in their perception of threatening words. On the other hand, those who had a high failure-to-success ratio in the first situation perceived the threatening words as quickly as they did the non- threatening words.

Eriksen was also able to show that subjects favouring successes over failures in the first type of situation described above also required longer to learn and to relearn paired associates when one of the pair was a word having a long reaction time in a word association test. On the other hand, the subjects who favoured the incompleted tasks learned words with long association times just as quickly as words with short association times.

Spence, on the other hand, failed to find such consistency in the learning and recognition of failure words. Absolute threshold difference rather than *direction* of difference was related to anxiety in his experiment.

However, Lazarus and Longo were also able to show that when individuals favouring successes to failures in the recall of interrupted tasks were required to learn and relearn pairs of nonsense syllables, some of which had been associated with electric shock, then they recalled and relearned a higher percentage of the unshocked syllables. Those who had recalled more failures in the first situation, however, were able to recall and relearn a higher percentage of the shocked syllables

Lazarus and Longo note that:

> The primary finding of this experiment is that subjects who recalled their successes in one situation also tended to recall material not associated with painful stimulation in another. This relationship occurs in spite of the fact that the two tasks employed are essentially different and the two experiments which are being compared utilized apparently different kinds of threat (viz. failure *v.* physical pain produced by electric shock). It is impossible to account for the correspondence in the performance of the subjects in the two situations in terms of task or ability variables. In order to explain the relationship, it appears reasonable to think in terms of some *intervening process* or some concept like habit or style of responding to threat.

Such apparent "consistency of response" seems to the writer to be of considerable interest since it indicates, as has been noted by a number of authors, including Walton, an important link between avoidance in simple perceptual tasks *and* in more complex ones. It also appears that the common mechanism of mediation avoidance, and similar effects of stress and personality on this mechanism, can also be adduced, for example in the work on memory for incompleted tasks, instances of which have been mentioned above. Such experiments have, of course, been commonly placed under the label of "studies in the Zeigarnik effect," and before the suggested relationships are further explored some of the findings made in this latter area may be briefly discussed.

Studies of the "Zeigarnik Effect"

Description of the Phenomena

Zeigarnik reported a series of experiments concerning the performance and recall of simple paper-and-pencil tasks. In these experiments she allowed her subjects to complete some of the tasks but interrupted their performance on others before they had finished them. When they were later asked to recall the names of the tasks Zeigarnik found that most of her subjects recalled more of the uncompleted than of the completed items. This kind of differential recall has been labelled "the Zeigarnik effect." This effect was originally measured in terms of the proportion and it can be seen that if $P = 1$ then there is no differential preference; if $P > 1$ then the interrupted *I* tasks are favoured in recall, and if $P < 1$ then the completed *C* tasks are favoured. The actual means of the ratios obtained by Zeigarnik in one experiment with thirty-two subjects averaged 1.9. This represented an advantage of 90 per cent to the *I* tasks. In another experiment with different items and fifteen different subjects the mean ratio was 2.0. Following upon the work of Zeigarnik other investigators have criticized and have attempted to improve upon her methods and techniques.Pachauri argued the importance of better controls in the experimental study of the effect. This author reported a study which took into account such variables as the nature and duration of the tasks (showing the longer the task the more likely it was to be recalled), and which also examined the effects of the difficulty of the tasks and the influence of repetition. On the whole, the results of this study were in remarkable agreement with Zeigarnik's original findings; *I* tasks being recalled on the average 90 per cent better than C tasks.Other authors who have confirmed Zeigarnik's original findings include McKinney who studied the effect in relation to maze- and nonsense-syllable learning; Martin who examined the effect of the time-span between task completion or incompletion and recall, and Cartwright and Gebhard who studied the effects of interruption on the rated "attractiveness" of activities.Marrow used an experimental procedure with thirty subjects and twenty tasks takinginto account such factors as serial position effect and individual differences in remembering. He was also able to show that the Zeigarnik effect was a function of "experienced failure" rather than of interruption or incompleteness *per se*. He also criticized the kind of ratio used in the first studies and suggested a more adequate measure in the form De Monchaux showed that this reduced Zeigarnik's original ratio from 1.9 to 1.6. She also studied the effects on the recall ratio of the relation between item completion and serial isolation; showing the interaction between these factors to be significant.

Variations in the Phenomena

Despite the ample confirmation of the effect achieved by many investigators, certain variations and even contradictions have emerged from other studies. These have been commented upon by Prentice, Boguslavsky and Guthrie, Crafts, Schneirla, Robinson and Gilbert and Boguslavsky among others. The main contradiction has emerged from experiments which have found a preponderance of C over *I* tasks in recall. It should be noted, however, that Zeigarnik herself was aware of the possibility of obtaining such reversals. This happened in an experiment of hers when the subjects were fatigued. Rosenzweig and Mason however, secured more recall for C than for *I* tasks in subjects not suffering from fatigue. They used forty crippled children between the ages of 5 and 14 approximately. The tasks they gave them were jigsaw picture puzzles, and these were presented as a "test" with a prize for the one who did best. Each child was allowed to succeed on half the puzzles he attempted and prevented from completing the other half. At the end of the session each was asked to recall the names of the puzzles attempted. The scores obtained were "recall difference" scores, expressed as percentages from the formula. Altogether more C than *I* puzzles were recalled. The authors found, in fact, that the subjects could be divided into three groups:

i. Those who remembered more *C* than *I* tasks;
ii. Those who remembered more *I* than *C* tasks;
iii. Those who remembered equal numbers of each.

They also found that those in group (i) were different from those in group (ii) in that they tended to have a higher M.A. and also a higher average rating, as made (fairly unreliably as it proved) by their teachers, in the trait of "pride."

Further work by Rosenzweig showed that this discrepancy with Zeigarnik's original results could be considered due, in part at least, to differences in ego involvement, or, as the present writer would prefer to say, to differences in the amount of stress in, or to the amount of anxiety aroused by, the test situation. Thus, in one study sixty college students were each given a series of jigsaw puzzles to solve but were only allowed to finish half of them. One half of these subjects were given the tasks under informal conditions (*i.e.*, non-stressful) which were "task-oriented" in the sense that the experimenter implied that he wanted to find out certain facts about the material used. The remaining subjects had impressed on them that the results would reflect their own ability; that is to say, the conditions were formal, "ego-oriented," stressful, or anxiety-arousing. When the subjects were asked to recall what they had been doing, the results of this experiment, using the notation already described, could be tabulated as follows:

Table 7.2.

	$P < 1$	$P > 1$	$P = 1$
Informal conditions	7	19	4
Formal conditions	17	8	5

These results not only showed that the relative stressfulness of the situation plays a part in differential recall, but also that individual differences in reaction can be demonstrated.

The effect of such individual differences has received a good deal of attention from Alper. In one of her studies, Alper examined the general hypothesis that if in the completed-interrupted task situation the group of subjects is *unselected* for personality factors, then the ratio *P* will approximate unity. The subjects used in this study were twenty undergraduates (ten experimental, ten control).

The main experimental tasks were the rearrangement of twenty-four twenty-word scrambled sentences; half of which were solvable in the time allowed and half of which were not. The control subjects were used only to measure performance on the tasks under *informal* conditions. The experimental group, on the other hand, were given twelve of the sentences (some solvable, some not) first under informal conditions, together with other tasks, and, second twelve different sentences (some solvable, some not) under the *formal*, "pseudo-intelligence-test" conditions, together with the other tasks. The control results served to ensure that the two sets of twelve sentences were of comparable difficulty.

For the experimental group it was shown that *fewer* sentences were solved under formal than under informal conditions; in other words, the ego-orienting circumstances were shown to be, in fact, more disrupting or stressful. Actual memory for the sentences was also found to be significantly poorer for the formal than for the informal conditions. There was, however, no significant difference in selective recall *within* the sessions. This finding Alper interprets as supporting the hypothesis that when subjects are unselected for personality factors then there will be no statistically significant difference between the incidental recall of an equal number of *C* and *I* tasks.

Alper then went on to examine two further hypotheses. The first of these stated that under conditions where equal numbers of *I* and C tasks are to be recalled, then subjects who recall more C tasks will show consistent differences in personality from subjects who recall more *I* tasks. This hypothesis was tested on the basis of data gathered in the previous investigation. It should be noted that the ten experimental subjects had, in that investigation, been intensively investigated, in terms of personality, at the Harvard Psychological Clinic, along lines similar to those recounted in Murray's *Explorations in Personality*.

The second hypothesis examined by Alper was that the *direction* of selective recall would differ systematically between the formal and the informal situations. Examination of the data permitted both these hypotheses to be upheld and Alper went on to suggest that the differences found could be explained in terms of "ego-strength." Those individuals characterized as strong egos preponderantly recalled *I* tasks in the informal situation and *C* tasks in the formal situation; while the converse was true of those with weak egos. According to the personality investigations conducted, those with strong egos were high on traits like self confidence and low on dejection and pessimism; the opposite being true of those with weak egos.

Alper notes that:

> Two major patterns of selective recall were isolated by studying the recall of the same Ss under two objectively different experimental conditions, a large body of personality data being available for interpreting the behaviour of each S. The recall of incompleted tasks when self-esteem is not objectively threatened is a pattern characteristic of the "strong ego" who needs to protect his self-esteem only when it is objectively threatened. The recall of completed tasks in an objectively non-self esteem-involving situation and of incompleted tasks when self-esteem is objectively threatened is characteristic of the "weak ego" who can protect his self esteem only when the threat is not objectively present.

A critical review of these studies by Rosenzweig and by Alper has been written by Glixman who points out that the type of "recall ratio" used by these authors (*i.e.*, of the type *I*/*C*) confounds a number of variables and makes interpretation of their results extremely difficult. For example, any decrease noted in the ratio *I*/*C* might be due to (i) a decrease in *I* task recall alone, or (ii) to an increase in C task recall alone, or (iii) to an increase in *I* task recall accompanied by a greater increase in C task recall. Glixman advocates instead the use of separate recall ratios for completed tasks and for incompleted taskswhich avoids these difficulties.Such points as he made have been further discussed by Rosenzweig and by Alper. Alper has recently reported further validating evidence for her hypotheses. Two groups of nine subjects were chosen as being, respectively, strong and weak egos. She demonstrated that it was then possible to predict correctly, significantly beyond chance, their ego-group membership from the direction of their recall patterns on *I* and *C* tasks over two sessions, one task- and the other ego-oriented.

The Zeigarnik Effect and the Mediation-Avoidance Hypothesis

Relationships between certain of the phenomena elicited in experiments on perceptual defence and recall of completed and incompleted tasks has already been traced for example, in the experiments of Eriksen and Lazarus and Longo. Postman and Solomon have also examined the notion that common motivational principles may govern behaviour in the two situations.These latter authors conducted an experiment in order to ascertain the speed with which a subject would recognize stimuli representing C and *I* tasks. The subjects were eighteen students and they were required to solve a series of ten seven-letter anagrams, word-frequency being taken into account. The subjects were stopped, in each case, as soon as half of them had completed any given anagram. After this part of the experiment the recognition thresholds for these words were measured tachistoscopically. It was shown that, for the group as a whole, there was no significant difference in recognition thresholds for C and *I* tasks. Postman and Solomon note, however, that individual differences were evident in that the greater proportion of their subjects showed a significant difference of sensitivity for one or the other. In fact, this result is not inconsistent with Alper's notion about the lack of differences which may be expected in such experiments when subjects are *unselected* for personality factors. An interesting corollary of the suggested connexion between the Zeigarnik phenomena and perceptual defence is that the selective recall noted in the former may be due to faulty *registration;* whereas, of course, the explanation put forward in terms of "repression" usually emphasizes poor *retention.* A recent study by Caron and Wallach shows that the effects are, in fact, mainly due to selective learning rather than selective remembering. Following the lead of these experimental attempts to unite these two areas it seems feasible to try to bring them together within the conceptual framework already employed in this chapter.Since the main hypothesis has been expounded already, it will be sufficient to outline the main points here:

1. The conditions of differential ego-involvement (*e.g.*, "formal v. informal" conditions of testing) may be regarded as lying on a continuum of differential stress.
2. The personality variables which are important are those which are related to susceptibility to stress (*i.e.*, neuroticism) and to the development of socialized anxiety (*i.e.*, introversion-extraversion). It seems likely, therefore, that the relevant dimension described by Alper in terms of a dichotomy of strong ego and weak ego may well be a "continuum" through *NE-NI*.

3. Differential recall may be explained in terms of differences in efficiency of recall in situations of high, as compared with situations of low, stress. This is such that while it may be quite efficient to recall incomplete tasks in a low-stress situation it may be relatively inefficient (*i.e.*, anxiety-provoking) to do so in situations of high stress, where the reduction of such anxiety-mediators may be preferable, while, on the other hand, too great avoidance may also be maladaptive.

As before, the "Low Stress" half of the represented dichotomy is already a situation of differential stress for individuals of differing status on the personality continuum *NE-NI*. At the *NE* end individuals have not yet begun to initiate the avoidance of mediators involved in the recall of either *C* or *I* tasks. For the *NI* individuals, however, the situation has already come to be one of considerable stress so that they have already begun to suppress the recall of anxiety producing mediators (*i.e.*, the *I* tasks).

In the situation objectively involving high stress the *NE* individuals now avoid the recall of *I* tasks. Individuals at the *NI* end, however, have reached and passed such anxiety-level so that their avoidance behaviour breaks down and *I* tasks again preponderate in their recall.

Consideration of Some Further Evidence

The earliest experiments in the field were founded no theories of Lewin's, so that, implicitly at least, the notion of "personality" has had some part in the interpretation of experimental results. Perhaps the earliest attempt to relate such results to independent, objective personality measurement was made by Pachauri who obtained no very conclusive results. More recently, however, studies using various techniques have elicited information which may be interpreted in terms of the hypothesis outlined. As in the previous section of this chapter the relevant studies may be examined under headings provided by the principal factors taken into account in their design, as follows.

Stress and Personality

Eriksen nas reported an experiment which is almost equivalent to a direct test of the present hypothesis, which is, of course, fairly similar to his own way of conceptualizing the found relationships. In this study he set out to test three general hypotheses, as follows—

a. That "ego–strength" (measured in this experiment partly by a Rorschach conformity score not unlike that found by Eysenck to be a fairly good measure of neuroticism) should be *directly* related to the tendency to recall *I* tasks under task oriented (*i.e.* "low stress") conditions and *inversely* related to the recall of *I* tasks under ego-oriented (*i.e.*, "high stress") conditions.
b. That" hysteria," as measured by the M.M.P.I., should be inversely related to the recall of *I* tasks under ego-oriented conditions.
c. That "psychasthenia," also as measured by the M.M.P.I., should be directly related to *I* task recall under ego-oriented conditions.

Eriksen himself goes on to cite the relevance of these hypotheses to Eysenck's dimensional analysis of personality.

The results of his experiment show, in line with the hypothesis advanced, that the *less* introverted the individual the more *I* tasks will he recall in a non-stressful situation; whereas the more C tasks will he recall in a stressful situation.

Table 7.3. Correlations between the Ego-strength Scale and Completed-incompleted Tasks Recall Score for the Experimental and Control Groups

	Experimental (ego-oriented)	Control (task-oriented)
N	43	19
r	- 0.60	0.38
p	0.001	0.055

Analysis of the results of this experiment also showed that the higher the individual scores on the hysteria scale the *less* will be the tendency for him to recall more *I* tasks in the threatening (*i.e.*, high stress) situation. Also, before neuroticism was partialled out of the psychasthenia score, the higher an individual's score was on this scale, the *greater* was the tendency to recall relatively more *I* tasks in the threatening situation.

Another study by Jourard failed to discover consistent relations (in terms of his own hypothesis) between certain Rorschach responses which were taken as measures of ego-strength and the recall of *I* tasks. However, the hypothesis outlined above would produce almost the opposite expectations from those predicted by Jourard. Thus, in terms of the notions outlined above, the present writer (like Alper) would expect little or no significant difference between the recall of *I* and C tasks in a population unselected for personality variables (since individual differences would tend to reduce the mean difference). Jourard, on the other hand, did predict differences, but his results were not in accord with his own prediction. Also, since the tests used were presented under formal, intelligence-test (and hence presumably stressful) conditions, the present author would predict that the strong egos would recall more C tasks, unlike Jourard, who predicted that they would recall more *I* tasks. In any case the Rorschach indices used by Jourard in this study have never been validated, whereas the one used by Eriksen as has already been pointed out, was very similar to that derived from the multiple choice Rorschach, which has been shown to be a valid test of neuroticism. It is therefore hardly surprising that Jourard was unable to report any consistent results arising from his study.

Two studies have been reported using the "Schneider index" which is an index of neurocirculatory efficiency, found to be low in neurotics, the results of which agree with the current hypothesis. Thus, Abel showed that, in a low stress situation requiring the recall of *I* and C tasks individuals with high Schneider indices (*i.e.*, good neurocirculatory efficiency) recalled more *I* tasks, whereas those with low indices recalled more C tasks. Strother and Cook using the same index report results in striking agreement with Abel's in the performance of a test under conditions of differential stress. Those individuals with high neurocirculatory efficiency tended to show a gain in performance under conditions of increased stress while those with low efficiency showed a marked decrement.

The reaction to frustration, as represented by the Zeigarnik situation, has been explored by Rosenzweig and Sarason and Sarason and Rosenzweig. These authors were concerned to evaluate Rosenzweig's "triadic hypothesis" which he had enunciated as follows: "Hypnotizability as a personality trait is to be found in positive association with repression as a preferred mechanism of defence and with impunitiveness as a characteristic type of immediate reaction to frustration,". The main measure of "repression" which these authors employed was the differential recall of *I* and *C* tasks in a situation of fairly mild stress. They were able to show that the correlations between the forgetting of *I* tasks and suggestibility (as measured by the "Body Sway" apparatus) in two groups for whom both these measures were available was 0·25 and 0.47 respectively. For another group for whom a correlation was obtained between forgetting of *I* tasks and ability to be hypnotized the correlation was 0.66.

Atkinson and Raphelson studied the relationship between "n-Achievement" as measured by responses to the T.A.T., to differential recall of *I* and *C* tasks under conditions differing in stressfulness. From previous formulations regarding the processes of socialization it is to be expected, on the present hypothesis, that those highest on n-Achievement will, in fact, be those individuals nearer the *NI* end of the *NE-NI* continuum. The results of these experiments show that those subjects high in n-Achievement do, in fact, show an increasing tendency to recall more *I* tasks as stress increases and that the opposite is true of subjects low in n-Achievement who, as stress increases, tend to recall fewer *I* tasks. In addition, and again in line with the predictions of the present hypothesis, under conditions of relaxed orientation (*i.e.*, low stress) the low n-Achievement group recalled *more I* tasks than the high n-Achievement group under the same conditions although the difference was only "near significance."

The present hypothesis is further confirmed by Alper's demonstration of an *inverse* relationship between n-Achievement and ego-strength in a group of twenty-eight college leaders.

Variations in Stress

Some studies have paid attention only to stress variables, ignoring factors of personality. Differences in the recall of tasks would only be expected in such cases if the subjects used were fairly homogeneous in terms of personality since, as Alper has suggested, the results of heterogeneity may be to cancel out differences.

Most of the studies have been, in fact, carried out on normal undergraduates and it would therefore be expected, in terms of the present hypothesis, that, overall, an increase in stress would produce the recall of a preponderance of *C* tasks, since most of such studies operate in the area of low-stress.

Such results have been reported by Walsh who investigated, in several experiments, the differential recall of various groups of school children. On the whole most of the work confirmed Zeigarnik's main finding, her general *I*/*C* ratio being 1·7. In view of the present hypothesis, however, it is interesting to note that one of the principal occasions when this ratio fell below unity, indicating superior recall of *C* tasks, was just after an air-raid when the children had been under considerable strain.

Lewis showed, in an experiment with fourteen students, each working with a "planted" co-worker in an "informal atmosphere," that co-operative completion was as good as "self-completion" so far as differential recall was concerned. She also went on to show that an increase in stress (*i.e.*, through ego-orientation) resulted in the recall of more *C* than *I* tasks.

A report by Sanford and Risser showed that, when twenty-five mothers were tested in the presence of their daughters, and were failed on six out of fifteen difficult tasks, recall produced a preponderance of *C* tasks. It should be noted that most of these women found the proceeding very embarrassing. A somewhat similar experiment with children, on the other hand, produced recall preponderance of *I* tasks, but the circumstances of administration were not nearly so stressful. Sanford and Risser conclude that such "self-defensive forgetting" is likely to occur when the need to regain self-respect is greatest and the possibility of doing this by constructive striving is at its lowest.

Glixman examined the recall changes for *I* and *C* tasks as a function of stress. This author showed in an experiment with college students, under three different degrees of anxiety arousing situation, that as stress increases the recall of *I* tasks decreases. He also showed, however, that there was no significant increase in the number of *C* tasks recalled with increase in stress.

This table shows clearly that, as the stress increases so the recall of *I* tasks decreases. There can also be seen a tendency, as stress increases, for fewer tasks altogether to be remembered and for a greater proportion of these to be *C* tasks.

Table 7.4. Means for Recall Ratios for Completed and Incompleted Tasks and for the Recall Difference Score Over Situations I, II, and III, and The F-values Associated with Variations among the Means

Situation I	Situation II	Situation III	F	F at 5 per cent	
Recall Ratio: *C*	0.60	0.62	0.52	2.44	3.13
Recall Ratio: *I*	0.57	0.52	0.44	3.42	3.13
Recall Differences m	0.03	0.10	0.08	0.50	3.13

The greater recall of *C* tasks under conditions of stress has also been confirmed by Kendler in a situation in which twenty-two college students were given sixteen jigsaw puzzles as an intelligence test and their recall compared with that of ten students given the same puzzles under neutral conditions. The former remembered more successful than unsuccessful tasks, to a significant degree, whereas the latter remembered more, though not significantly more, unsuccessful tasks.

Hays found that the effect, suggested here to be a function of stress, could be produced by interpolating a complex rather than a simple task between performance and recall. He was also able to show that, under both conditions, recall of stimuli selected as likely to arouse anxiety were recalled to a lesser degree than were the neutral stimuli.

An interesting cross-cultural verification of the effects of stress comes from a study by Ito who obtained with Japanese subjects the kind of results predicted.

As well as attempting to encompass such additional evidence, the present formulation enables the resolution of an apparent discrepancy between the findings of Rosenzweig and Mason on the one hand, and those of Sanford on the other. It will be recalled that Rosenzweig and Mason found among their crippled children subjects that those of greater maturity tended to remember more *C* than *I* tasks. Sanford, however, using normal children, found the reverse, namely that those of more advanced M.A. tended to remember more *I* than *C* tasks. It should be noted, however, that in the first study the tasks were set under formal, test-like, competitive and presumably stressful (or ego-orienting) conditions, whereas in the second study the tasks were given under much less stressful conditions. Thus, if we suggest that those who appeared to be of greater maturity in each study were those nearer the *NE* end of the *NE-NI* continuum, then, given the differential stress, the results are as predicted by the present hypothesis and the contradiction vanishes.

One of the few studies examining the effect of *recall* of completed and uncompleted tasks in psychotic individuals is that by Winder who reports that while paranoid schizophrenics tend to recall more *I* than *C* tasks, non-paranoid schizophrenics show a slight but significant tendency to recall more C than *I* tasks.

Another study, by Tamkin, showed that a group of schizophrenic subjects remembered more *I* than *C* tasks under ego-involved conditions.

It may be claimed, therefore, that in situations in which the anxiety component is provided by failure experience we find results which are consonant with the hypothesis originally elaborated to relate findings in the adjacent field of perceptual defence.

Credence is further lent to this hypothesis by its ability to relate certain facts within this new area which at first seemed quite contradictory one to another. It will be of considerable interest to see if the same hypothesis can be extended to relate together data from yet another adjacent area, namely that comprising studies in the phenomena known by the label of "Level of Aspiration." The tasks which are commonly used to elicit such phenomena are, of course, concerned to provide experience of performance in situations of success and failure so that it would seem reasonable to expect the current hypothesis to apply, at least in part.

Such a link has explicitly been suggested by Eriksen who notes that:

> Eysenck reports that in level-of-aspiration experiments Ss high on the extraversive pole tend to overestimate their performance and are little bothered by failure, while Ss falling on the introversive pole tend to underestimate their performance and are preoccupied by failure. Such reaction to failure and threat would, at least superficially, seem to be related to differential memory for completed and incompleted tasks. By emphasising the successful tasks and ignoring the failed ones, extraverted Ss would be expected to recall relatively more completed than

incompleted tasks, while for the introversive Ss the tendency would be reversed.

Some aspects of level of aspiration studies may now be considered.

Studies of Level of Aspiration

Description of the Phenomena

The first reference to "level of aspiration" to appear in the literature was in a study which used the concept only incidentally. Dembo used the term "momentary level of aspiration" in an experimental study of anger and Hoppe next took over this concept and experimented with it, being especially interested in the relationship between goal setting and the feelings related to experience of success and failure.

The first objective definition of the notion, however, was provided by Frank, who defined it as: "*... the level of future performance in a familiar task which an individual, knowing his level of past performance in that task, explicitly undertakes to reach.* By *level of past performance* is meant *the goodness of the individual's past performance, as he knows it.*" The last phrase of this definition covers the fact that the subject may, in certain experiments, be given a false score.

Rotter has mentioned seven characteristics which such a task should have: it should be (1) novel, (2) neither too easy nor too difficult, (3) neither have too wide a variance, nor (4) be too stable; it should be (5) interesting, (6) not much influenced by learning, and, finally, (7) be convenient and adaptable. To these considerations Eysenck adds the suggestion that it should (1) show moderately high correlation between successive trials, so as to permit fair anticipation of future scores and that (2) success as shown in scores should not be too readily evaluated by the subject himself, but only by the experimenter.

Gardner and Rotter have further critically examined the use of the notion and methods employed for its study. Eysenck has described in some detail one piece of apparatus which has been used to derive level of aspiration scores. This is the "Triple Tester," which, he says, is:

An adaptation of the pursuit meter, constructed by the late Dr. Craik of Cambridge University. The apparatus consists of a brass drum carrying an ivorine cover, rotating towards the subject. This ivorine cover is marked out as a helical "road" with holes punched in it. A "vehicle" in the form of a bronze ball moved sideways on a rack is steered along this road by a steering wheel. The purpose is to keep the ball on the line of holes; each "hit" is scored on an electric counter. The steering wheel operates the rack through an integrating gear instead of directly. Instantaneous deflection of the vehicle from its path is impossible with this method of transmission, and the subject is forced to anticipate the necessary moves. The more he anticipates, the smoother will be the path which he describes, whereas rapid movements made at the last moment will result in violent oscillation or wobbling of the vehicle which requires correction and leads to still worse scores. The test resembles in some ways the penny-in-the-slot machines seen at fun-fairs and has a certain fascination for most subjects which often makes them loath to abandon the machine after the testing session is over.

A variety of other devices has, of course, been employed, prominent among them being the so-called "Aspiration Board" devised by Rotter. For example, in the "Triple Tester" task described above, the Judgement Discrepancy Score (J.D.) is obtained as follows: after a few practice runs the subject may be told what the best possible score is and then given his initial test trial. He is then asked what he thinks his first score was. The difference between his actual score, and his judgement of it constitutes a J.D. score. He is now *told* his actual score and is then asked to say what he will get next time. The difference between this estimate and his past actual performance is his Goal Discrepancy (G.D.) score. The difference between what he says he will get next time and what he actually does get is his Attainment Discrepancy (A.D.) score. Other secondary measures which have been used include the *Affective Discrepancy*, or difference between G.D. and J.D.; the *Index of Flexibility*, the sum of all shifts made in level of aspiration throughout the test, and the *Index of Responsiveness*, or the measure of typical response, *i.e.*, the number of times bids are raised after success, and lowered after failure. More detailed examination has been accorded to scoring practices and the measurement of interrelationships by Preston, Lezak and Raskin, Sutcliffe, and by Siegal. who relates the phenomena to a theory of games model. It is evident that the notions employed can only be useful in so far as they have some kind of generality. They must, for example, be relatively independent of the actual tests employed. Examples of the range and types of generality which have been found are given, in chronological order.

J.D. = Judgement discrepancy
= Difference between what you did get and what you then think you got.

G.D. = Goal discrepancy
= Difference between what you did get and what you think you are going to get.

A.D. = Attainment discrepancy
= Difference between what you think you are going to get and what you do, in fact, get.

As Eysenck has pointed out in his review: "The actual size of the correlation would appear to depend upon three points:

1. The similarity of the two tests, as regards the ability measured.
2. Similarity of the scale on which goodness of performance is measured.
3. Similarity of the experimental situation, *i.e.*, whether the two tests are given in the same experimental session or not."

Differences in aspiration expressions have also been noted between situations using different kinds of instructions. For example, Frank found that the achievement of subjects who were asked, "What do you think you will do " were likely to be closer to their guesses than those who were asked, "What do you intend to do?" Festinger also found that discrepancy scores of subjects who were asked, "What score would you like to make next time?" were likely to be significantly higher compared with those of subjects who were asked, "What score do you expect to get next time?" The influence of different kinds of instructions has also been examined in other studies.

Variations in the Phenomena

From the beginning most studies have demonstrated high "Indices of Responsiveness" in most subjects. That is to say, the most "typical" responses have involved raising aspirations after success and lowering them after failure. For example, Jucknat showed that, in the case of children's performance on a maze task, 76 per cent shifted their aspirations upward following success and 84 per cent downward following failure.However, besides such "typical" reactions, variations in level-of-aspiration phenomena have been described in the literature from time to time and it is these latter results which are of most interest in the present context. Such phenomena may be considered under two main headings:

a. Variations due mainly to *environmental* factors (principally changes in environmental *stress*) and
b. Variations due mainly to *personal factors* (principally differences in *susceptibility* to stress).

Environmental Factors

This category may itself be subdivided as follows:

i. The Effect of "Reference Scales". It has been shown that the expressions of level of aspiration may be altered by making the subject aware of the status of his performance, either in relation to his own group or in relation to members of other groups. An example of the latter kind of study is provided by Chapman and Volkmann. These authors were able to show an inverse relation between level of aspiration and the social prestige value of the reference group. They gave eighty-six students a multiple choice test of literary knowledge. These subjects were divided into four groups: (1) control subjects, who were given their own scores as a base-line for their aspirations; (2) subjects who were given their scores in terms of a comparison with a fictitious group of "literary critics"; (3) subjects given their scores in comparison with a fictitious group of students; (4) subjects given their scores in terms of a comparison with a group of "workers." The lowest discrepancy scores were obtained in the case of group 2, next for group 1, then for group 3, and the highest were obtained for group 4. That is to say, comparison with the "worker group" produced most "challenge to self esteem." resulting in higher discrepancy scores. Similar effects of differential social prestige have been observed elsewhere. The effect of "intellectual prestige" has been neatly demonstrated by Gilinsky. She attempted to make the position of the comparison group more precise in relation to the individual. Ten groups of ten students were each told the (fictitious) average I.Q.s and average scores of another group of students. They were then asked to state their I.Q. and their level of aspiration on the test. The results demonstrated that the greater the perceived difference in ability between the individual and the group, the further the level of aspiration diverged from the group norm.

ii. Social Factors. Gould divided eighty-one students into two extreme groups showing high and low discrepancy scores respectively on six different tasks. She was able to show that members of the low discrepancy group had better economic and social backgrounds than the high discrepancy group. The author suggests that the latter group are subject to more social and economic stress than the former. A similar difference in social circumstance has been found between high and low discrepancy groups by Klugman.

Differences between the sexes have been explained on similar grounds; less social pressure is put on women to "get ahead" so that they find a goal-setting situation less stressful. Smaller discrepancy scores for female normal and neurotic subjects have been reported by Himmelweit, for negro women by Sumner and Johnson, for schoolgirls by Walter and Marzolf, and for female stutterers by Sheehan and Zelen. Bruner and Rotter found differences in "shifting behaviour" between male and female Navaho Indians, the males shifting significantly more often. This difference was not confirmed in a study by Himelstein on white Americans. That such social differentials may result in part, at least, from parental influence is demonstrated in a study by Little and Cohen who showed that a group of thirty asthmatic children who set high positive goals, compared with control children, had mothers who also set high positive goals for them, compared with the mothers of the control children.

iii. Success and Failure. The effect of failure-stress *within* the experimental situation has been examined by several authors. Sears, for example, studied the effects of success and failure on the goal discrepancy scores of thirty-six school children performing reading and arithmetic tasks. She was able to show that under failure-stimulated (and therefore presumably more stressful conditions) there were, generally, larger discrepancy scores and also greater variability of discrepancies.

Steisel and Cohen also showed, in a study using forty students, that while the level of aspiration itself decreased markedly following severe failure, the discrepancy scores for their subjects under this condition were extremely high and positive. Somewhat similar results have been reported in a study of fifty students by Ausubel and Schiff. They note that goal discrepancy scores were significantly more positive after cumulative than after variable failure.

Personal Factors

The earlier workers who were concerned with level of aspiration phenomena, such as Hoppe and Frank mainly attempted to *deduce* personality traits from the phenomena rather than to try to relate these effects to independent measures of personality. The first attempts to do this failed to show significant results. Gardner using a digit-symbol substitution test on fifty-one adolescent subjects, correlated a version of the G.D. measure with ratings made on the subjects' personality traits by four independent judges. When the correlations between these variables were examined none were found to be significant. Gould and Kaplan correlated the G.D. scores of eighty-two students on various tasks with certain personality variables, including extraversion as measured by Guilford's S, E and M scales; only insignificant relationships were found.

Sears however, found more promising results in a further examination of data secured in her study of schoolchildren under conditions of success and failure. She made what amounted to further "clinical" assessments or ratings of various discrepancy groups (these were composed respectively of individuals showing low positive, high-positive and negative discrepancies). At this descriptive level she found that the low positive group were well adjusted socially, confident, adaptable, well oriented. The high-positive group, on the other hand, were not very well adjusted socially, tense, insecure, worried. The negative discrepancy group showed strong social reactivity and desire to impress others.

There is a suggestive relationship between these findings and Jucknat's earlier work. The latter author had three groups of subjects divided in terms of their school work into good, medium and poor students. The poor students tended to show either very low, or very high, aspirations, compared with the other two groups.

Contrary evidence, however, comes from a study by Hanawalt, Hamilton and Morris who found, in a study of forty college women, that it was the leaders and dominant individuals who tended to have the higher discrepancy scores.

Other workers have discriminated "patterns" of scores in which very high or very low discrepancy scores appeared to be related to personality difficulties. These include Gruen who found that, in adolescents, the maladjusted subjects tended either to keep their estimates *below* performance level or to make gross compensatory over-estimates. Ax divided twenty-five subjects into two groups, the "better integrated" and the "less integrated." The second group fell into two subgroups, one of these with high positive aspiration scores the other with large negative discrepancy scores. Klugman has reported positive correlation between a Psychosomatic Inventory and discrepancy scores, which he interprets as indicating that the more stable individuals tend to have lower discrepancy scores.

An interesting study by Berkeley related level of aspiration behaviour, on the Rotter Aspiration Board, to the activity of the adrenal cortex as measured by 17-ketosteroid excretion. He found the greater discrepancies were related to increase in steroid excretion (multiple $R = 0 \cdot 70$). This author writes that: "The response, in which a wide discrepancy is maintained between aspiration and achievement, is the response of the individual who is stressed by the situation, as indicated by increased activity of the adrenal cortex." Cohen studied the relation, in fifty patients in a general hospital, between goal-setting behaviour and feelings of self-acceptance. He showed that there was a curvilinear relationship between the two; both very high and very low goal-setting being related to self rejection, only those who could accept themselves were able to set low positive goals.

Rahuls and Steiner also report studies concerned with relations between self-rating and level of aspiration behaviour.

Level of Aspiration and the Mediation-Motivation Hypothesis

It remains to be seen whether the level of aspiration phenomena already presented can be systematized in relation to an extension of the explanatory hypothesis already put forward in this chapter.

Aspirations

It can be seen from this figure that there has been added to the conceptions which have so far been used another variable which is a curvilinear function related to the setting of the levels of aspiration with increase in anxiety (induced, for example, by experience of failure). This notion derives plausibility from the findings of Steisel and Cohen who demonstrated that, whereas failure experiences were in general followed by *lowering* of the level of aspiration, this level, under several degrees of failure, does not continue to be reduced proportionately, thus resulting in *increase* in discrepancy scores with increasing failure. Similarly, Rao showed that the *rate* of decrease in level of aspiration, with an increase in the duration of failure stress, was not constant, but became negligible after a certain point.

Judgements

It can be seen that this aspect of level of aspiration performance is held to be in accordance with the relationships presumed in the examination of the phenomena of both perceptual defence and the Zeigarnik effect. Thus, at low levels of stress, recall is fairly indiscriminate. At moderate stress level it is focused on success mediation as an anxiety-reducing technique, which then at high stress levels breaks down, once more admitting the anxiety-mediating self-produced stimulation which in turn increases anxiety level even further.

Performance

The evidence for the application of the "Yerkes Dodson effect" to motor performance has been adduced elsewhere. The notion of a set of curvilinear relationships between performance and aspiration has previously been propounded by Holt. This author points out that, "Bayton found some positive relation between levels of aspiration and achievement in the more ego-involved of two tasks, with previous performance held constant. Yet when, in line with his suggestion, ego-involvement was increased considerably in this experiment, the relation fell back to zero. I have been able to reconcile his results and mine only by the hypothesis of a curvilinear relation between the degree of ego-involvement in a task and the extent to which levels of aspiration measure achievantmotivation." Holt describes this hypothesis in terms of three propositions:

1. "When ego-involvement is minimal, levels of aspiration have little motivational significance, being primarily rational judgements.

2. When ego-involvement is present but at low intensities, levels of aspiration have little defensive meaning, but reflect to some extent the intensity of motivation.
3. When ego-involvement surpasses a certain limit, defensive considerations become paramount, and the level of aspiration becomes more complexly determined."

The same author had previously reported a study in which after it had been empirically determined which of the two tests was the more ego- involving, subjects were given two level of aspiration tests. When he examined the correlation between aspiration and improvement for the less involved tasks the correlations were significant and *positive*. On the other hand for the more stressful task this correlation became *negative*.

Consideration of Some Further Evidence

In the case of the level of aspiration phenomena and their relation to personality, data are available which constitute a direct test of the hypothesis advanced. It should be noted, however, that such studies have commonly provided a good deal of stress and the results mainly lie in the right-hand area of the proposed "stress dichotomy". Eysenck and Himmelweit have reported on certain relations between level of aspiration phenomena and the introversion-extraversion dichotomy as defined by two groups of fifty neurotic patients, dysthymics and hysterics respectively. The situation employed the "Triple Tester" described above. Although the two groups were quite comparable in age and intelligence, as well as in actual performance on the test, striking differences emerged in, for example, the G.D. and J.D. measures.

Dysthymics' aspirations are significantly higher, compared to performance, than are the aspiration scores of the hysteric group; also the judgement scores of the dysthymic group are significantly lower, compared to performance, than are the judgement scores of the hysterics. Similar differences have been reported for such groups by Himmelweit on a different test.

Differences between neurotics in general and normals in general have also been reported by Himmelweit. The principal difference between these groups lay in the fact that the actual performance of the normals was significantly superior to that of the neurotics. Some of the most interesting results obtained, however, were concerned with *relationships* between various kinds of scores. For example, whereas the correlation between G.D. and J.D. scores was significantly *positive* for the normal groups, it was significantly *negative* for the neurotic groups. That is to say, while the members of both the neurotic and normal groups tended, on the whole, to overrate their future performance and underrate their past performance, in the normal group those who overrated their future performance more than others tended to underrate their past performance less. In the neurotic group, on the other hand, those who overrated their future performance more than others also underrated their past performance more. The findings of this study, in relation to the normal group, is in accordance with the results obtained by Hilgard and Sait who tested fifty students on a card sorting and on a pursuit-learning task. In the case of both these tests the correlations, for this normal group, between G.D. and J.D. scores were significant and positive.

Given the relationships expressed between aspirations and recall, or judgement, however, it may be suggested that the reversal of the sign of the correlation noted by Himmelweit may be a function of the part of the curve at which the various groups lie.

Studies of the performance of psychiatric groups conducted independently of the above findings have been reported. For example, Hartogs studied the level of aspiration in two hundred and fifteen cases of anxiety neurosis and found an unduly high initial level in 81·2 per cent of these cases. Miller tested five groups of twenty-five patients including one group of conversion hysterics, one of neurasthenics, one of character disorders, one of paranoid schizophrenics and one of normal controls. On the basis of their G.D. scores on the Carl Hollow Square test Miller was able to divide these subjects into three groups. The neurasthenics, whom Eysenck would, of course, call dysthymics, obtained high discrepancy scores, while the character disorders and hysterics (*i.e.*, neurotic extraverts) fell together with low discrepancy scores, the normals falling in between the two. Ausubel, Schiff and Goldman also found significantly higher level of aspiration and goal tenacity scores in a high-anxiety as compared with a low-anxiety group of college students in performance on a stylus maze test. A study by Raifman also suggests that patients suffering from peptic ulcer, who are commonly conceived as over-driven personalities, also show high goal-discrepancy scores.

Confirmatory data from normal subjects has also been provided by Gately who found level of aspiration behaviour was related to extraversion introversion measures obtained from analysis of questionnaire and projective measures of personality. Here again the introverts showed the higher discrepancy scores.

Results on level-of-aspiration measures have also been obtained for abnormal groups of other kinds. So far as psychotics are concerned Escalona showed that manic patients demonstrated greater "mobility" than did depressed patients and were also more sensitive to success and failure. Miller found the scores of paranoid schizophrenics to lie nearer his normal control groups than did the groups of conversion hysterics, character disorders or neurasthenics. Winder found that paranoid schizophrenics showed positive, and non-paranoid small negative, discrepancy scores on a pursuit-rotor task. Jost found differences between a group of twenty-nine normal subjects and twenty-nine schizophrenics, carefully matched for age, occupation and education. The schizophrenics showed significantly higher reaction-times and frequency of high goal discrepancies. The response score mean on the other hand, was lower for the schizophrenics; they also forgot to make verbal statements of their goal more often than the normal subjects.

Level-of-aspiration phenomena have been examined in epileptic subjects by Arluck and in mentally defective persons by Shaw and Bensberg, but in neither case did very striking results emerge.

Conclusion

A review of the results secured by various investigators in three adjacent experimental areas suggests that certain common elements may be distinguished in them. An attempt has been made to trace the relationships in terms of interactions between stress and the susceptibility to stress, and the effect of such interactions upon mediation-avoidance behaviour.

The kind of investigations which have been considered form part of that body of data associated with the label ego-function. This examination of the literature has been conducted from that point of view which regards such a label as referring merely to one *kind* of behaviour rather than to a *source* of behaviour, as seems to be implied by some writers or to an "upper member" in some hierarchy of behaviour, as seems to be suggested, for example, by McDougall in his notion of the "self-regarding sentiment."

In common with the general policy of this text attention has been focused on interrelationships among psychological data. Over twenty years ago J. McV. Hunt pointed out that:—

> Almost blind acceptance of existing nosology has also been an unfortunate tendency (*i.e.* in psychological experiments with disordered persons). All too frequently this has led to the vain hope of supplying the psychiatrist with rule-of-thumb diagnostic tests for his own categories of disorder. As most of these diagnostic categories have been derived from rough clinical observation of gross symptoms, usually without even statistical check, they should not remain dogma. The experimental psychologist must proceed critically in his use of diagnosis. He should attack problems independently, achieving his own psychological classification inductively from experimental results.

The attack on "real life problems," through such inductive principles as have been presented, has, as yet, hardly begun; although, for example, Kleinman has attempted to relate the conceptions of perceptual defence to the phenomena of "psychogenic deafness." It may be hoped, however, that the practice of clinical psychology may benefit from such an approach to abnormal psychology at least as much as it has benefited from an uncritical acceptance of psychiatric models.

Bibliography

Abramson, L. Y., Metalsky, G. I. and Alloy, L. B. (1989). "Hopelessness depression: A theory based subtype of depression." Psychological Review, 96: 358-372.

Abramson, L. Y., Metalsky, G. I. and Alloy, L. B. (1989). "Hopelessness depression: A theory based subtype of depression." *Psychological Review*, 96: 358-372.

Abramson, L., Seligman, M. and Teasdale, J. (1978). Learned helplessness in humans: critique and reformulation. *Journal of Abnormal Psychology*, 87, 49-74.

Achenbach, T. (1991). *Integrative Guide for the 1991 CBCL/4-18, YSR and TRF profiles*. Burlington, VT: University of Vermont Department of Psychiatry.

American Psychiatry Association (1994). Diagnostic and Statistical Manual of Mental Disorders. 4th ed. Washington, D.C.

American Psychiatry Association (1994). Diagnostic and Statistical Manual of Mental Disorders. 4th ed. Washington, D.C.

Barkley, R. (1994). Impaired delayed responding: a unified theory of attention deficit hyperactivity disorder. In D. Routh (ed.), *Disruptive Behaviour Disorders in Childhood: Essays Honoring Herbert C. Quay* (pp. 11-57). New York: Plenum Press.

Barkley, R. (1998). *Attention Deficit Hyperactivity Disorder: A Handbook for Diagnosis and Treatment* (2nd edn). New York: Guilford.

Campbell, D., Draper, R. and Crutchley, E. (1991). The Milan systemic approach to family therapy. In A. Gurman and D. Kniskern (eds), *Handbook of Family Therapy* (vol. 11, pp. 325-362). New York: Brunner Mazel.

Carr, A. (1999). *The Handbook of Child and Adolescent Clinical Psychology*. London: Routledge.

Carr, A. (2000a). *What Works with Children and Adolescents? A Critical Review of Research on Psychological Interventions with Children, Adolescents and their Families*. London: Routledge.

Dishion, T., McCord, J. and Poulin, F. (1999). When interventions harm: peer groups and problem behaviour. *American Psychologist*, 54, 755-764.

Estrada, A. and Pinsof, W. (1995). The effectiveness of family therapies for selected behavioural disorders of childhood, *Journal of Marital and Family Therapy*, 21, 403-440.

Eysenck, H. (1979). The conditioning model of neurosis. *The Behavioural and Brain Sciences*, 2, 155-199.

Eysenck, H. (1987). The definition of personality disorders and the criteria appropriate to their definition. *Journal of Personality Disorders*, 1, 211-219.

Friedman, E. (1991). Bowen theory and therapy. In A. Gurman and D. Kniskern (eds), *Handbook of Family Therapy* (vol. 11, pp. 134-170). New York: Brunner Mazel.

Gadow, K. (1992). Paediatric psychopharmacology: a review of recent research. *Journal of Child Psychology and Psychiatry*, 33, 153-195.

Gray, Peter. Psychology. 3rd ed. New York: Worth Publishers, 1999.

Hauser, P., Zametkin, A., Martinez, P., Vitiello, B., Matochik, J., Mixon, A. and Weintraub, B. (1993). Attention deficit hyperactivity disorder in people with generalized resistance to thyroid hormone. *New England Journal of Medicine*, 328, 997-1001.

Hilke, I. (1998). The playing through of selfobject transferences of a nine-year-old boy. In A. Goldberg (ed.), *Progress in Self Psychology, Volume 14*, 71-84.

Kane, J. (1995). Current problems with the pharmacotherapy of schizophrenia. *Clinical Neuropharmacology*, 18 (Supplement), S154-S180.

Kaslow, N. and Rehm, L. (1991). Childhood depression. In T. Kratochwill and R. Morris (eds), *The Practice of Child Therapy* (pp. 43-75). New York: Pergamon.

Katz, R., and McGuffin, P. "The genetics of affective disorders." Progress in Experimental Personality and Psychopathology Research. New York: Springer, 1993.

Katz, R., and McGuffin, P. "The genetics of affective disorders." Progress in Experimental Personality and Psychopathology Research. New York: Springer, 1993.

Leonard, H., Swedo, S., Allen, A. and Rapoport, J. (1994). Obsessive-compulsive disorder. In T. Ollendick, N. King and W. Yule (eds), *International Handbook of Phobic and Anxiety Disorders* (pp. 207-220). New York: Plenum.

McFarlane, W. (1991). Family psychoeducational treatment. In A. Gurman and D. Kniskern (eds), *Handbook of Family Therapy* (vol. 11, pp. 363-395). New York: Brunner Mazel.

McNeal, E. T., and Cimbolic, P. (1986). "Anti-depressants and biochemical theories of depresssion." Psychological Bulletin, 99: 361-374.

McNeal, E. T., and Cimbolic, P. (1986). "Anti-depressants and biochemical theories of depresssion." Psychological Bulletin, 99: 361-374.

Newnes, C. and MacLachlan, A. (1996). The antipsychiatry placement. *Clinical Psychology forum*, 93, 24-27.

Newnes, C., Hagan, T. and Cox, R. (2000). Fostering critical reflection in psychological practice. *Clinical Psychology Forum*, 139, 21-24.

Oltmanns, Thomas F. and Emery, Robert E. Abnormal Psychology. 2nd ed. New Jersey: Prentice Hall, 1998.

Oltmanns, Thomas F. and Emery, Robert E. Abnormal Psychology. 2nd ed. New Jersey: Prentice Hall, 1998.

Oltmanns, Thomas F., Neale, John F., and Davison, Gerald C. Case Studies in Abnormal Psychology. 5th ed. United States: Malloy Lithographing Inc., 1999.

Oltmanns, Thomas F., Neale, John F., and Davison, Gerald C. Case Studies in Abnormal Psychology. 5th ed. United States: Malloy Lithographing Inc., 1999.

Paris, J. (1996). *Social Factors in the Personality Disorders. A Biopsychosocial Approach to Etiology and Treatment.* Cambridge, UK: Cambridge University Press.

Patterson, G. (1982). *Coercive Family Process*. Eugene, OR: Castalia.

Rauch, S. and Jenike, M. (1998). Pharmacological treatment of obsessive compulsive disorder. In P. Nathan and J. Gorman (eds), *A Guide to Treatments that Work* (pp. 358-376). New York: Oxford University Press.

Robins, L. (1966). *Deviant Children Growing Up*. Baltimore, MD: Williams and Wilkins.

Stolorow, R. (1999). The phenomenology of trauma and the absolutisms of everyday life: A personal journey. *Psychoanalytic Psychology, 16*, 464-468.

Storr, Anthony. Freud: Past Masters. Britain: Oxford University Press, 1989.

Storr, Anthony. Freud: Past Masters. Britain: Oxford University Press, 1989.

Taylor, E. (1994b). Physical treatments. In M. Rutter, E. Taylor and L. Hersov (eds), *Child and Adolescent Psychiatry: Modern Approaches* (3rd edn, pp. 880-899). London: Blackwell.

Thomson, M. (1990). *Developmental Dyslexia* (3rd edn). London: Whurr.

Wada, H. (2003) The applicability of self psychology to psychotherapy with the elderly: With emphasis on twinship selfobject needs and empathy as a mode of observation. In *Progress in Seif Psychology, Vol. I 9* (M. Gehrie, ed.), 331-343.

Walker, T. & Dudley, S. (2004). Trauma and recovery: A story of personal transformation and healing amidst the terror of September 11. In W. Coburn, (ed.), *Transformations inSelf Psychology: Progress in Self Psychology, Volume 20*, Hillsdale, NJ: Analytic Press, 109-123.

Whaley, A. (1998). Racism in the provision of mental health services: a social-cognitive analysis. *American Journal of Orthopsychiatry*, 68, 48-59.

Widiger, T. (1993). The DSM III R categorical personality disorder diagnoses: a critique and an alternative. *Psychological Inquiry*, 4, 75-90.

INDEX